Gathering Together

Gathering Together

Baptists at Work in Worship

Edited by Rodney W. Kennedy
and Derek C. Hatch

PICKWICK *Publications* · Eugene, Oregon

GATHERING TOGETHER
Baptists at Work in Worship

Pickwick Publications
An Imprint of Wipf and Stock Publishers
199 W. 8th Ave., Suite 3
Eugene, OR 97401

www.wipfandstock.com

ISBN 13: 978-1-61097-758-6

Cataloguing-in-Publication data:

Muhlhan, Brett.

    Gathering together : Baptists at work in worship / edited by Derek C. Hatch and Rodney Wallace Kennedy.

    xii + 194 pp. ; 23 cm. Includes bibliographical references.

    ISBN 13: 978-1-61097-758-6

    1. Public worship—Baptists. 2. Worship 3. I. Title

BX6337 G37 2013

Manufactured in the U.S.A.

Contents

Contributors

C. Randall Bradley is Professor of Church Music at Baylor University in Waco, Texas

Scott Bullard is Professor of Theology at Judson College in Marion, Alabama

Amy Butler is Senior Pastor of Calvary Baptist Church in Washington, DC

Kyle Childress is Pastor of Austin Heights Baptist Church in Nacogdoches, Texas

Derek C. Hatch is Professor of Christian Studies at Howard Payne University in Brownwood, Texas

Cameron Jorgenson is Professor of Theology at Campbell University Divinity School in Buies Creek, North Carolina

Rodney W. Kennedy is Senior Pastor of First Baptist Church in Dayton, Ohio

Elizabeth Newman is Professor of Theology and Ethics at Baptist Theological Seminary of Richmond in Richmond, Virginia

Michael D. Sciretti Jr. is Minister of Spiritual Formation at Freemason Street Baptist Church in Norfolk, Virginia

Sharlande Sledge is Associate Pastor of Lake Shore Baptist Church in Waco, Texas

Philip E. Thompson is Professor of Theology at Sioux Falls Seminary in Sioux Falls, South Dakota

Introduction

THE JOURNEY OF THIS book arises not from an idea, but from lives immersed in the practice of worship. Both editors, in various contexts, have come to discover the rich depth within the Christian liturgical tradition and have worked in both lay and clerical capacities to bring those to life within our congregations. This has not always been easy because, along the way, we have encountered a relative dearth of resources for Baptists in the United States related to the practice of worship. In other words, with a few exceptions, we have found that Baptists have not often thought intentionally about the activities of Christian worship. This book, and all of the voices within it, humbly aims to relieve some of that deficit.

As a collaborative effort by a team of ministers and teachers, all of whom have serious commitments to the primacy of worship, the essays in this book underscore our conviction (nurtured in congregations and classrooms) that worship, the primary Christian practice, is essential to the formation of faithful disciples of Jesus Christ. To be formative, though, requires participation in the rhythm of Christian liturgy. Thus, within the parameters of the practice of worship, there are multiple activities that develop, energize, and shape the Christian believer, not only as an individual, but as a participant within the gathered community of faith, the *ekklesia*. We hope to examine those in order to take seriously the ways that worship molds genuine Christian faith.

As Marva Dawn has well reminded us, God is the subject and object of worship.[1] Augustine of Hippo wrote in his *Confessions*, "[Y]ou have made us for yourself [O God] and our heart is restless until it rests in you."[2] Worship, with its focus on God, is the activity of our restless hearts pursuing God, though this is a communal task above all else. The Greek root of the word *liturgy* means "work of the people." Thus, all Christians (including Baptists) *do* liturgy. Nonetheless, the description of what liturgy entails certainly varies from one congregation to another. Some are often described as "high

---

1. Dawn, *Reaching Out without Dumbing Down*, 75ff.

2. Augustine, *Confessions* 1.1.

church" and others as "low church," but liturgy remains the work of worship. It is what congregations do when they gather together in the name of the Tri-une God to praise and give thanks. This book has been written to celebrate the powerful ways that Baptists praise and love God. As John Chrysostom says in his sermon on Ephesians 1, "The Divine nature knoweth no want. And wherefore then would He have us praise and glorify Him? It is that our love towards Him may be kindled more fervently within us."[3] Chrysostom is gesturing toward what it means to be human. Similarly, James K.A. Smith writes that human beings are not thinkers or believers primarily, but lovers (*homo liturgicus*), "embodied agents of desire or love."[4] Thus, forming our desires becomes a central part of the practices of Christian worship.

From every corner of the globe, with the embedded memory of Pentecost in our hearts, Christians gather to worship God. We gather with the words of a promise of Jesus precious to all Baptists: "For where two or three are gathered in my name, there I am among them" (Matt 18:20). In myriad ways, Christians gather in worship to meet God and to be met by God. Carlyle Marney said,

> This is the meaning of the Sabbath, the Temple, and worship. One keeps coming by to be sure it is still there. This is the prophet's cry. 'Turn, turn, return!' Keep coming by! God has been met with! And here you have an appointment – at the Tent of the Eternal – and it is a come and go affair. It is a constant reminder of what has gone by. One comes here in order to pass by again.[5]

Undergirding this work is a passionate devotion to Scripture as the book of the church. We affirm that the Bible is the organizing center of all worship. We are interested here in the nature and will of God. What we offer in this book is reflections on the way that the Bible informs and forms the worship practices that we find so meaningful and important. We hope that the readers will be able to sense that we are Christians at work in worship and glean what they can learn from the acts and practices of worship.

In short, this book is intended for the church and is gifted to her servants, those who have committed themselves to lives of ministry. Each of the essays found in this book emerges from the ties that bind the assembly of faith together as a gathered community, but also as part of the body of Christ across space and time. Because of this, the essays in this work all form an argument that invites you into a conversation that views worship as

---

3. John Chrysostom, *Chrysostom: Homilies on Galatians, Ephesians, Philippians, Colossians, Thessalonians, Timothy, Titus, and Philemon* (NPNF1 13:52).

4. Smith, *Desiring the Kingdom*, 47.

5. Marney, "A Come-and-Go Affair," 136.

something like a seamless garment where music, sermon, prayer, reading, confessing, and silence interpenetrate one another and provide a multifaceted yet singular direction to worship. Like any conversation, however, debate is welcome. What is most important in this volume, then, is not the diversity of positions, but a rich and engaging conversation about what occurs in Baptist liturgy. Within these chapters, for example, there are challenges to Baptists' ways of thinking about baptism and communion that can expand the significance of these acts for Baptist congregations. There are discussions of recovering practices that Baptists previously lost or abandoned, not for the sake of nostalgia, but because these practices offer resources for forming disciples of Jesus. There are also patterns and practices of worship that are designed to produce intentional discussion among seminarians, pastors, and worship committees about the shape of our worship.

Thus, rather than quibble about whether or not one style of worship "reaches" or appeals to more people or is the "right" way to worship, we have partnered this collection of essays with an appendix of resources that can be used in Sunday worship, perhaps in small, subtle ways. What we attempt is the elevation, celebration, and magnification of the ways, the means, and the practices of worship available to Baptists. In other words, as this book was birthed in the practices of Christian worship, it certainly must maintain its focus there as well. British Baptist theologian Christopher Ellis writes that "worship is embodied theology."[6] This, in concert with the ancient church's emphasis on *lex orandi, lex credendi* (or "the law of prayer/worship is the law of belief"), provides the impetus for thinking deeply about the work of worship. Not surprisingly, then, while this book's chapters have a Baptist audience in mind, they will certainly appeal to a wider group of readers, especially those with free-church affinities and background (i.e., those whom James McClendon called "baptists").

In the end, as part of the Body of Christ, we enter liturgy with the great cloud of witnesses mentioned in Hebrews. Worship, then, is inextricably a corporate act that occurs in the company of the gathered assembly and in the company of the gathered saints across the generations. We must always remember that Baptists draw from and participate in the depth and breadth of the Christian tradition. Thus, we are all the children of St. Peter and the Jerusalem Church, of St. Paul and the churches of Colossae, Galatia, Ephesus, Thessalonica, and Philippi. Indeed, we are the children of Augustine, John Chrysostom, Thomas Aquinas, Martin Luther, John Calvin, Jakob Arminius, John Wesley, Karl Barth, Martin Luther King, Howard Thurman, and Gardner Taylor. Baptists certainly did not appear full-grown in the seventeenth century, but while our historical journeys may not have involved Anglican

---

6. Ellis, *Gathering*, 14.

prayer books or liturgical rituals, this does not mean that we cannot learn from these elements and cultivate a deeper memory of the practice of the worship of Triune God. As worship is at the heart of the church, we offer these essays in order that Baptists might consider how we might worship God more fully and become the people of God more faithfully.

Overview of Chapters

The first two chapters give broader context for considering the depths of Christian worship. The first, written by Kyle Childress, addresses Sunday worship as liturgy. That is, what does it mean to think intentionally (and even theologically) about what happens in worship. If worship is essential to the formation of the Christian life, then the shape of that worship deserves attention. In the second chapter, Michael Sciretti discusses the sweep of the Christian liturgical year. For generations, Christians old and young followed a calendar of seasons that gave form and rhythm to the practices of worship. Sciretti examines these seasons and the manner in which the calendar as a whole becomes a crucial resource for thinking well about worship and the narrative that shapes all Christians.

The next seven chapters address specific practices within worship, discussing how to approach these theologically and suggesting ways to better embrace them within the warp and woof of Christian worship. Amy Butler examines many congregations' subtle, though significant, practices of building ties of community (whether through an informal welcome or a formal litany or response). Sharlande Sledge addresses prayer in worship by discussing how it contributes to and draws from worship as a whole. Philip Thompson contends that affirmations of faith, such as the Nicene and Apostles' Creed, could have a robust place within Baptist worship (even if they do not presently). Rodney Kennedy discusses the art of preaching and its role as a contributor to an entire worship service. Scott Bullard and Elizabeth Newman address the depths of the two commonly practiced Baptist sacraments: Communion and Baptism. Randall Bradley argues that music, while not coterminous with worship altogether, nonetheless facilitates the fullness of authentic Christian worship.

The book concludes with a chapter by Cameron Jorgenson that situates worship within a broader context—the mission of the church in the world. Thus, rather than seeing intentional consideration of liturgy as a insular activity that shields a congregation from the outside world, this book, and Jorgenson's chapter, contend that better thinking about what Baptists do in worship will also shape better practice of the Christian life and better pursuit of God's mission for the world.

1

Worship and Becoming the Body of Christ

Kyle Childress

There's a saying I've heard around Baptist clergy circles for years that goes, "There are all kinds of Baptists: everything from those who burn incense to those who bay at the moon."[1] We Baptists have a history of worshiping God in all sorts of ways. Some have followed dignified order, with classical sacred music, and sermons carefully prepared and thoughtfully expressed. Some have celebrated the Eucharist every week on Sunday morning while other Baptists observe the Lord's Supper once a quarter on Sunday nights. Others have had nothing printed for guidance in worship and instead relied on the spontaneity of the moment, ever sensitive to the moving of the Holy Spirit and sermons preached with powerful emotion on whatever verse happened to open in the Bible. As an old-time rural preacher told me a long time ago, "If you're not hoarse and standing knee-deep in sweat when you've finished preaching, then you haven't preached."

In my own context of the western edge of the American South early in the second decade of the twenty-first century, Baptists who in times past might have leaned toward the baying-at-the-moon end of the worship spectrum have in recent years joined the wide-spread evangelical movement toward an entertainment model of worship with emphasis on praise bands, contemporary choruses, short snappy sermons focused on practical advice, and, when affordable, the use of sound and lighting special effects. And while there is a church or two which still has a service with a printed

1. I first heard this from Don Burke, pastor emeritus of the Highland Baptist Church, Louisville, Kentucky, and H. Stephen Shoemaker, senior minister of the Myers Park Baptist Church, Charlotte, North Carolina.

Order of Worship and sings traditional hymns or gospel songs, it's a service relegated to second-class status to the primary contemporary praise service. Even among people who are not church-goers I've noticed over the last twenty years a shift in their generalized cultural assumptions of what goes on inside of churches, from expectations of hard preaching on sin and hell and salvation to expectations of praise bands and sermonettes on "five hints for a happy family."[2]

What I'm describing can be loosely associated with what Baptist historians call the "Sandy Creek Tradition" of worship among Baptists in the American South. Walter Shurden gave it the short hand description "ardor" for its revivalistic emphasis on faith as feeling and focus upon conversion.[3] And with all its variations and developments into the early twenty-first century, the central question still tends to be how might worship speak to the individual?

My own congregation, Austin Heights Baptist Church of Nacogdoches, Texas, was founded in 1968 asking different questions. While it expressed much of the turmoil of its time by questioning racism and segregation and the war in Vietnam, it tended to give different answers from the social norm of white churches in East Texas. Founded with an open membership policy on race set the church apart from the beginning and its willingness to engage in dialogue and even debate about the teachings of Christ and the war in Vietnam definitely labeled the church as "liberal," which usually meant we were "different." The congregation also looked for and found a pastor who preached thoughtful sermons and led the congregation to understand worship as primarily about God, moving it away from the predominant "Sandy Creek" model and in the direction of what Shurden calls the "Charleston Tradition" of Baptist worship with emphasis on dignity and "order."[4] The three subsequent pastors over the next twenty years before me continued the same tradition.

When I became pastor I knew that I wanted to work within this tradition but their version of it had become worn and they were exhausted. I knew they needed change if they were going to survive. There's an old rule of thumb for a new pastor arriving in a congregation—a congregation will give you one big change your first year without undue debate and push-back, so choose wisely what that change will be. And there's a second rule, which is more important than the first: work with what is good that is already going on with a congregation. Probably the best single bit of pastoral advice I ever

2. For your information they're "happy, helpful, healthy, holy, and heaven-bound."
3. Shurden, "The Southern Baptist Synthesis"; McBeth, *The Baptist Heritage*, 234.
4. Shurden, "The Southern Baptist Synthesis."

received came from Kentucky farmer and writer Wendell Berry as he wrote about a farmer looking over and day-dreaming about a new farm:

> When one buys the farm and moves there to live, something different begins. Thoughts begin to be translated into acts . . . It invariably turns out, I think, that one's first vision of one's place was to some extent an imposition on it. But if one's sight is clear and one stays on and works well, one's love gradually responds to the place as it really is, and one's visions gradually image possibilities that are really in it.[5]

Berry's wisdom about a farm goes for a church, too. A new pastor's first vision can be an imposition on it, so one must be careful and humble about the changes one seeks to bring, instead of imposing change, seeking to learn and understand what changes God is already bringing about. The distinction between the change the pastor wants and learning to pay attention to the change God is bringing is no small thing. When pastors seek to impose change it tends to be hasty, but it takes patience to discern the work of God already present. The challenge comes when we are patiently seeking what changes God is already making while also remembering the first rule named above, that usually a congregation will grant the new pastor one big change the first year without significant disagreement. The new pastor is trying to do both within the first year.

For me, an obvious strength of the congregation was its counter-cultural identity. Though sometimes acted out as contrariness for the sake of contrariness, it could be recovered, redeemed, properly understood, and rooted in Jesus Christ and Christ's kingdom, resulting in a way of life embodied counter to the predominant ways of this world. What was essential was helping the congregation re-root and recover its life together in the God we know in Christ.

Because the congregation was small, they might be more flexible, making consensus-building easier. It also meant that cultivating a sense of oneness and community might bear fruit much sooner than if I were working with a larger and more diverse church. And with a small church, when good things happen, there is little confusion that it comes from the grace of God instead of the congregation's power, wealth, or size.

There were other gifts to work with as well. The so-called "Charleston Tradition," like the other gifts in the church, needed a lot of pastoral work of recovery and healing, but it was definitely a gift God had given us. One

---

5. Berry, *Standing by Words*, 70. Berry's writings are an invaluable pastoral theology as one learns to see "congregation" every time Berry writes "land" or "farm." See Peterson, *Under the Unpredictable Plant*, 131; and Childress, "Proper Work."

other specific gift we had was that even though the 1970s bare-bones sanctuary multi-purpose space was not all that pleasant to the eye, it was beautiful to the ear—the acoustics for congregational singing were outstanding. I
remembered the words of a veteran front-line pastor from the civil rights
movement years before: "You show me a church that sings and I'll show you
a church on the move." Austin Heights was a singing church and those good
acoustics only helped make it better.

Here were places where God was already present and here was where I
made my big change: worship. The church already sang well and knew that
worship was about God rather than the individual. It was small and over-
whelmed, fragmented and exhausted, and its only renewal possible would
be found in God. But not just any God but the God we know in Christ as
Triune, the God known over time in the traditions of the Church. My hope
was that traditional liturgy would help transform isolated individuals into
the Body of Christ, a community of faith that was larger and deeper and
older than they were. As I talked to the congregation about these changes I
soon learned that they were hungry and thirsty for such change. They knew
they were missing something, but didn't know what.

This God we worship is not some generalized or spiritualized Deity
but the God known as Father, Son, and Holy Spirit. This God is perfect
communion, perfect relationship. The One God known as Father, Son, and
Holy Spirit practices community within the Godhead. And as the church
has taught for centuries we end up looking more like that which we adore.
The more we worship the God we know as Trinity the more we move from
discrete individuals to a community, a single Body of Christ. At the same
time, as we learn to practice a shared life with each other, we also come to
know this Trinitarian God in deeper and more profound ways.[6]

Furthermore, the gospel reminds us that salvation itself is a communal
affair. In Matthew 27:42, for example, Jesus is on the cross and the onlook-
ers shout "He saved others; he cannot save himself." And even though they
mean it as mocking, they speak the truth. Right here in this simple assertion, these mockers encapsulate what Mark Heim calls the transitive nature of
God's redemption. The one who brings salvation cannot deliver himself. This
is the way God works. Salvation, redemption is not an autonomous achievement. Always salvation is dependent on others. Heim calls this the "wonderful exchange" of atonement in which mutuality is the condition of salvation.[7]
Based then on the nature of God and what salvation is I believed then and

6. Charry, *By the Renewing of Your Mind*, 120–42. See also Cunningham, *These
Three are One*; Newman, *Untamed Hospitality*; and Marshall, *Joining the Dance*.

7. Heim, *Depth of the Riches*, 56–68.

still believe that my central pastoral task is helping form a shared life in Jesus Christ among a small band of Christians who live in an otherwise hyper-individualized society. Doing so has taken constant teaching, reinforcement, paying attention and making connections, persistence, and most importantly, Sunday morning worship focused and rooted in this Triune God.

My first Sunday we began ending worship with a benediction I first learned from the African-American church historian Vincent Harding, which begins, "Let's take each other's hands . . . Now look who you're holding hands with, and hold on tight! Because we're going to need each other this week" before proceeding into the traditional Aaronic blessing found in Numbers 6:24–26, "The LORD bless you and keep you; the LORD make his face to shine upon you, and be gracious to you; the LORD lift up his countenance upon you, and give you peace."[8]

Every Sunday for twenty-two years we have held hands and had this benediction. And several times over the years I've had church members in unexpected crisis tell me later, "When I first heard the news, I didn't know what to do or who to call. Then it hit me, who was I holding hands with Sunday? And that's who I called." I want my people to think in terms of God and each other, each other and God—that we can't have one without the other until it forms as habit, practice, and instinctive way of life. Now, there is a practical aspect to this. If our people are going to live the Christ-like life, then they had better do it as a body or else they'll never make it. Lone individuals trying to live faithfully cannot stand against sin, death, the Powers, and the overwhelming pressure of society. Both we and our people, as individuals, are easy pickings for the Powers of Death; they'll separate us, isolate us, dis-member us, pick us off one at a time and grind us down into the dust.

Only a community nurtured in the Triune God known in Jesus Christ, together worshiping, working, living, serving and witnessing in the same direction, seeking to cultivate the same habits in order to live for Christ can stand against the Powers. Community, the commonplace life, is the nature of the Triune God; it is the nature of salvation; it is the nature of the church and the Christian life; and it is the nature of simple survival. How we worship and whom we worship is no small thing.

After introducing the Benediction, I had a new member, who had joined the church the week after we had joined, make a large cross from local dogwood and hang it in the baptistry, providing the central focus for the sanctuary/multi-purpose room. Next I introduced the liturgical year

---

8. I recall that Vincent Harding said that he learned this benediction from his father who learned it from his father, and his father before that.

or calendar to the congregation with its colors and symbols and a rhythm based upon the life of Christ, along with reading Scripture and preaching based upon the Revised Common Lectionary. I soon revised the Sunday morning Order of Worship, incorporating more congregational responsive readings and prayers, seeking to increase a sense of communal participation rather than the older habit of isolated individuals who happen to show up at the same time on Sunday morning. We began to use the standard English translation of the Latin traditional *Sursum Corda* rite: "The Lord be with you. / And also with you. / Lift up your hearts. / We lift them unto the Lord." Then the congregation went to one another repeating "The Lord be you," responding with "And also with you."

Our church was already vigorously warm and inviting and loving. And we were comfortable with one another to the point of being casual. I wanted worship to gather us from being isolated individuals to becoming once again the Body of Christ, but I also wanted to remind us that the worship of the One True God was not something done carelessly. We were a church in which many would have been comfortable worshiping in pajamas, house-slippers, and sipping a cup of coffee, so I sought to move us to becoming intentional about what we were doing while retaining our warmth. In short, when we greeted and hugged one another I hoped that we would learn that our love was formed and rooted in God's love for us in Christ; instead of a simple "Good morning!" we learned to say "The Lord be with you." Furthermore, here was a greeting and liturgical practice dating back in one version or another to the third century so when we greeted one another we were joining with the Communion of the Saints, the whole church stretching across millennia and around the globe—something important for a small, tired, counter-cultural congregation to practice, learn, and remember.[9]

Each change in the liturgy was accompanied by much conversation and teaching, some of it in formal sessions held at the church but much of it occurring around kitchen tables or on porches. And over the years, I've learned that it is important to occasionally explain what and why we do something in worship while we're practicing it. The teaching task within a congregation never ends. I also learned another rule of thumb when changing worship: always accompany changes with the familiar, especially by singing favorite hymns. While we added a Corporate Confession we also invited prayer requests from the congregation. Both methods of prayer reinforced the sense that we were a single body of believers while also retaining warmth and comfort.

9. I am aware that the *Sursum Corda* is used in the Preface to the prayers before the Eucharist in the churches that observe traditional liturgies. However, my practice in leading a Baptist church is "one small step at a time."

There has been disagreement and conflict at times. When we moved the Lord's Supper from once a quarter to the first Sunday morning of the month, we had disagreement. The deacons had passed out the bread and cups to the seated, but we moved to the congregation coming forward, forming half-circles around the Table while the deacons served from the Table and then the people served one another. During one of the dialogue forums, one of my church members put it well: "When I have the bread or cup passed to me while I sit, I can think about Jesus and never have to pay attention to anyone else. When I come forward I notice everyone else." She thought this was a bad thing which interfered with her worship while this was exactly what I wanted to convey—this meal *is* about those other people; we are all in this together in Christ.

Early on I began to wear a clergy robe and stole when I led worship but I soon discovered that this was one step this congregation was not ready for, so I put it aside. Six or seven years later I re-introduced the practice, emphasizing that it was about worship and not about my own ego; in fact, it was the very opposite of my ego at stake. It said to us all that worship is not about me, my clothes, or my wishes. When I put on that robe and stole it's about God. This time the practice was welcomed.

Over the years my conviction about practicing a traditional liturgy on Sunday morning has become something to which I'm more committed than ever. The people coming through our doors for the first time on Sunday mornings know less and less about the Christian faith than people coming for the first time twenty years ago. Plus, we have less and less time to teach the faith than we used to. Only a small number avail themselves of the multiple opportunities for Christian formation and education in comparison to a generation ago, so I have to try to pack as much Christian formation and teaching into that one hour on Sunday morning when the Body of Christ is gathered together in one place. Therefore, every symbol, color, piece of music, reading, and movement needs to convey as much of the faith as possible in as many ways as possible. Traditional liturgy does that.

We had been at this for several years when one of our pillars-of-the-church suddenly went down with a massive heart attack and was transported to one of the major medical centers in Houston. For a week he lingered after surgery with the best medical care available. Nevertheless, it became apparent that he was not going to survive. On a Sunday morning I received a call that he wouldn't make it through the day and I had better come now. The deacons of the church led the morning worship with an extended time of prayer, while I went on to Houston, about a three hour drive away. As soon as worship ended most of the church loaded up and followed me down, and that afternoon about twenty-five of us gathered around him in the cardiac-care unit while the nurses disconnected hoses and machines. His brain-wave activity was already flat and slowly his heart-rate slowed and his breathing grew shallower as we prayed, read Scripture, and sang hymns.

The doctor pronounced him dead, and after lingering and hugging and crying for awhile, we began to make our way out. As I passed the supervising nurse, she turned to me and said, "I've never seen anything like this before from a church." And I mumbled something about how good a man he was and that we were going to miss him. She paused, grabbed my hand and said, "The Lord be with you!" and then reached over and hugged me. Every one of us immediately turned in response and said, "And also with you." No longer were we just a small, tired, grief-stricken band of Christians. We were surrounded by a cloud of witnesses, the Communion of the Saints, stretching across the centuries. Thanks be to God.

How and whom we worship is no small thing.

2

The Christian Year

Practicing the High Priesthood of Believers

MICHAEL D. SCIRETTI JR.

MANY BAPTIST CHRISTIANS HAVE been spiritually formed in churches that observed a reduced version of the Christian Year, possibly only celebrating Christmas and Easter. Today, a growing number of Baptist congregations choose to follow the Christian Year in worship, education, and mission. Yet even in churches that celebrate the Christian Calendar to some extent, misunderstanding remains concerning the meaning and purpose of the Christian Year. Over the course of the first three centuries of Christianity, the high festivals of the Christian Year emerged from the three ancient temple pilgrimage festivals that anchored the Jewish calendar.[1] *Sukkoth* (Tabernacles), with its twin themes of revelation and judgment soon after the ancient autumnal *Rosh Hashanah* (New Year), evolved into the feast of Epiphany—the manifestation of God at Christ's birth and baptism. *Pesach* (*Pascha* or Passover), already a central commemoration of Jews, easily evolved into the central Christian feast of Easter because of the suffering, death and resurrection that historically took place at this time of the Jewish year and which theologically celebrated Christ's passage (*pesach*) from

---

1. For example, after mentioning the importance of almsgiving every Sunday, Athanasius (d. 373) exhorted bishops to celebrate "three seasons each year: the Paschal feast . . . a feast at the end of the Fifty Days [Pentecost] and the New Year's feast [Epiphany]." In the Jewish calendar, New Year's Day was in the autumn and was associated with the enthronement of the king. However, for Athanasius the New Year occurred in January. In one of his Festal Letters, Athanasius relates Epiphany (January 6) with the Jewish festival of Tabernacles.

death to life.[2] *Shavuot* became the feast of Pentecost, celebrating the union of Spirit with matter and the birth of a new humanity. Finally, *Yom Kippur* (Day of Atonement), although not appearing in standard lists noting the correspondence of Jewish and Christian feasts, is hidden in plain sight—the atonement myth and ritual formed the basic template of Sunday worship that culminates in Holy Communion.

Rather than simply commemorating certain events in Jesus' life, the Christian Year has been used to initiate believers into the life, teachings and mission of Christ. As the Church's yearly calendar moves through one full cycle of the solar year, remembering the Christ event, so we too move through phases of awakening to divine light, resurrection into eternal life right now, and union with the Spirit of love—in order to be "ministers of reconciliation," people who embody God's light, life, and love in this world. To use language familiar to Baptists, the Christian Year can be a way of embracing the full meaning of the Protestant tenet of "the priesthood of believers." When we use the title "Christ," we enter the realm of the temple and its priesthood. According to the early Christians, Jesus was the Christ ("Anointed One"), the Great High Priest.[3] As those "in Christ," we have entered the high priesthood too. This means we have access to the heavenly holy of holies, a reality experienced in the *sanctuary*—of the church and of the heart.[4] Yet the high priesthood of believers also means that like Jesus we become incarnations and epiphanies of God in this world, healer-priests who continue Jesus' Jubilee mission. The Christian Year, for Baptists and all Christians, can facilitate this process of Christian formation. This chapter presents one Baptist's historical-theological interpretation of each of the major "seasons" of the Christian Year as it relates to the great "High Priesthood" of Jesus and the high priesthood of all believers.

From Temple to Christ:
Remembering the High Priesthood of Jesus

> For if Christ had not been born into flesh he would not have
> been baptized, which is the Theophany [Epiphany], he would

2. Although English-speakers do not easily ascertain the close relationship between *Pascha* and Easter, many other Western languages such as Italian, Spanish and French still use words derived from *Pascha*. Hickman et al., *New Handbook*, 20.

3. See Heb 3:1, 4:14—15:10, 10:19–25.

4. 1 Pet 2:5, 9; Rev 1:6, 5:10, 20:6. At the end of Revelation, the city descending from heaven is a perfect cube, which signifies the Holy of Holies. This heavenly Holy of Holies is accessible to all of God's servants.

not have been crucified [and risen], which is the Pascha, he would not have sent down the Spirit, which is the Pentecost.

~ John Chrysostom (d. 407)

Jesus of Nazareth was a faithful Jew who lived by the Jewish calendar. We see this clearly in the New Testament. We know he observed the Sabbath, even though he taught a more contemplative meaning of it. We also know he went on pilgrimages to Jerusalem with his family, such as when he was twelve years of age.[5] According to John, Jesus went to Jerusalem for Passover, Tabernacles, and Hanukkah.[6] The early followers of Jesus also continued to observe the Jewish calendar, e.g. Passover, Unleavened Bread, and Pentecost.[7] However, they soon established a new day of celebration—Sunday. For them it was the Day of Resurrection and Day One—not only of the week but of the new creation. As early as the first century, Sunday was the Lord's Day and was the day Christians celebrated the Lord's Supper.[8] According to Adolf Adam, both of these references are "essential to Sunday as the day commemorating the paschal mystery."[9] Thus, this day was not only a day to remember the resurrection of Jesus; it was also the Day of the Lord, the fulfillment of *Yom Kippur*, the Day of Atonement.[10] Early Christians interpreted the events that happened at *Pascha*—Christ's crucifixion, entombment, resurrection and later ascension—in light of the Day of Atonement.[11]

5. Luke 2:41–51.

6. Passover: John 2, 6, 12; unknown feast: John 5:1; Tabernacles: John 7; and Hanukkah: John 10:22.

7. Passover: 1 Cor 5:7–8; Unleavened Bread: Acts 20:6; and Pentecost: Acts 2, 20:16; 1 Cor 16:8.

8. The word *kyriakos* only appears in two places in the New Testament in reference to Christ—in Rev 1:10 (*kyriake hemera*, Lord's Day) and 1 Cor 11:20 (*kyriakon deipnon*, Lord's Supper).

9. Adam, *The Liturgical Year*, 40.

10. "The day of the Lord was the time when the Kingdom was established on earth . . . The Book of Revelation is a vision of the day: 'I was in the Spirit on the Lord's day . . . (Rev 1:10). John's vision describes the judgment, the coming of the Lord, and establishing the Kingdom on earth" (Barker, *Temple Themes*, 180–81). Each Sunday was a remembrance and recommitment to this vision of already "standing in the kingdom" and "seated with Christ in the heavenly places." See Mark 9:1; Eph 2:6.

11. These two festivals (*Pascha* and *Yom Kippur*) are based on the spring and autumn equinoxes respectively, which may have contributed to the conflation of themes. For the earliest Jewish Christians, their confession "Jesus is Lord" probably meant they believed Jesus was the incarnation of *YHWH*, the Son of *El Elyon* (God Most High, the Heavenly Father), just as Melchizedek in Gen 14 was Priest of *El Elyon*. Although mainstream scholarship might still contend Jesus never claimed to be the Messiah, a growing number of scholars are beginning to question this. Based on texts found at

Gathering Together

When Christianity is placed back into its original temple context, most notably the Day of Atonement, then the central themes of the life of Christ and the Christian Year emerge in their full splendor: incarnation and manifestation, sacrifice and resurrection, union and atonement. Each Sunday, celebrated as the Day of Atonement and the Lord's Day, we can experience these truths as the gathered community. The earliest Jewish Christians celebrated all of these at each worship gathering, but over the course of the first four centuries these great themes were divided out into seasons of the year: incarnation and manifestation were commemorated during the cycle we now know as Advent-Christmas-Epiphany, sacrifice and resurrection during Lent-Easter, union and atonement at Pentecost and beyond. Each of these cycles celebrate Jesus' "fulfillment" of the ancient Jewish pilgrimage festivals of *Sukkoth*, *Pascha*, and *Shavuot* in his High Priesthood ministry.

The Manifestation of God in Christ

The first cycle of the Christian Year, practiced as a meditation on the life and mission of Jesus, centers on the manifestation of God to humanity in Christ and thus could be called the *cycle of light*. The foundational themes for this cycle come from the Jewish festival of *Sukkoth*. The word *Sukkoth* literally means "booths" or "tabernacles." Through this festival, Rabbinic Judaism remembered the time when Israel wandered in the wilderness and dwelt in booths for shelter. Yet the more ancient understanding comes from priestly circles where the festival was related to judgment of evil, enthronement of the Anointed King, and the renewal of the Eternal Covenant—symbolized by the gift of promised rain in Zechariah 14:16–17. Rituals of blessing and drawing water, mixing water and wine, and procession of lights were also practiced.[12]

A brief review of the gospel texts suggested by the Revised Common Lectionary for the seasons of Advent, Christmas and Epiphany demonstrate how Christians have used these priestly themes and practices to interpret the Nativity and Epiphany. In Advent we are urged to wakefulness and *metanoia*

Qumran, such as the Melchizedek text, it is now clear that certain priestly Jewish circles were anticipating the return of the Melchizedek priest who would usher in the year of Jubilee around the very time Jesus began his ministry. When the gospels are read in light of such texts, it becomes likely that Jesus did understand himself to be this longed-for anointed one who would bring to completion the great Day of Atonement, the great Day of the Lord. At the very least, this is how early Jewish Christianity interpreted Jesus and his mission.

12. Cobb, "History of the Christian Year," 466.

for the coming of the Son of Man and God's kingdom.[13] We hear that Jesus will be the Anointed One as well as God-with-us.[14] Each Christmas we celebrate the birth of the "Firstborn."[15] We marvel how the Word and Light that was with God in the beginning has now "tabernacled" among us through God's Son, disclosing the heart of God.[16] We remember how the Firstborn emerged into the world with angels' song (outside the Temple where it should have been), was brought to the Temple to be presented as a babe, and went on pilgrimage to his Father's house (the Temple) at the age of twelve.[17]

While the manifestation of God to humanity was more secret and protected at the nativity and his first epiphany to the magi, this changes when Jesus begins his High Priestly mission of reconciliation and Jubilee that Christians mark with the beginning of Epiphany.[18] In Epiphany we observe Jesus' baptism by John, when the heavens opened and Jesus received a revelation and a word from God—"You are my Son, the Beloved."[19] After his baptism and wilderness ordeal, in Luke 4 Jesus reads from Isaiah 61, claiming that the Spirit was upon him and had anointed him to inaugurate the year of Jubilee.[20]

---

13. Advent means "coming." *Metanoia*, typically translated "repentance," literally means to "change (*meta*) your mind (*nous*)" or to "go beyond the mind." Year A: Matt 24:36–44; 3:1–2. Year B: Mark 13:24–37; 1:1–8; Year C: Luke 21:25–36; 3:1–6.

14. Year A: Matt 1:18–25. Year B: Luke 1:26–38. Year C: Luke 1:39–55.

15. When the Gospel of John says the Word "tabernacled" among us, he may be alluding to the rabbinical significance of *Sukkoth*, which early Christians related to Christ's birth. The phrase "Christ's Mass" comes from the Latin Western tradition.

16. Years A, B, C for Christmas: Luke 2:1–20; John 1:1–18.

17. Luke 2:22–40 (Year B), Luke 2:41–52 (Year C).

18. Each year the gospel reading from the lectionary for the Sunday of the Epiphany is Matt 2:1–12, the epiphany of God in Christ to the magi. Historically, the Epiphany first celebrated Jesus' baptism. The magi and their gifts are probably veiled allusions to Temple mysteries: gold, frankincense and myrrh. See Barker, *Christmas*, 118–19 and *Creation*, 233–34. The word *epiphany* means "manifestation," and so the celebration of Epiphany is the culmination of the first cycle of the Christian Year—the manifestation of God.

19. Matt 3:13–17 (Year A), Mark 1:4–11 (Year B), Luke 3:15–17, 21–22 (Year C). According to Syriac scholar Gabriele Winkler, the earliest layer of Epiphany centered on Jesus' pneumatic birth in the Jordan River where, according to Syrian and Armenian texts, the Spirit rested on him and the heavenly voice and fire manifest the moment of his birth as the Son of God. See Winkler, "Appearance of the Light," 330. Eastern Christianity continues the practice of blessing the water at Epiphany (a *Sukkoth* practice), in association with the baptism of Jesus. See Barker, *The Gate of Heaven*, 82–86.

20. Luke 4:14–21 (Year C). In the Qumran Melchizedek text (11QMelch), Isaiah 61 is also applied to the heavenly High Priest Melchizedek, the incarnation of the Lord, who will usher in the year of Jubilee that culminates in the great Day of Atonement. It is likely that Jesus knew of this Qumran document or a similar prophecy, and that he believed he was fulfilling it in his fourfold mission of teaching, healing, empowering, and casting a vision of God's Kingdom.

Throughout the rest of Epiphany we see the multifaceted mission of Jesus at work: we watch as Jesus transforms water into wine, wonder about John's testimony of the anointed Lamb and Son of God who has come to make atonement, hear Jesus call his first disciples, listen to Jesus teach and proclaim the Good News of God's Kingdom for those who experience *metanoia*, marvel at his healings and exorcisms, attend to his contemplative wisdom teaching (the beatitudes, being salt and light), before the final epiphany of his glory at the Transfiguration where Peter wishes to set up "booths," not realizing that he is in the presence of the fulfillment of *Sukkoth*.[21]

The *Pascha* of Christ, from Death to Life

The second cycle of the Christian Year, which might be called the *cycle of life*, centers on Jesus' teaching and personal experience of the "paschal mystery"—the secret of dying and rising. The foundational themes for this season come from the Jewish festival of *Pesach* or *Pascha*, which also provides the cultic context for the final days of Jesus' High Priestly earthly mission of atonement and reconciliation. The "paschal mystery" is the heart of the Christian liturgical year. From this center the rest of the liturgical year expanded and grew.[22] The word *pascha* literally means "passage" and was associated with the "passage" of the angel of death over the Hebrew houses marked with the blood from the sacrificed lamb (the "passover" of Ex 12) as well as the "passage" of the Hebrews through the Red Sea (Ex 14). Some believed the world was created on this day and that the Anointed One would come on it.[23] In the first century many were hoping and expecting

21. Year A: John 1:29–42, Matt 4:12–23; 5:1–20 and depending on the year Matt 5:21–48 (interior Judaism); 6:24–34 (seeking the kingdom first); and 7:21–29 (the good foundation of Jesus' teaching). Year B: John 1:43–51; Mark 1:14–39 and depending on the year Mark 1:40–55 (healing the leper); 2:1–2 (healing the paralytic); and 2:13–22 (healing "sick" sinners, feasting and fasting, new and old wineskins). Year C: John 2:1–11, Luke 4:21–30; 5:1–11 and depending on the year Luke 6:17–26 (teaching & healing, blessings & woes); 6:27–38 (loving enemies); 6:39–49 (parables about inner condition of heart; good foundation); 7:1–10 (healing and faith and spiritual authority). The last Sunday of Epiphany is Transfiguration Sunday: Matt 17:1–9 (Year A); Mark 9:2–9 (Year B); Luke 9:28–43 (Year C).

22. Historically, it is difficult to unravel the last weeks of Jesus' life because of the various calendar systems used in the first century. In the synoptic chronology Jesus celebrates a Passover feast on 14 Nisan and crucified on 15 Nisan, but the Johannine chronology places the crucifixion on 14 Nisan. Paul seems to adhere to this latter Johannine tradition (1 Cor 5:7), and the evolution of the Christian *Pascha* presupposes it.

23. In addition to these three events, the binding of Isaac was also remembered on this day ("Poem of the Four Nights" in the Palestinian Targum). See Talley, *Origins*, 3.

the Messiah's imminent *advent*; thus in *Pascha* memory and hope come to-gether. In this theological context Jesus died on the Jewish *Pascha*, fulfilling the earliest hopes and dreams of many Jews who saw in his death both the fulfillment of *Pascha* and *Yom Kippur*.

A cursory look at the gospel texts suggested by the Lectionary for the seasons of Lent and Easter demonstrate how Christians have used these paschal themes and practices to interpret the Christian *Pascha*. In Lent[24] we first overhear Satan tempting Jesus to doubt the Sonship he experienced at his baptism and to abandon his mission.[25] Rising victorious, Jesus begins teaching his transformative wisdom concerning the passage from death to life.[26] Over the course of Lent in Year A, Jesus teaches about being born from above in order to see and enter God's kingdom, thirsting for the inner waters of eternal life, moving from blindness to sight, and passing from death to new life.[27] In Year B we see Jesus cleansing the Temple when the Jewish *Pascha* was approaching, using a whipping motion as was done on the Day of Atonement by the high priest.[28] We also overhear him teaching how the temple of his being would be destroyed but rise again, and how trust in the Son leads to eternal life and the salvation of the *kosmos* (world). On his final temple pilgrimage to *Pascha*, we begin to understand the contemplative meaning of the paschal mystery: one must die in order to be born into true

---

24. The word *Lent* means "lengthen," referring to the lengthening of days in Spring. It has come to be used for the forty days (excluding Sundays) preceding Easter. To call this season *Lent* is to use a much later way of identifying an ancient practice of preparing for the Christian *Pascha*, which included extended fasting and the preparation for the baptism of catechumens. In Greek it is known as *Tessarakoste* while in Latin it is *Quadragesima*; both mean "fortieth." This preparatory season became formal at the Council of Nicaea, but it was practiced previously in various ways. The number forty was later chosen because of Christ's fast in the wilderness, although this kind of fast was originally related to Epiphany and not *Pascha* since Jesus fasted immediately after his baptism and not prior to his crucifixion. The length varied originally: sometimes including Sundays and sometimes excluding Saturdays and Sundays, in some places including and some places excluding Holy Week. In the West, Lent begins with Ash Wednesday, excludes Sundays, but includes Holy Week. In the East, Lent begins on the previous Monday, includes Sundays, but ends the Friday before Palm Sunday and thus does not include Holy Week.

25. Matt 4:1–11 (Year A); Mark 1:9–15 (Year B); Luke 4:1–13 (Year C).

26. John 3:1–7 (Year A); 8:31–38 (Year B); 13:31–35 (Year C).

27. Year A: John 3:1–7; 4:5–42; 9:1–41; 11:1–45. The epistle readings in Year A help us deepen our understanding of this *pascha* from darkness to light (Eph 5:8–14) and from the flesh to Spirit (Rom 8:6–11).

28. Barker, *Temple Themes*, 179.

life.[29] Finally, in Year C Jesus teaches us about *metanoia* through his parables and how consciously preparing for death is part of the paschal process.[30]

The climax of the Christian *Pascha* is a remembrance (*zkr* in Hebrew, *anamnesis* in Greek) of the last week of Jesus' life. In this Holy Week, Christians are immersed into the climactic fulfillment of Jesus' atoning self-sacrifice.[31] Holy Week begins with Jesus' planned, anti-imperial entry into Jerusalem; people waving palm branches greet him as he makes his way to the Temple. The gospel writers interpreted this event through the lens of *Sukkoth*—this was the time for the enthronement of the coming Anointed Davidic King.[32] The Revised Common Lectionary uses the Gospel of John for the rest of Holy Week.[33] On Monday we see Mary anointing Jesus for his

29. Year B: John 2:13–22; 3:14–21; 12:20–33. The epistle reading for the final Sunday before Palm/Passion Sunday is Heb 5:5–10, which summarizes the High Priestly mission of Jesus.

30. Year C: Luke 13:1–9; 15:1–3, 11b–32; John 12:1–8. In Luke 15, the *metanoia* moment is when the younger son "comes into himself" and begins the return journey to the father who welcomes him home as one who has journeyed from death to life. In John 12, Mary anoints Jesus six days before *Pascha*, and challenges Judas' thinking about the matter. The epistle readings for the two Sundays prior to Palm/Passion Sunday are 2 Cor 5:16–21 and Phil 3:4b–14. These texts continue the themes of old and new creation, reconciliation, suffering, and resurrection.

31. Some churches observe the Sunday prior to Easter as "Passion Sunday" (emphasizing the passion and death of Jesus) while others observe it as "Palm Sunday" (commemorating the anti-imperial entry of Jesus into Jerusalem). Both have ancient precedent. What we know of Holy Week can be traced at least as far back as fourth-century Jerusalem which, because of the many pilgrims flooding the Holy City each year during the days leading up to the Christian *Pascha*, was easily able to provide enhanced worship experiences by linking the final events of Jesus' life with the days of the week and historical places in which his last days occurred. In fourth-century Jerusalem, "Palm Sunday" began with a palm procession from the Mount of Olives back into city in the afternoon. The practice was soon imitated in other areas, always beginning in some place outside the main church. Also in Jerusalem, "Good Friday" was kept as a commemoration of the Cross—through the veneration of a relic of the cross in Jerusalem, along with readings and hymns in the afternoon.

32. Matt 21:1–11 (Year A); Mark 11:1–11 or John 12:12–16 (Year B); Luke 19:28–40 (Year C).

33. Visitors to Jerusalem in the fourth century would have been immersed in Matthew's description of Jesus' final days. Those in Alexandria would have closely followed Mark's account. According to Talley, the Eastern Orthodox liturgy was greatly influenced by both of these traditions. From Jerusalem, the Byzantines inherited their gospel readings for the Great Week from Matthew, and from Alexandria the practice of Lazarus Saturday and Palm Sunday. See Talley, *Origins*, 213. Many Baptist churches have experimented with various ways of observing Holy Week. For example, Freemason Street Baptist Church (Norfolk, VA) has observed Holy Week services for over eighty-five years and, for the past several decades, has partnered with a local Epworth United Methodist Church for daily worship and fellowship.

burial. On Tuesday, we hear him teaching again how the *pascha* from death to life is like a grain of wheat that must die to bear fruit. On Wednesday we watch as Jesus foretells his betrayal at the Last Supper and releases Judas to begin what is inevitable. Knowing that death is approaching, on Holy Thursday Jesus demonstrates his love for his disciples at the Last Supper and gives them the new commandment to love one another.[34] On Good Friday, we follow Jesus as he is betrayed, arrested, denied by Peter, questioned by the high priest, sentenced to death, crucified and buried. The Epistle for Good Friday transmits the ancient Jewish and priestly understanding of this event as the fulfillment of *Yom Kippur*.[35] On Holy Saturday, we watch with Mary Magdalene as Jesus is buried, and at the Easter Vigil—the "mother of all vigils" according to Augustine—the history of salvation is rehearsed before culminating in the reading of the good news of the resurrection and the celebration of baptism and holy communion.[36] With the joy and celebration of Easter morning, the Christian *Pascha* cycle—passing from death to life—is complete.[37]

The Union of Spirit and Flesh by Christ

The third cycle of the Christian Year centers on the loving union of Spirit and flesh—in Christ (originally at his baptism) but now in his disciples at Pentecost—and therefore might be called the *cycle of love*. The foundational themes for this season come from the Jewish festival of *Shavuot* or Pentecost. The Hebrew root of the festival's name, *sh-b-e*, has multiple connotations

34. Maundy Thursday, a commemoration of the Last Supper, receives its name from Jesus' new commandment to his disciples as it appears in Latin: *Mandatum novum do vobis ut diligatis invicem sicut dilexi vos*—"A new commandment I give to you, that you love one another as I have loved you" (John 13:34).

35. There are two options for the Epistle Reading: Heb 10:19–22 or Heb 4:14–16; 5:7–9. Both use imagery derived from the Day of Atonement myth and practice to interpret the life and death of Jesus, the Great High Priest.

36. Holy Saturday: Matt 27:57–66 (following the Byzantine lectionary) and John 19:38–42. The Old Testament readings for the Easter Vigil clearly demonstrate the paschal mystery of passing from death to life and retain readings used for the Jewish *Pascha*. This is especially true for the fourth-century Jerusalem liturgy. See Talley, *Origins*, 48–49. Gospel readings for Easter morning: John 20:1–18 or Matt 28:1–10 (Year A); Mark 16:1–8 (Year B); Luke 24:1–12 (Year C). The readings for the Easter Vigil could be incorporated into Easter sunrise services, with which Baptists might be more familiar.

37. *Easter* comes from "Eostre," the name of a Germanic dawn goddess celebrated in April by Anglo-Saxons prior to the eighth century AD. In Semitic, Romance, Celtic, and Germanic languages, Christians use some version of *Pascha*.

of oath, testimony, covenant, and week.[38] The Torah reading for the Jewish festival comes from Exodus 19 (the Sinai theophany to Moses) and the Prophetic reading comes from Ezekiel 1 and 10 (the *merkavah* theophany to Ezekiel). In the former, the Jewish people are betrothed to God—in the midst of wind and fire—in order to become "a priestly kingdom and a holy nation." In the latter, the exiled prophet-priest beholds the *merkavah* (Throne of God), the fiery Spirit in the midst of the thunderous cherubim, and a rainbow—the only other appearance of a rainbow mentioned after the Covenant with Noah.[39] Based on these theophanies that took place on *Shavuot*, various traditions in ancient Jewish spirituality linked *Shavuot* "with the perception of the Covenant between heaven and earth as a pact or oath of betrothal, matrimony, and sacred conjugality in the supernal worlds."[40] In this light, *Shavuot* or Pentecost is a Covenant of marriage between heaven and earth, divinity and humanity, spirit and flesh. All of these images are foundational for an understanding of the Christian Pentecost.[41]

During the Great Fifty Days of Easter, also known as the Season of Pentecost (50th), we hear from the Resurrected Christ almost exclusively from the Gospel of John. The first two weeks of the season are post-resurrection appearances. First, Jesus reappears to his disciples, speaking *shalom* to them. Breathing on them, he imparts the Divine Breath/Spirit so that they might begin their priestly ministry of forgiveness.[42] On the journey to Emmaus we encounter the hidden Christ—who enlightens our hearts by

38. Elior, *The Three Temples*, 226. The Book of *Jubilees* associates *Shavuot* with the fifteenth of the third month, relating it to the beginning of the Rainbow Covenant with Noah and the angels, the Covenant between the Pieces made with Abraham, and culminating with the Sinai Covenant with Moses. The Covenant was to be renewed annually in 3rd month and with first fruits of wheat harvest.

39. His vision, according to Michael Chyutin, was on the "eve of Shavuot, the fourteenth of the third month, or on the festival itself, on the fifteenth, as believed by the members of the Qumran sect." *Shavuot* is "the festival of pilgrimage to the earthly Temple which the exiled prophet-priest transformed into a heavenly Chariot Throne." See ibid., 155.

40. Ibid., 157–58. "These traditions are associated with the time of the theophany at Shavuot, that is, with the theophany at Sinai, with Ezekiel's Merkavah and the Chariot Throne of the cherubim in the Holy of Holies. Shavuot, one of the three pilgrimage festivals, is explicitly associated with the first fruits and thereby with fertility and the cycle of crops and procreation" (ibid.).

41. In Ezek 2, after the *merkavah* vision, the Lord speaks to Ezekiel and the Spirit enters him. This results in Ezekiel "standing to his feet" (resurrection imagery) and being called to go to Israel, prophesy and speak the Lord's words. In Ezek 10, the cherubim give fire. A case could be made that the original Christian Pentecost was the experience of the *merkavah*, with Christianity being one early expression of ancient Jewish *merkavah* mysticism. See deConick, "What is Early Jewish and Christian Mysticism?," 1–24.

42. John 20:19–31 (Easter 1 for Years A, B, C).

opening the scriptures concerning the paschal mystery and opens our eyes at the breaking of bread—and we leave filled with love to proclaim *metanoia* and forgiveness to the nations.[43] On the seashore, after eating bread and fish with the risen Lord, we overhear Jesus asking Peter if he loves him and, like Peter, we receive Christ's commission to minister out of the love with which we are capable.[44] In the remaining weeks of this season, we listen to Jesus' teachings about life and love anew—through the prism of the Resurrected Christ: the Good Shepherd through whom we receive abundant life and the Living Word who embodies the way, truth, and life. As the season of love moves towards its ultimate fulfillment at Pentecost, we are invited into the loving union of the Trinity and encouraged to manifest the same love to one another that Christ did for us.[45]

In the arc of the Christian Year, these are Jesus' post-resurrection teachings before his ascension. Since these intimate encounters with Jesus are in the context of life and love, Jesus' ascension was seen as the "day the bridegroom was taken away."[46] For Ascension, the lectionary uses the same readings all three years. In Acts 1 the resurrected Christ teaches the apostles during the forty days of Easter/Pentecost about God's kingdom, and he commands them to wait in Jerusalem to receive the baptism with the Spirit in a few days. In the final verses of Luke, the living Christ further teaches his disciples about the paschal mystery before telling them they will soon be "clothed with power from on high"—priestly vesting imagery. As the Great High Priest, Jesus blesses them with grace and peace, and he ascends into the heavens—like the high priest on *Yom Kippur* who ascended through the clouds of incense as he entered into the Holy of Holies.[47] The Gospel ends by stating, "They were continually in the Temple blessing God."

43. Luke 24:13–48 (Year A and B).

44. John 21:1–19 (Year C).

45. John 14:15–21 (Year A); John 15:1–17 (Year B); John 13:31–35; 14:23–29 (Year C). The epistle readings for this cycle support the life and love themes in the context of the atoning sacrifice of Christ and our continuing of Jesus' ministry of reconciliation of all things. For more, see the final section of this chapter. In the Christian West, Holy Trinity Sunday follows the Pentecost Sunday.

46. Talley, *Origins*, 66. Originally, Ascension was celebrated on Easter Day or the fiftieth day. Some early traditions link the ascension with the resurrection (Luke 24:50–53; John 20:21–22; *Barn.* 15:9). In the second half of the fourth century, Ascension was commemorated as a separate historical event on the fortieth day and the descent of the Spirit on the fiftieth. These developments were the result of following the chronology of Acts, the development of a theology of the Spirit by the Cappadocians in the fourth century, and the influence of holy sites in Jerusalem. After its split from Pentecost, fasting was permitted after the commemoration of Ascension. See Cobb, "History of the Christian Year," 463.

47. In light of John 20 (the reading for Easter 1 in all three years), we know the

The cycles of light, life, and love culminate in the Day of Pentecost—the union of Spirit and flesh as well as the birth of a new humanity in Christ. Each year Acts 2 is read, with its subtle hints of Moses' and Ezekiel's theophanies of wind and fire.[48] Again, as in most of the Easter/Pentecost season, the Gospel readings come from John, in which Jesus discusses the coming Spirit of Truth, commissions his disciples with a ministry of witness and reconciliation, and blesses them with his peace.[49] As the season of Easter/Pentecost is lived in the light of Christ's passage from death to life that makes true love possible, so the season after Pentecost (about half of the Christian Year) is lived in the afterglow of this sacred union of Spirit and flesh.

From Christ to Christian:
Entering the High Priesthood of Believers

> What a multitude of high festivals there are in each of the mysteries of Christ; all of which have one completion, namely my perfection and return to the first condition of Adam.
>
> ~ Gregory of Nazianzus (d. 389)

According to this great pastor-theologian, all of the great "high festivals" of the Christian Year have one goal: our return to the completion of Adam, who was the first great high priest in Eden—the Lord's Temple. But

---

living Christ spoke words of peace, one of the main blessings in the high priestly payer found in Num 6:24–26: "The Lord bless you and keep you; the Lord make his face to shine upon you, and be gracious to you; the Lord lift up his countenance upon you, and give you peace." Might it be we are meant to believe this is how Christ blessed his disciples as he left them? Margaret Barker elucidates the fact that these same blessings form a central place in the salutations of Paul found in all of the letters attributed to the apostle, and thus were central to early Jewish Christianity: "Grace to you and peace." See Rom 1:5; 1 Cor 1:3; 2 Cor 1:2; Gal 1:3; Eph 1:2; Phil 1:2; Col 1:2; 1 Thess 1:1; 2 Thess 1:2; 1 Tim 1:2; 2 Tim 1:2; Titus 1:4; and Phlm 1:4. These blessings are also found together in 1 Pet 1:2; 2 Pet 1:2; Jude 1:4 (with mercy in the place of grace); and Rev 1:4. In Jesus the Christ, the Great High Priest, they were experiencing the fulfillment of the great high priestly blessing.

48. In Year A Num 11:24–30 can be read, and we hear how the Lord filled seventy elders in the Tabernacle with the same Spirit that was upon Moses, leading to his hope that "all the Lord's people were prophets, and that the Lord would put his Spirit on them!" In Year B Ezek 37 is the alternative reading, in which at the Lord's command Ezekiel prophesies to dry bones in a valley to come together, be clothed with flesh, receive breath, and stand to their feet (resurrection imagery). The Lord says he will raise his people and put his Spirit within them. In Year C Gen 11 can be read, which casts Pentecost as a reversal of the effects of building the Tower of Babel.

49. John 20:19–23 or John 7:37–39 (Year A); John 15:26–27; 16:4b-15 (Year B); John 14:8–17, 25–27 (Year C).

the question arises—How do these festivals facilitate our "completion" and "return"? Two images for the Christian Year can help answer this question: the circle and the spiral. The Christian Year is circular: each and every year we move through the cycles of light (Advent-Epiphany), life (Lent-Easter) and love (Easter/Pentecost and beyond) as we move around the wheel of the Christian Year.[50] However, we are not meant to merely repeat the same rites and practices of the previous year. The ancients spoke of spiritual transformation as *helikos tropon* ("in the manner of a spiral"). So in following the Christian Year, we remember the life of Jesus in time; but as we move through time as transformed by the paschal mystery, we progress through ever-deepening cycles of awakening to divine light within and around us, interior soul surrender in order to rise to eternal life now, and uniting with the Spirit of love—that we might continue the ministry of reconciliation as the Body of Christ in this world.

From this standpoint, the Lectionary from Advent to Pentecost leads us into a *lectio divina* ("holy reading") of the life and mission of Jesus so that the cycles of manifestation, resurrection, and union become an inner roadmap for the Christian spiritual pilgrimage.[51] In *lectio divina* we come to see that the scriptures are not only about Christ but also about us. Similarly, a *lectio divina* of the Christian Year leads to the discovery that Jesus' life can become a teaching (*theoria*) as well as a practice (*praxis*), a spiritual exercise whereby we are transformed into the likeness of Christ the second Adam.[52] As it went for Christ, so it must go for us. Although often interpreted as only relating to some future event, early Christian tradition is emphatic that the

50. According to Thomas Keating: "The whole panorama of the mysteries of Jesus' life is condensed in a single Eucharistic celebration. The Liturgical Year divides up all that is contained in that single explosion of divine light, life and love so that we can more easily assimilate the significance of these theological ideas by experiencing them one by one" (Keating, *The Mystery of Christ*, 6).

51. The root word of *lectionary* is *lectio*, and the early Christian practice of *lectio divina* was a way one read (*lectio*) and reflected (*meditatio*) on scripture, responded to it in prayer (*oratia*), and rested in God (*contemplatio*), allowing God to use the images of the scripture to do a hidden, interior work.

52. "Is the problem of sacred history in the Christian calendar so different from the problem of meditating on sacred history in the Bible and proclaiming it day in and day out in the liturgy of the word?" (Taft, "The Liturgical Year," 18). According to Cynthia Bourgeault, "Jesus' life . . . is a sacrament: a mystery that draws us deeply into itself and, when rightly approached, conveys an actual spiritual energy empowering us to follow the path that his teachings have laid out. This sacramental life of Jesus rests on four cornerstones which are both historical events and cosmic realities: his incarnation, passion, resurrection, and ascension. Together they compose the foundation of the Christian mystical and devotional life, and to open oneself fully to the meaning of these great mysteries is to be able to read the inner roadmap of the Christian path" (Bourgeault, *The Wisdom Jesus*, 92).

"coming of Christ" is also through us—we are the new temple and priest-hood, we are the Body of Christ now here on earth.[53] Thus Christ becomes a *double revelation*, revealing who God is as well as what we are to be.[54] Like the Christian Scriptures, the whole point of the Christian Year is to usher in the New Age and the New Human through us, for humanity to return to the perfection and oneness of Adam.[55]

In this light Advent is not simply a preparation for the coming of Christ 2000 years ago or in some imminent or distant future, but a preparation for his spiritual coming within us that will complete our hope for fulfillment.[56] Christmas is not only celebrating the birth of Christ in Bethlehem, but the

53. Christians throughout the centuries have intuited from these sayings timeless truth relevant for contemporary living. Understood contemplatively, "watchfulness" is only possible if we are also in the process of "awakening." If we are awake, re-oriented to God, we are able to watch for our Master's appearance and do God's will in our daily lives. The Divine Presence is active and working, but if our hearts are not awake we will not perceive it. If we are not attentive to our inner being, the outer events around us, and our reactions to them, we will inevitably "fall asleep" and "forget God." When we practice "watchfulness" from the place of an awakened heart, we will intuitively know what to do in the present moment. The "watcher" and "worker" for the kingdom of God will unite to welcome the coming of the Anointed One.

54. According to Taft, Christ is "the personalization of all that went before, and the recapitulation and completion and model and foretaste of all that will ever be. As such, he is not just the mystery of the Father's love for us, 'image of the unseen God' (Col 1:15); he is also the revelation of what we are to be (1 Cor 15:49; 2 Cor 3:18; Rom 8:29). His life is the story of entering sinful humanity and returning it to the Father through the cross, a return that was accepted and crowned in Christ's deliverance and exalta-tion (Phil 2:5ff). And this same story, as we have seen, is also presented as the story of everyone, the archetype of our experience of returning to God through a life of death to self lived after the pattern Christ showed us . . . The whole point of the New Testament rewrite of Christ's life is to make it speak to this new awareness: that the new age was to be not a quick end but a new holy history . . . the eschaton is not a time or a thing, it is a person, the new Adam, Jesus Christ (2 Cor 5:13–19)—or rather, his life in us (Gal 2:20)" (Taft, "The Liturgical Year," 21–22).

55. Taft also quotes Paul Regan in this regard: "The death and resurrection of Jesus brings to fulfillment not only history but creation as well . . . In him, man and the world have, for the first time, come to be what they were meant to be. Hence the eschatological 'last days' join the protohistorical 'first days.' The kingdom is the garden. Christ is Adam. The eschaton is the Sabbath; the day on which God rests from his work and delights in its perfection" (Regan, "Pneumatological and Eschatological Aspects," 346–47).

56. In the historical evolution of the liturgical year, Advent developed last. Connell tentatively suggests "in some places the period that became the pre-Christmas Advent may well have been originally a time of preparation for Epiphany baptism, a period of preparation reorganized and reinterpreted when the December 25 feast of Christmas, a latecomer in the West outside of Rome, was finally accepted" (M. Johnson, *Between Memory and Hope*, xxiii).

birth of the New Human—the Christ Self—within each believer.[57] More than merely remembering magi visiting Jesus or his baptism in the Jordan, Epiphany celebrates the dawning manifestation of God in us—through our birth into new life, symbolized in our own baptism.[58] Thus, the first great cycle of the Christian Year concerns the preparation, birth, and manifestation of God in those who are becoming the New Humanity, the Body of Christ on earth, priests and mediators between Spirit and flesh.[59]

Through Lent, we intentionally enter a time of wilderness, a time of purgation, to "reflect on, affirm, remember, and reclaim that baptism" which symbolized our intention to "pass over" (*pascha*) from the *kosmos* into the life of the kingdom of God right now, for we are currently entering the New Age (the heavenly Holy of Holies) through Christ.[60] Thus, what

57. Christmas is not about baby Jesus in a manger "but *our* baptismal birth in the adult Christ *today* as He is born anew in us" (ibid., xii, 23). Salvation history does not go on in the sense that we are somehow making Christ's birth present again at Christmas. Rather, what is "present is *our* being born anew in Christ, *our* entrance into new life through this coming of God to us *now*" (Taft, "The Liturgical Year," 22).

58. For the Sundays that follow, the Revised Common Lectionary uses readings from 1 Corinthians to help us practice being the transformed body of Christ in the world. Like *Sukkoth* and its allusions to sacred marriage, both Christmas and Epiphany celebrate two unions, which prefigure the gift of Pentecost: the marriage of humanity and divinity, both in Christ and in Christians. During Epiphany, three manifestations are remembered: (1) of divinity in humanity, made to the Gentiles and symbolized by the magi; (2) of divinity in humanity, made to the Jews at Jesus' baptism; and (3) of humanity divinized, like water into wine at Cana. Historically, after *Pascha* and Pentecost, Epiphany is the oldest Christian celebration, pre-dating Christmas by one or two centuries. Originally, Epiphany was a dual celebration of Jesus' birth and baptism. Only later (possibly with the popularity of the gospels of Matthew and Luke) did the infancy account of Jesus' birth lead to a separation of these earliest themes of Epiphany into two distinct celebrations—Christmas on December 25 and Epiphany on January 6, the two dates suggested for Jesus' birth based on the date of his conception/death on March 25 or April 6.

59. This is beautifully portrayed by Jeremy Taylor: "After the holy Jesus was baptised, and had prayed, the heavens opened, the Holy Ghost descended, and a voice from heaven proclaimed him to be the Son of God, and the one in whom the Father was well pleased; and the same ointment that was cast upon the head of our High Priest, went unto his beard, and thence fell to the borders of his garment; for as Christ, our head, felt this effect in manifestation, so the church believes God does to her, and to her meanest children, in the susception of the holy rites of baptism in right, apt, and holy dispositions" (quoted in Porter, "Day of the Lord," 56).

60. Lent is "about *our* annual retreat, our annual re-entry into the catechumenate and order of penitents in order to reflect on, affirm, remember, and reclaim that baptism" (M. Johnson, *Between Memory and Hope*, xii). In contrast to popular assumption, recent liturgical scholarship has demonstrated that the origins of Lent are not based within "a gradual backwards development of the short preparatory and purificatory fast held before the annual celebration of Pascha." Rather, according to Johnson,

English-speakers call Easter is not only about an empty tomb in Jerusalem around 2000 years ago but "*our* death and resurrection in Christ *today*, our passover from death to life in his passover, through water and the Holy Spirit in baptism."[61] Thus, the second great cycle of the Christian Year facilitates our dying to egoic living according to the values of the *kosmos*, the re-alignment of our hearts according to the values of God's kingdom, so that we might live as resurrected ones today.[62]

As the Easter season progresses and we are immersed in the light, life, and love of God through contemplation of the lectionary readings, we are being fully prepared for the grace of Pentecost. When celebrating the 50th day of Pentecost, Christians have tended to emphasize only the birthday of the church, following rabbinic tradition that interprets the Lord's Covenant with Moses at Sinai as the time when Israel was born. However, the ancient priestly tradition understood Pentecost to be a celebration of the betrothal of Israel to the Lord. Therefore, the Christian Pentecost celebrates the sacred marriage between the divine and human, out of which the birth of the New Humanity issues.[63] Thus, the third great cycle of the Christian Year culminates in the Day of Pentecost, a marital covenant between Spirit and flesh, resulting in the birth of the New Humanity in Christ in the summer season of love.

The Christian Year, understood and practiced contemplatively, becomes an indispensable tool for facilitating the formation of Christians—*anointed*

---

summarizing Thomas Talley, the forty-day observance is based in the Alexandrian tradition where "the forty-day prebaptismal fast" was "associated with Jesus' temptation in the wilderness (see Mark 1:12–13), commencing on January 6, led to the celebration of baptism six weeks later on the sixth day of the sixth week of this fast (i.e., sometime in mid-February)" (M. Johnson, *Between Memory and Hope*, xix). Once the decision was made to observe the Christian *Pascha* only on a Sunday (the day of resurrection)—regardless of the day of the Jewish *Pascha*—and extend a fast backwards to Friday (the day of crucifixion), the seeds were planted for the further "refraction of the single mystery of redemption into a series of commemorations of discrete historical moments in that mystery" (Talley, *Origins*, 39). The current practice of Lent appears to be a blending of these two traditions coming from Alexandria and Jerusalem.

61. Johnson, *Between Memory and Hope*, xii. Taft says Easter is the "reawakening here and now of my baptismal death and resurrection in Christ" ("The Liturgical Year," 23).

62. Using the imagery from Eph 5:14, as we awaken to God's light we begin to stand up (resurrection) out of those things that lead to death, which leads to enlightenment: "Wake up, sleeper. Rise from the dead and Christ will shine on you."

63. Incidentally, in the Jewish tradition during this Pentecost season (what Christians call the Great Fifty Days), the Song of Solomon and the Book of Ruth are read—books that reflect a high view of both physical and spiritual love. Song of Solomon is read on the seventh day of *Pesach* (21 Nisan). Ruth is read on the actual day of Pentecost (15 Sivan). Ruth was betrothed to Boaz during the season of *Shavuot*/Pentecost.

ones, royal priests.[64] It provides both a *vision* and a *path* of initiation into high priestly service.[65] Historically, there have been two central ways to initiate people into this path: baptism and catechesis. In the ancient Church across various regions, there were three preeminent times to practice baptism: Epiphany, *Pascha* and Pentecost.[66] As we have seen, each of these "high festivals" encapsulates a major movement in the arc of becoming a Christian in this world. These are "high and holy" times for Baptists to also practice baptism. For a group of Christians that are defined by the practice of believers baptism, Baptists have historically been known for a very weak theology of baptism. Administering baptism on or around these days—as ways for the baptized to enter more deeply into these mysteries—could greatly enrich a Baptist theology and practice of baptism as more than "just a symbol."[67]

64. Robert Taft summarizes the ramifications of such a vision for those entering into the high priesthood of Christ: "Christian vision is rooted in the gradually acquired realization of the Apostolic Church that the parousia was not imminent, and that the eschatological, definitive victory won by Christ must be repeated in each one of us, until the end of time. And since Christ is both model and source of this struggle, the New Testament presents both his victory and his cult of the Father as ours; just as we have died and risen with him . . . so too it is we who have become a new creation . . . a new circumcision . . . a new temple . . . a new sacrifice . . . and a new priesthood . . . This is why we meditate on the pattern of his life, proclaim it, preach it, celebrate it: to make it ever more deeply our own. This is why the Apostolic Church left us a book and a rite, word and sacrament, so that what Christ did and was, we too may do and be, in him. For this reason, sacred history is never finished. It continues in us" ("The Liturgical Year," 21).

65. This understanding was part of the Jewish priestly tradition as transmitted by Philo, a contemporary of Jesus: "If, however, you are worthily initiated, and can be consecrated to God and in a certain sense become a spiritual shrine of the Father, (then) instead of having closed eyes, you will see the First (things), and in wakefulness you will cease from the deep sleep in which you have been held. Then will appear to you that manifest One, Who causes incorporeal rays to shine for you, and grants vision of the unambiguous and indescribable things of nature and the abundant sources of other good things. For the beginning and end of happiness is to be able to see God. But this cannot happen to him who has not made his soul, as I said before, a sanctuary and altogether a shrine of God" (Philo, *Questions on Exodus* 2.51; quoted in Barker, *Creation*, 32).

66. Taft, "The Liturgical Year," 29–30. "These are the great festivals observed and honored throughout the eastern church and frequently paralleled to the pilgrim festivals of the Old Testament" (Talley, *Origins*, 128). The usual chant at holy communion, the Trisagion, was changed on these baptismal days to the baptismal troparion, "As many as have been baptized into Christ have put on Christ" (ibid.).

67. For example, Syrian baptismal liturgies at Epiphany used a plethora of birthing imagery in light of the belief that Jesus' baptism was the moment he was "born" as God's Son. Just as Jesus heard the voice from heaven naming him as God's beloved child, Baptists could develop baptismal liturgies intentionally echoing the themes from Jesus' baptismal experience. Like the Syrian baptismal liturgies, Epiphany is a very appropriate time

However, these rich images and theological truths cannot be adequately transmitted without periods of preparation that lead up to baptism and that continue afterwards. The Christian Year provides this opportunity for the entire congregation. For ancient Christians, a primary means of being initiated into the high priesthood of Christ was through *lectio continua*, a process of scriptural "course readings." At an early period the Gospels were "read continuously" (*lectio continua*) in light of the arc of Christ's high priestly mission and in light of the three "high festivals" of Epiphany, *Pascha* and Pentecost.[68] Certain events in Christ's life and mission were meant to coincide with these commemorations, e.g. birth and baptism at Epiphany, death and resurrection at *Pascha*, and the sending of the Spirit at Pentecost.[69] Through the practices of *lectio divina* and *lectio continua*, followers of Christ were formed into "anointed ones" (Christians), through the reading of a Gospel that followed the arc of Christ's ministry of atonement. This implicitly communicated that each Christian was awakening to their true calling and being initiated into the life, death, and priestly mission of Christ.[70]

---

to transmit the teaching of the process of "being born again," which is the appropriate way during Christmas and Easter of dealing with the truth of resurrected living.

68. For distinctions between *lectio continua*, *lectio selecta* and *lectio semicontinua* in the Lectionary, see Bonneau, *The Sunday Lectionary*, 45–47, and West, "Readings, Scripture," 491–96.

69. There is evidence that some of the earliest course readings began in the autumn, around the time of the autumn equinox and/or *Sukkoth*. Course readings that began in the autumn may have been influenced by the practice in Jewish synagogues of beginning the Torah after *Sukkoth*. In Constantinople, the reading of Luke commenced with the beginning of the "New Year" (September 23) while other churches began the Lukan readings on the autumn equinox (September 24)—which was also the commemoration of the conception of John the Baptist, the Forerunner. Originally, the Jewish "New Year" began around *Sukkoth* and was thus associated with the Day of Atonement myth and ritual when all creation was "renewed." The eventual connection between *Sukkoth* and Epiphany may have led to the commencement of course readings in the winter at Epiphany. See Talley, *Origins*, 131, 134. Although Asian Christians in Ephesus originally began their course reading of John in the autumn, they later moved its commencement to Epiphany. The Cana wedding feast occurs in John 2, a story associated with Epiphany. Alexandrian Christians apparently used Mark, which begins with the Epiphany at Jesus' baptism, for their Spring course reading, while Jerusalem used Matthew, which begins with Nativity. See Talley, "Liturgical Time," 40–44.

70. The Revised Common Lectionary continues this tradition to a degree with the synoptic gospels, but unfortunately the RCL leaves no place for this with John and seriously truncates Acts, some of the Epistles, and the Old Testament. *Year A* follows the gospel of Matthew, but the Sermon on the Mount is practically left out. For years that Easter is early, possibly no portion of it will be read. Other than that, Year A is a semi-continuous reading of Matthew, beginning in Advent and ending on Christ the King Sunday with Matt 25:31–46 (The Son of Man who judges the nations). Throughout Year A, there are semi-continuous readings of the following Epistles: the first three

As Christians within the Free Church Tradition, Baptists can use the Christian Year and Revised Common Lectionary in ways they discern best continue the vision and spirituality of the ancient Church. Creative possibilities that use John, Acts, the Epistles, and Old Testament books for course readings can emerge that still have as their intent the initiation of Christians into the paschal mystery and, consequentially, priestly ministry.[71] One solution may be to primarily use the Revised Common Lectionary during the

---

chapters of 1 Corinthians (during the season after the Epiphany); 1 Peter (during the Easter/Pentecost season); Romans (the season after Pentecost), Philippians (late September, around autumn equinox); and 1 Thessalonians (mid October—Sunday before Christ the King). There is also the semi-continuous option for Old Testament readings: Genesis (season after Pentecost) and Exodus (beginning late August). *Year B* follows the gospel of Mark. After commencing in Advent and following the arc of Christ's life until the resurrection, the Markan readings pick up again at Mark 2:23—3:6 on the second Sunday after Pentecost. Throughout Year B, Mark is supplemented with Johannine readings, before ending with Mark 13:1–8 on the Sunday before Christ the King. A contemplative reading of this final passage suggests the priesthood of all believers for in it Jesus teaches that David and his friends ate the Bread of the Presence that only the priests were to eat, thus implying that all believers have access to the Bread of Divine Presence, the holy Bread that sanctifies the eater (which is an image of Holy Communion). Throughout Year B there are semi-continuous readings of the following Epistles: 1 Cor 6–9 in the season after the Epiphany and 2 Cor 1–4; 1 John, during the Easter/Pentecost season; the remainder of 2 Corinthians, ending in early July; Ephesians, beginning early-mid July and ending in late August; James, beginning late August-early September and ending late September; and Hebrews, beginning in early October and ending with chapter 10 on the Sunday before Christ the King. There is also a semi-continuous option for Old Testament readings: 1 Sam 3, 8, 15–16,17–18, ending in late June; 2 Samuel, beginning late June with chapters 1, 5, 6, 7, 11, 12, 18 ending early-mid August; and 1–3 weeks each from 1 Kings, Song of Solomon, Proverbs, Esther, Job, and Ruth. *Year C* follows the Gospel of Luke. The semi-continuous reading of Luke begins in Advent and, after the Easter interlude that follows John, picks up again on the Sunday after Trinity Sunday with Luke 7:1–10 and ends on Christ the King Sunday with Luke 23:23–43—Jesus' crucifixion as the "King of the Jews"). There are semi-continuous readings of the following Epistles: 1 Cor 12–15 in the season after the Epiphany; selections from the book of Revelation for the Easter/Pentecost season; Galatians, beginning with the first Sunday after Trinity Sunday; Col 1–3 beginning in mid July; Heb 11–13 beginning in early August; Philemon; 1 and 2 Timothy beginning in mid-September; and 2 Thessalonians beginning in late October and ending the Sunday before Christ the King. There is also a semi-continuous option for Old Testament readings: selections from 1 and 2 Kings in June and July; two Sundays each for Amos, Hosea, and Isaiah; Jeremiah, commencing at the end of August and ending mid-October (interrupted with one selection from Lamentations); and one Sunday each from Joel, Habakkuk, Haggai, Isaiah and Jeremiah.

71. When John is used in the RCL, it tends to be thematically driven with the unfortunate result that the reader or hearer is not able to fully experience its coherent beauty and symmetry, the tightly connected Johannine *mandala*. For a contemplative course study of John, see Barnhart, *The Good Wine*. For a contemplative reading of the lectionary gospel readings for all three years, see Shea, *Spiritual Wisdom*.

"Temporal Cycle" of Advent-Epiphany, Lent-Easter, and Pentecost for the first half of the Christian Year and develop a course reading unique to each individual Baptist church that can be followed for the second half of the Christian Year.[72]

From Christian to Creation: Continuing the Ministry of Reconciliation

> You have made them to be a kingdom and priests serving our God, and they will reign on earth.
>
> ~ Revelation 5:10

> For in [the Anointed One] all the fullness of God was pleased to dwell, and through him God was pleased to reconcile to himself all things, whether on earth or in heaven, by making peace through the blood of his cross.
>
> ~ Colossians 1:19–20

Each Christian participates in the high priesthood of Christ in two ways, both of which are reflected in the Liturgical Year. Through a process of *en-templing* (going into the inner temple of our being), we experience the inward meaning of the three great Christian feasts: the manifestation of God within us, inner resurrection into new life, and intimate union with the Spirit. This is the usual understanding of the word "contemplative," with caricatures of navel-gazing and excessive introversion. However, the full meaning of "contemplative" includes both inward and outward orientations. Thus, having experienced divine manifestation, a taste of resurrection and union with God, like the magi we are meant to carry these gifts into the temple of creation—completing our return to the state of Adam (the first high priest of Eden) and assuming our place as high priests in creation.[73]

72. For example, any of the gospels (but especially John) could be read continuously during the weeks between Pentecost and Advent. A congregation could do this as well with entire Epistles, immersing themselves in Hebrews with all of its priestly themes, or a series of smaller Epistles, such as the Johannine letters, with the exegetical aim of unlocking the contemplative meaning of these texts for those who are entering the high priesthood of the believers. In imitation of the ancient churches that began course readings around the autumn equinox and the "new year" in September (and also in conjunction with their "Fall Kick-off"), Baptist churches could choose certain passages (e.g., the Sermon on the Mount in Matt 5–7) or entire Epistles (e.g., Ephesians) to reflect on in light of the paschal mystery until the commencement of Advent. Another option for the month of September is the "Season of Creation," discussed below.

73. For an excellent study of Adam (and all humanity) as high priest of creation,

This is the process of *con-templing*—the inter-relationship between the heavenly temple, the temple of our being, and the temple of creation. In Christ we become mediators of heaven and earth, "hybrid worshippers," conduits whereby God's light, life and love flow into creation to heal and restore.[74] If the "Temporal Cycle" of the Christian Year immerses us into the life of Christ, then the rest of the Christian Year can be seen as further training in fulfilling the mission of Christ—reconciling all things to God as we continue the fourfold mission of Jesus through inspiring, teaching, healing, and liberating ministries.[75]

This is the over-arching vision of the Liturgical Year—every Sunday the Day of Atonement, each year the Year of Jubilee.[76] In the Jewish tradition, ev-

---

see Barker, *Creation*, 193–236. For example, she shows the priestly meaning behind the command to "subdue" (*kabash*) the earth and "have dominion" over living creatures. The word translated "subdue" can also mean atonement (e.g., Mic 7:18–19), which in the Day of Atonement myth implies renewing the broken bonds of the eternal covenant and restoring creation. The word translated "have dominion" (*radah*) is also used to describe Solomon's reign that resulted in peace. Interestingly, in the Dead Sea Scrolls the verb instead is *mashal*, which also means a proverb or parable that transmits wisdom, which Solomon used to impart the wisdom he acquired through contemplation of creation (1 Kgs 4:32–34). See Barker, *Creation*, 214–16.

74. Gregory of Nazianzus, in *Oration 45, For Easter*, says, "The great Architect of the universe conceived and produced a being endowed with both natures, the visible and the invisible: God created the human being, bringing its body forth from the pre-existing matter which he animated with his own Spirit . . . Thus in some way a new universe was born, small and great at one and the same time. God set this 'hybrid' worshipper on earth to contemplative the visible world, and to be initiated into the invisible . . . He created a being at once earthly and heavenly, insecure and immortal, visible and invisible, halfway between greatness and nothingness, flesh and spirit at the same time . . . an animal en route to another native land, and, most mysterious of all, made to resemble God by simple submission to the divine will" (quoted in Clément, *The Roots of Christian Mysticism*, 77).

75. Jesus cast an inspiring vision of God and God's kingdom. Jesus transmitted this vision through contemplative teachings (parables, aphorisms). He embodied his vision and wisdom through healing people of diseases and releasing people from various powers. This fourfold mission of Jesus (prophet, sage, priest, king) was often practically experienced in the context of an inclusive meal practice.

76. According to Mark Searle, Jesus proclaimed that "the sabbath represented a vision whose time had come. The 'rest' of God and the definitive liberation from slavery to work have arrived in the messianic age, present in the person and work of Jesus. The new age, which he inaugurated by this death and resurrection, has a sabbatical character and is properly understood as a new creation and a new exodus in which we are all invited to share . . . But the consensus that generally came to prevail in the early decades of the Church is that what the sabbath represented had actually been realized in the whole new age ushered in by Christ, of which the first day of the week became the symbol." Thus the Sabbath was a symbol of the Christian life, not just a weekly practice: "Christians were to exercise their new-won freedom and celebrate the "rest" of God after the new creation by their total life-style, seven days a week" (Searle, "Sunday,"

ery fifty years on the Day of Atonement the high priest proclaimed Jubilee—the Sabbath of Sabbaths (Lev 25:9). The atonement ritual restored the eternal covenant and brought nature and humanity to its original, Edenic state. In this mythology, the temple was creation: what happened in the temple affected all of creation. Thus, the Jubilee was a practical implementation of the atonement.[77] In like manner, every year believers perform their high priestly duties of continuing the ministry of reconciliation and Jubilee as the Body of Christ. Therefore, the high priesthood of believers does not only mean we have direct, immediate access to God; our vocation includes blessing, healing, restoring, and facilitating the earth's full union with the Divine Realm—"Thy Kingdom come, thy will be done, as in the heavens so on earth."

The second half of the Christian Year (often called the "Season after Pentecost" or "Ordinary Time") follows this outward and missional trajectory. This longest season in the Church Year begins the week after Pentecost with Trinity Sunday and ends on the final Sunday of the Christian Year—Christ the King Sunday, which can serve as a prism through which to examine this often confusing and lengthy season. On this day, the psalmist inspires us to join all the earth in worshiping the Lord, to enter the King's presence (his temple), to be still before his power, and as priests be clothed with robes of righteousness and salvation.[78] The prophets Ezekiel, David and Jeremiah exhort us to justice and proclaim the coming of an Anointed Just One whose rule will bring both refreshment and judgment.[79] Following in the tradition of Daniel, first-century prophets cast a new *merkavah* (throne) vision—all believers are priests, serving God the Father and seated in the heavenly places with Christ, through whom God has reconciled to himself all things.[80] In the Gospel, we glimpse what kind of justice the Son of Man desires, learn the true nature of Jesus' kingship and its relationship to truth, and listen to his comforting words that we are returning to Paradise, the Kingdom of God.[81] According to the Christian Scriptures, Christ's

---

62–63). Thus, the images of Sabbath, *Yom Kippur*, Day of the Lord, and Jubilee reflect the same vision of the high priesthood of all believers and *con-templing* ministry.

77. "The key figure in the rite of atonement," according to Margaret Barker, "was the high priest who was the visible presence of the Lord on earth, and, just as the Lord had ordered the creation at the beginning, so he recreated it on the Day of Atonement at the New Year. The Jubilee recreated society by restoring people to their own land and by removing the burden of slavery and debt" (Barker, *The Great High Priest*, 35).

78. Year A: Ps 100 or 95:1–7a; Year B: Ps 132; Year C: Ps 46.

79. Year A: Ezek 34:11–16, 20–24; Year B: 2 Sam 23:1–7 or Dan 7:9–10, 13–14; Jer 23:1–6.

80. Year A: Eph 1:15–23 (Eph 2:6 teaches that we are seated with Christ in these heavenly places); Year B: Rev 1:4b-8; Year C: Col 1:11–20.

81. Year A: Matt 25:31–46; Year B: John 18:33–37; Year C: Luke 23:33–43.

reign and reconciliation program begins through us; we participate in the sanctification of the world.[82]

The Catholic tradition practices this truth through the "Temporal Cycle" of Advent-Pentecost and a "Sanctoral Cycle" that commemorates the heroes and heroines of the faith on the day they passed over into eternity. In light of the cosmic vision of reconciliation presented in the Christian Scriptures, Baptists can expand this "Sanctoral Cycle" to include additional elements of creation. Particularly, the Christian Year can help "priests of creation" practice reconciling all things to God in three primary arenas: time, nature, and people.

Listening Attentively to Events

Throughout the Christian Year we commemorate the manifestation of God to humanity through events in time. This is obvious for the half of the solar year in which we celebrate how God acted in history through Christ (Advent-Pentecost). During this period we are initiated into Christ's life and mission, which radically shapes our understanding and living of time now. But what about other events of the past, whether it be the past of our family, church, community, city, country, or world? Christians affirm that God has always worked in history and continues to work in our personal and communal lives. So how can we see the events of the past and present in the light of Divine Presence?

For all of us, our experience of time is shaped by many calendars, e.g. liturgical, school, civic, and seasonal to name a few. Throughout Christian history, churches have sought to understand the events of their lives, communities, cities and countries in light of the paschal mystery. Cities such as tenth-century Constantinople held a plethora of outdoor liturgical celebrations that sought to help Christians understand their faith in relation to events in the history of the city. According to John F. Baldovin, many of these celebrations were related "to crucial moments in the social experience: the birthday or dedication of the city, a plague, an earthquake, the defeat of invaders in a siege. Here, God's power was made manifest and commemorated year after year in a tangible way to which people could relate; it was liturgy at its most popular."[83]

This ancient perspective and practice is fundamental for Baptists commemorating events that may not appear related to Christianity, e.g. Mother's Day, Father's Day, Memorial Day, Independence Day, Labor Day, Veterans

82. E.g., 2 Cor 5:17–19 and Rev 5:9–10.
83. Baldovin, "The Liturgical Year," 436.

Day, Thanksgiving Day or 9/11. Some Baptist congregations struggle with how best to commemorate these important yet often emotionally charged days. Each local Baptist congregation must find its own way to help congregants learn to see events through the lens of the cycle of light—how God manifests to and in humanity, in the events of history and of our lives today. This requires what the monastic tradition called "obedience" (*ob-audire*), which essentially means, "to listen attentively." In its broadest sense, obedience is radical openness of the whole person to the meaning of all events in one's life situation.[84] By attentively listening to the events of the past and present, we might awaken to how God was present (and absent) in the event being commemorated and how God may use it to guide the faith community for continuing the teaching, healing, liberating, and inspiring mission of Christ. Such a practice of listening attentively to events can help redeem the past, present and also aid in the redemption of the future. As the eyes and ears of our hearts are opened and we are able to hear and see more clearly God's Presence in the events of the past, we are given wisdom and strength to be priests in our time, working towards social justice and peace.

Living Simply With Creation

The Christian Year facilitates the redemption and healing of creation. This was the most ancient understanding of the Jewish calendar, which formed the foundation for the Christian Calendar. Some scholars suggest that the two great sacrifices of the Jewish Tradition—Passover and the Day of Atonement—occurred at the time of the spring and autumn equinoxes, respectively.[85] As we have seen, *Yom Kippur* shaped the earliest (and most priestly) understanding of Jesus' life, mission, and death, resulting in the belief that they continued Christ's ministry of reconciling all things (time, nature and people) to God as priests of God. Christians endowed the turning of the seasons with new meaning. Some early Christians believed John the Baptist was conceived on the autumn equinox and born at the summer solstice, while Jesus was conceived at the spring equinox, born on the winter solstice, and died at the spring equinox.[86] Christians used imagery from pagan festivals

84. According to Adrian van Kaam, "This respectful reading of events is the safeguard and basis of human development . . . Because I am incarnated spirit, listening to the possible meaning of events implies my willingness to listen to the whole and Holy to which all events are related" (*Vowed Life*, 25–26).

85. Barker, *The Gate of Heaven*, 38. For a summary of the structure of the temple and its sacrifices, see chapter 1, "The House of the Lord."

86. This is the "Computation Hypothesis." The celebration of the birth and death of Jesus were determined by the early identification of March 25 as the date of Jesus'

based on these solar events to celebrate the paschal mystery, such as the feast of the Unconquered Sun-god at the winter solstice. There is no denying the great symbolic power of the birth of Christ for those celebrating Christmas in the Northern Hemisphere. In Christmas sermons from such theologians as Ambrose, Leo the Great, and the Cappadocian fathers, Christ is the "Sun of Righteousness" that has risen and has experienced a rebirth (implying both the resurrection and the "rebirth" of the sun at the winter solstice).[87]

We can learn from these ancient Christians who sought to understand the inner meaning of nature, which required the respectful, wise and simple use of the creation. The monastic tradition called this *poverty* which, "in its deepest sense signifies the wise use and celebration of things [including nature]. It aids my openness to all dimensions of their meaning."[88] This call to poverty and sacrifice, to "living simply with things," is part of the vocation of all Christians as "priests of creation." According to Ecumenical Patriarch Bartholomew, "There can be no salvation for the world, no healing, no hope for a better future, without the missing dimension of sacrifice. Without a sacrifice that is both costly and uncompromising, we shall never be able to act as priests of creation in order to reverse the descending spiral of ecological degradation."[89] Thus the redemption of creation is closely linked to the Christian concept of *pascha*—the passage from death to true life.

---

crucifixion and the belief that the day of his death was also the day of his conception. Logically then, the day of his birth would have been nine months later, on December 25. Based on Luke 1:26, Jesus was conceived six months after John's conception, which logically would have occurred at the autumn equinox, resulting in his birth at the summer solstice. See Adam, *The Liturgical Year*, 123. If this "Computation Hypothesis" is correct, then such feasts as the Nativity and Epiphany are not primarily (if at all) dependent upon the Christianization of pagan festivals like that of the dedication of a temple to Sol Invictus on December 25, 274, a Julian winter solstice date. Some support for this "computation hypothesis" can also be found in the tractate *De solstitiis et aequnoctiis*, which probably originated in the Syriac (Aramaic) Christian community sometime in the early fourth century.

87. See Roll, "The Origins of Christmas," 289. The "history of religions" approach to this season notes the similarities between Christmas/Epiphany and pagan festivals: December 25 was celebrated as the birthday of the sun and January 6 was celebrated as the virgin-birth of Aion/Dionysus who on this day revealed his presence by transforming water into wine.

88. van Kaam, *Vowed Life*, 33. "The man who is truly alive grows daily in presence to the possibilities and limitations of the gifts of culture and nature. Increasingly, he comes to a deep comprehension of the manifold ways in which they can be used by him and others without destroying the harmonious unfolding of human life . . . Everywhere in culture and nature the mystery of the Holy is waiting to reveal itself to the man no longer burdened by the need to possess things disrespectfully" (ibid., 32, 34).

89. Ecumenical Patriarch Bartholomew, "Sacrifice," 217–20.

Some contemporary Christian denominations and churches have attempted to make this call to redeem nature a part of their liturgical practice through observance of what is called the "Season of Creation." The World Council of Churches has encouraged the practice of this new season, which began as a call in 1999 from the Ecumenical Patriarch Dimitrios I of Constantinople. The season begins on September 1, the day the Eastern Orthodox Church commemorates God's creation of the world. For the next four Sundays of September, some aspect of creation becomes the focus for the Christic ministry of reconciliation, e.g. earth, humanity, sky, oceans, mountains, fauna and flora. The season continues through October 4, the feast day of St. Francis of Assisi (with a possible Blessing of the Animals ceremony) and ends on World Communion Sunday (the first Sunday in October).[90] Like the Revised Common Lectionary, there is a three-year cycle.[91] The use of the "Season of Creation" is one practical way Baptists can join the wider Christian Church to overcome the American "privatization of religion" for therapeutic purposes and recapture the Christian eschatological vision of the redemption and healing of all creation.[92]

Remembering Embodiments of Love

Finally, Baptist Christians can use the Christian Year to remember "embodiments" of God's love, i.e., "saints." Baptists are quick to recognize that all Christians are considered saints in the New Testament, but we also realize we often do not live up to our high calling. Thus, early Christians found great value in models and manifestations of God's presence in history. These were individuals to whom people could relate, great Christians who could embody in "contemporary cultural circumstances what it means to be *in Christ*, to be grasped by the power of God."[93] Such persons were not mere examples for moral imitation but tangible epiphanies of Christ's power and presence, channels of Christ and incarnations of Christ's paschal mystery and priestly ministry. Like Jesus the Anointed, they reveal what it means to be fully human,

90. For more on the "Season of Creation," see Habel et al., eds., *The Season of Creation*, and the Season of Creation website, online: www.seasonofcreation.com.

91. Year A: The Spirit in Creation (forest, land, wilderness, river); Year B: The Word in Creation (earth, humanity, sky, mountain); Year C: Wisdom in Creation (ocean, fauna and flora, storm, cosmos).

92. Recent studies show how modern American worshippers "have engaged in common worship for therapeutic purposes. It is difficult to step outside this scenario because the therapeutic life is as common as the air we breathe, as real to us as angles and demons were to our forebears" (see Baldovin, "Liturgical Year," 429, 430).

93. Ibid., 436

for the love they extend has been "chastened or purified of self-centered purposes, anxious needs, over-dependency and isolated passions," helping us to remember that only "when our love is chaste can we diminish the tendency to use and abuse ourselves and others in a disrespectful manner."[94] Regardless of whether they practiced physical celibacy, these faithful Christians can help us practice the inner meaning of *chastity*—a respectful and purified presence "to the call of the Holy in self and others."[95] One way to practice remembering tangible incarnations of God's love is by celebrating All Saints Day. As early as the second century, Christians celebrated the "birthday" of martyrdoms, "in commemoration of those who have already fought in the contest and also for the training and preparation of those who will do so in the future."[96] The practice extended to include other saints as early as the fourth century.[97] An easy entrance into this ancient practice might be to set aside a time on the Sunday closest to All Saints Day to remember a departed loved one during the morning worship service, e.g. vocalizing their name or writing it down on a piece of paper.

In addition to celebrating All Saints Day, Baptist Christians can experiment with commemorating the great heroes and heroines of the faith on their "feast day," remembering their birth into eternity (death) rather than their birth into time (birthday). Ancient churches began establishing a Sanctoral Cycle quite early to go along with the Temporal Cycle. Baptists could recover elements of the Sanctoral Cycle in many ways. First, begin using the prayers and meditations from the great saints of the larger Christian tradition in worship, prayer gatherings, and committee meetings. There are online resources that provide information on saint "feast days," as well as suggested Bible readings that relate to some aspect of their spirituality.[98] With a little research, appropriate selections from their writings could be used to facilitate Christian formation. Through this practice of remembrance, Baptists both claim their larger Christian tradition of which they are a part and allow ancient, medieval, and modern Christians to continue their

94. van Kaam, *Vowed Life*, 31.

95. Ibid., 101.

96. *Mart. Pol.* 18.3.

97. John Chrysostom assigned a specific date to celebrate all saints: the first Sunday after Pentecost, which remains the official Eastern Orthodox date for All Saints Day. Thus in the Christian East, the celebration of All Saints is closely related to the season of love that climaxes at Pentecost. In the Christian West, All Saints Day is celebrated toward the end of the Christian Year on November 1, preceded by "All Hallows' Eve" (Halloween).

98. See, for example, The Lectionary, online, http://satucket.com/lectionary/, and The Lectionary Page, online: http://www.lectionarypage.net/index.html.

formative influence today. This will require good education on the front end to begin this practice that might seem "too Catholic," but the formative fruits are worth the effort. For starters, on St. Francis of Assisi Day (October 4) or the closest Sunday, Baptist churches could develop a fun yet meaningful "Blessing of the Animals" service, which connects the spirituality of St. Francis with a tangible compassionate action—blessing and celebrating how animals can be little epiphanies of God's love.

Second, rediscover the "saints" within our own tradition. In some ways this is not new to the Baptist world—we have had our saints, too, even if we did not call them by that name. For example, Southern Baptists remember Lottie Moon as part of their annual Christmas offering around her "feast day" of December 24. In addition to incorporating meditations from "saints" within the larger Christian tradition, some communities might use contemplative readings from Baptists, e.g. John Bunyan, Benjamin Keach, Roger Williams, Anne Dutton, Henry Alline, Francis Wayland, Muriel Lester, Howard Thurman, or Martin Luther King Jr. For an Evening Prayer service, opening meditative quotes and benedictions could come from one of these Baptists whose "feast day" falls sometime that week.[99] This is one easy way to immerse contemporary Baptists in the stream of wisdom within our own Baptist tradition that is now four centuries old.

Finally, Baptists can commemorate the saints within their own local church. The Sanctoral Cycle began with local churches commemorating their local saints. Following this practice, Baptist churches can help shape the faith of the members by providing tangible epiphanies of God's love, people who may have sat in the same pews as they now sit. Celebrating local saints also provides the Baptist church the opportunity to shape both the church's identity and image of mature spirituality, for "'who' is commemorated on a sanctoral calendar suggests 'how' a particular church understands holiness and how such holiness is modeled, to be imitated, and so revealed to the world."[100] Some of these saints will be former pastors, so why not celebrate their "feast day" by including excerpts from a famous sermon, poem, hymn, or meditation they wrote? A church could even experiment with developing an entire worship service or prayer service using meditations and prayers from a former pastor as a way to immerse the congregation in the pastor's spirituality to learn and be shaped anew. Departed deacons or other lay members could be celebrated with

99. This is the current practice of Freemason Street Baptist Church in Norfolk, VA for Wednesday Evening Prayers. A sample service is provided in the appendix. For a collection of meditative readings from Baptists over the past four centuries, see Burleson and Sciretti Jr., *Entempling.*

100. M. Johnson, *Between Memory and Hope,* xxiii.

testimonies of how the individual showed God's love in the community. There are many possibilities to practice the Christian understanding of the "communion of saints"—that God's saving action in Christ continues through people (globally and locally) and that somehow, mysteriously, these "icons" are with us even now in Christ, yearning for us to become epiphanies of divine love while we walk on this earth.[101]

Conclusion

There is no one ideal Christian Calendar, especially for Baptists in the Free Church tradition. There is great freedom in how closely a Baptist church follows the Christian Year or the Revised Common Lectionary; understands the contemplative nuances of the seasons of light, life and love; and re-imagines its relationship with time, nature, and people. The "success" of the practice of the Christian Year is only determined on how it "builds up the body of Christ into a spiritual temple and priesthood by forwarding the aim of Christian life: the love and service of God and neighbor; death to self in order to live for others as did Christ."[102]

Jean Cardinal Daniélou articulately summarized this entire teaching of the Christian or Liturgical Year:

> The Christian faith has only one object, the mystery of Christ dead and risen. But this unique mystery subsists under different modes: it is prefigured in the Old Testament, it is accomplished historically in the earthly life of Christ, it is contained in mystery in the sacraments, it is lived mystically in souls, it is accomplished socially in the Church, it is consummated eschatologically in the heavenly kingdom. Thus the Christian has at his disposition several registers, a multi-dimensional symbolism, to express this unique reality. The whole of Christian culture consists in grasping the links that exist between Bible and liturgy, Gospel and eschatology, mysticism and liturgy. The application of this method to scripture is called exegesis; applied to liturgy it is called mystagogy. This consists in reading in the rites the mystery of Christ, and in contemplating beneath the symbols the invisible reality.[103]

101. Taft, "The Liturgical Year," 21.

102. Ibid., 23.

103. Daniélou, "Le symbolism," 17; English translation by Taft, "The Liturgical Year," 23.

What if we Baptists assumed the full meaning of the priesthood of all believers and saw the Liturgical Year as a yearly "work of the people" that goes on through (1) the work of remembering Christ's life, (2) the inner work of awakening, dying, rising, and communing with God, and (3) practicing Jesus' mission of healing and liberating all of creation? What if we saw each Christian Year as the Year of Jubilee, the Sabbath of Sabbaths? What if we understood this very year as the New Year, the New Age—and every Sunday celebrating the awe-full Day of the Lord, the Day of Atonement? What if we saw Sunday as the Day the Anointed One comes again in Holy Communion and in us, through his and our sacrifice, for the healing and renewal of the world? What if?

3

Liturgical Ties of Community

Amy Butler

One of the most important things I ever learned about worship I learned in a nursing home on a pastoral visit to an elderly member of our congregation. Mr. Smith seemed especially happy to see me that day. He was going home, he explained with a twinkle in his eye. I knew, of course, that there was no way Mr. Smith's wife could care for him at their home. Yet he kept insisting—he was going home. Before I left that day, as is my custom, I prayed with Mr. Smith. As I was getting ready to leave, he stopped me and told me again that he was headed home. I nodded and chalked his talk about home up to confusion. "Before I go home," he said, "can you sing our song?"

There are moments in the life and work of a pastor when the stress of the job lifts and you see clearly, if for just a moment, the presence of God in the ties that bind the community of faith. This was one of those moments for me. After wondering aloud what he meant by our song, I finally nodded in recognition when Mr. Smith looked at me incredulous that I didn't immediately understand, "You know, our song!," he said again. "The song we sing together in church every week! I want to sing it with you one more time before I go home."

At Calvary a few years before, we'd introduced the simple song, "Make Us One" into our liturgy, to be sung as we finished our tradition of Passing the Peace. When it was first introduced, some were disgruntled—it was something new and unfamiliar. Soon, though, it became one of those heart songs, a song to sing from memory and with feeling. Together. And as we sang it Sunday after Sunday, it somehow, gradually, became "our song."

And so Mr. Smith and I sang together, right there in the middle of the nursing home's common room. As I sang our song, Mr. Smith chimed in with enthusiasm, his quavering voice gaining strength as he sang out all the words, from memory. "Make us one, Lord, make us one. Holy Spirit, make us one. Let your love flow so the world will know we are one in you!" I hugged him goodbye then, and went on to my next appointment. The next day Mr. Smith died. He had been going home; he'd known it all along. And the one thing he wanted to be sure to do one more time before he left was to sing our song.

It's true—I finally learned through that experience that worship planned to include tangible opportunities for connection does connect us in new ways with each other. Worship that connects us with each other also ties us to God. Every element of worship has the potential and possibility to bring us together. A worship experience filled with intentionally placed opportunities for connection can lead us to deeper and more meaningful connection with each other and, in turn, with God. In the life of the community of faith, these opportunities for connection spread throughout the worship experience build a foundation of community that extends beyond the worship hour into our life together.

Why Are Liturgical Ties to Community Important?

Countless studies along with the modern experience of church have shown that church attendance and involvement are at an all-time low. In most modern communities, one can be a good person and never attend church at all; with busy lives and countless commitments, a leisurely Sunday morning is often the choice over church attendance. With this marked decrease in church-going, it's prudent to ask ourselves what motivates people to come to church. As human beings we are created to search for the Divine, but these days that search doesn't always take place in church. Some might even say church is the last place some would look for God. In his poem "Church Going," twentieth-century poet Philip Larkin describes the impression many contemporary folk have of church in general:

> Once I am sure there's nothing going on
> I step inside, letting the door thud shut.
> Another church: matting, seats and stone,
> And little books; sprawlings of flowers, cut
> For Sunday, brownish now; some brass and stuff
> Up at the holy end; the small neat organ;
> And a tense, musty, unignorable silence,

Brewed God knows how long. Hatless, I take off
My cycle-clips in awkward reverence,
Move forward, run my hand around the font.
From where I stand, the roof looks almost new—
Cleaned or restored? Someone would know, I don't.
Mounting the lectern, I peruse a few
Hectoring large-scale verses, and pronounce
"Here endeth" much more loudly than I'd meant.
The echoes snigger briefly. Back at the door
I sign the book, donate an Irish sixpence,
Reflect the place was not worth stopping for.[1]

What, then, makes the "place worth stopping for"? One might argue that ties to community are a key part of what draws people to church and keeps them there, as part of the community. But there is also a deeper, more profound reality that compels us to invest our lives in community. Our God is a God of community, of relationship, and we experience God in life-transforming ways when our lives connect with others' in the context of the worship of God. In his book *Life Together*, Dietrich Bonhoeffer is adamant about that deep and intertwined connection: "The more genuine and the deeper our community becomes, the more will everything else between us recede, the more clearly and purely will Jesus Christ and his work become the one and only thing that is vital between us. We have one another only through Christ, but through Christ we do have one another, wholly, and for all eternity."[2]

Jesus knew this truth and practiced it as the foundation of his ministry on earth. He touched people and healed them; he listened to them tell their stories; he engaged in the most mundane and at the same time the deepest, most meaningful interactions, like sharing a meal together or telling a story, pulling in a net of fish or attending a sickbed. There were many instances in which Jesus' acts of building community became profound experiences of worship.

Contemporary Christ-followers face the challenge and opportunity of emulating Jesus, who built his ministry around relationship. Whether he was teaching in the temple or wandering the hillsides of Galilee, Jesus knew that fostering deep connections between people helps to foster deep relationship with God. In a world bent on individualism, more narcissistic than relational, following Jesus' radical commitment to connection through

---

1. Larkin, "Church Going," 1015.
2. Bonhoeffer, *Life Together*, 26.

relationship can transform us; and this connection can begin and be fostered in the context of worship.

While the life of a faith community extends beyond corporate worship, it is in the context of the joint worship of God that we build and foster the deepest and most abiding connections to each other. Precisely because of the fraying fabric of community in society as a whole, worship that highlights, encourages, and empowers these connections is critical—not just for the future of the institutional church, but for the sharing of the Gospel message.

What Lets Us Connect

We cannot force people to connect with each other, of course; we can only make room for that connection to take place. And when we think about opportunities for connection in worship, it may be tempting to be prescriptive in our approach, to apply resources in an attempt to program community into our worship experiences. While it is true that resources for building community in worship are invaluable, a nuanced approach for worship leaders and planners may be more effective. Each community, each situation, differs, and there will be unique opportunities for community building if leaders stay attuned to the needs and opportunities presenting themselves in the life of the community. In other words, we must begin to understand what lets us connect with each other. One way to dream and imagine connectional opportunities is to keep in mind the qualities of connections and consider how these are experienced in your specific community. Here are a few:

When We Join Our Voices

Whether a worshipper comes to an experience of worship ready to interact with others or not, there is a simple way to underscore the idea of connection, of shared experience, by the opportunity to hear each others' voices. A foundational difference between a worship experience and any other group experience, like listening to a lecture for example, is the built-in, auditory act of raising our voices and hearing them in concert with the voices of others.

Whether a spoken call to worship, the recitation of a prayer, or the singing of a hymn, the quality of expression is not the important factor; rather, the lifting of human voices together is the goal. When your ears can hear the voices of others, an involuntary tie is formed and the worshipper knows: I am not alone. I am gathered with others. We are sharing this experience together. I recognize your voice. I hear you.

When We Experience Human Touch

Along with the primal assurance of hearing another voice, we human beings crave human touch. Numerous studies over the years have shown that human touch is necessary for physical growth and well-being, and some even suggest that peace and well-being are enhanced when we have physical contact with other human beings. A recent article on Beliefnet agrees:

> One simple way to improve your quality of life is to incorporate more touch into your daily activities. Something as simple as hugging family and friends hello and goodbye can help put them—and you—in a better frame of mind and may even provide a boost to physical health as well. And with virtually no negative side effects, a good dose of touching may be just what the doctor ordered.[3]

Recently a group from our church took a trip to San Salvador, El Salvador, to visit the intensive care unit of a maternity hospital there. Members of our church had been busily crocheting miniature caps for tiny premature babies to help them maintain their body heat. One of the groundbreaking programs the hospital was instituting while we were there was a program called the "Kangaroo Program." The idea behind this effort was to encourage human touch for the tiniest babies, as those who were held for significant periods made progress toward health and wholeness at a much quicker pace than those who stayed in the incubators. To learn about this program, we visited rooms lined with rows of chairs against each wall, each chair filled with a new mother or father who held a tiny baby to his or her chest. The hospital staff told us that seriously at-risk premature babies were making unprecedented strides in health and growth since the start of the Kangaroo Program. Human touch is a powerful healing tool that can foster deep ties between us.

In our increasingly transient, disposable, artificial society, we have less and less opportunity for a genuine hug, for a meaningful handshake, for intentional eye contact, or even for the sound of someone calling us by name. Worship that encourages the ties of community is worship that gives us opportunities for personal, individual human connection, the kind of experiences that lead us past the fear that we're alone and firmly toward an awareness that our individual lives matter. In a world where we can go days without the touch of another human being, worship can be a powerful and safe forum for connection and relationship. When we know we matter

---

3. Lain Chroust Ehmann, "The Health Benefits of Touch," Beliefnet, online: http://www.beliefnet.com/healthandhealing/getcontent.aspx?cid=13623.

enough for somebody to grasp a hand or give a hug, we can begin to form deeper connections and even flourish.

When We Feel a Part of the Larger Whole

Beyond the assurance that we are not alone is a deeper sense of connection found in knowing that we belong to a larger whole. Everyone is lonely, even in a world of fast paced, electronic interaction. Further, our society rewards individuality and independence. All of these trends can lead us to feelings of isolation and insignificance. Corporate worship, by contrast, can be an experience where our interaction with others tangibly demonstrates that we are part of something larger than our own individual selves. And this feeling of having a part in something larger than ourselves is a direct antidote to the feelings of isolation and insignificance that often fester in our modern lives.

Each year during a Sunday in January, our church celebrates a re-commitment Sunday. Acknowledging that our life circumstances change and that we live in a transient society and culture, we come together once a year to publicly recommit ourselves to the community of faith here at Calvary Baptist Church for the year ahead. We're reminded on that Sunday that being part of the larger whole means offering our presence, sharing our time and talents, giving our money, and tending carefully to the individual and corporate life of faith. Every year when we reexamine our commitment, we participate in a ritual that we make together. One year we each brought rocks to the front of the sanctuary and built an altar together as a reminder of our shared commitment. One year we created a piece of art together. Another year we each came forward and each tied a ribbon to a cross. In the act of ritual like that, we are connected to each other. We publicly commit to the life of faith together, and we can see that commitment as each one comes forward to be part of the whole. As we get up and take steps toward the altar to join the group, we experience a feeling of connection; we are part of a larger whole. Any ritual of worship that allows the worshipper to feel part of the larger whole and adds to the feeling of mutual interdependence is a ritual worth considering for its benefit of building and nurturing community ties.

Create Something Together

The ties that connect us in worship to each other and to God often result in corporate creation. That is, when we participate in rituals of worship that connect our lives to each others', we miraculously create something together. And in the process of creation, we are tied to each other in deep and abiding ways.

I recently was part of a conference worship service in which very few of the participants knew each other. During this service of worship the music leader got up and explained that, since we all came from different places and spoke different languages, we would commence to sing a song called "Jesus Christ is Present Here." He taught us the simple lyrics, then began singing them in different languages. The crowd had been trying to learn the song until the different languages started. You could hear the silence as the music leader forged ahead and sang the verses in a native language of the Republic of Congo, Spanish, German, French . . . but after each verse he would come back to the chorus: "Hallelujah, hallelujah, hallelujah, praise the Lord." Each time the chorus sounded, the congregation's singing got louder. By the final rendition of the chorus the congregation was singing at full volume, harmonies rising and falling, soaring all the way to the final note: "Hallelujah, praise the Lord . . . !"

As the final note faded, you could see the congregation looking at each other with amazement and recognition. Somehow, from this group of strangers who spoke many different languages and who did not know each other, a tremendous harmony rose to fill the sanctuary and there was suddenly a deep and abiding connection. This group of former strangers had created something together. Whatever the ritual may be—music or liturgy, art or movement—a group of individuals becomes connected to each other in the powerful act of creating something together. Worship should be filled with elements that help a group create something together.

Where We Invest

To be effective at creating connection, an element of worship should go even further. It should ask for personal investment. We can easily keep our positions as casual observers when nobody asks us to participate in such a way that we're called upon to give something up. Until we give something, we are not engaged; we are not connected. When something is asked of us and we respond, it is in that moment that the connection often happens. This act of sacrifice, of giving something, can take many different forms. For example, such a ritual could ask us to offer our time, to sacrifice a level of comfort or anonymity. Rituals of corporate connection ask us to offer resources we may not be inclined to offer on our own volition.

Rituals that ask us to sacrifice resources are powerful forces in connecting us to each other. When we offer our resources we are tangibly expressing our belief that the cause or the community at hand is worth our time or energy—whatever resource we happen to be investing. And when we participate in a corporate expression that asks the same sort of sacrifice from everyone around, we begin to feel some level of kinship with each other that perhaps we had not felt before.

One of the shared rituals members in my congregation often comment on is the passing of the peace. Toward the beginning of worship, as we are being drawn in to the act of worship, we encourage the entire congregation to pass the peace of Christ. The ritual begins with the pastor declaring, "The peace of the Lord be with you," to which the congregation responds, "And also with you." The ritual then continues with the pastors coming down from the dais and walking up and down the aisles, shaking hands, exchanging hugs, and passing the peace of Christ. Everyone present in worship participates by greeting those around them, especially those they identify as visitors. There is no individual in the entire room who is left out of this ritual; even visitors are approached and greeted with a handshake and a wish for peace. Sometimes the ritual lasts for quite awhile, as everyone present, young and old, is greeted and asked to greet each other.

We've heard from many worship attendees that this "aggressive" ritual of peace-passing can be a little bit scary or uncomfortable at first; many people are accustomed to a more sedate passing of the peace, where you briefly greet the person on either side of you. And while some have said the ritual is daunting the first time around, without exception people report loving this ritual of worship at Calvary perhaps more than any other. Everyone, from the littlest children to the pastors leading worship, is called upon to suspend a level of individuality and privacy, to move out of their seats toward others in the congregation, and to greet each another with a word of peace unavailable anywhere else in our frantic, weekday lives. We can suspend the discomfort of the ritual because we know that everyone in the group is offering up the same, and when we know that everybody is participating in some way, the ritual becomes a powerful source of community connection, tying us to each other in deep and meaningful ways we have perhaps never experienced before.

When We Affirm a Shared Conviction

My eldest son recently went through the process of choosing a college to attend. After years of attending college fairs, receiving piles of printed materials, going on numerous campus visits, and making lists of pros and cons, he finally decided where he would attend school. It was a huge decision, one that everyone in the family watched with interest and enthusiasm.

To celebrate his decision, our family had a dinner at which each of us was presented with a different t-shirt emblazoned with the name of the university my son will attend. Even the dog got a new tag with the university logo printed on it. We determined at dinner that night that we were now firmly fans of the university's sports teams, and we took a picture together with all of us wearing our university t-shirts. He's the first child in the family to go away to college, and it has become our family conviction to jointly cheer him on, even though we'll be cheering from afar. Through that simple ritual we managed to affirm a shared conviction.

One common practice at Calvary is the praying of The Lord's Prayer each Sunday. In the recitation of familiar words, often prayed in different languages all at one time, we affirm something together: "For Thine is the kingdom and power and the glory forever and ever. Amen." The bonds of deep connection are forged and fastened again when we participate in worship ritual or liturgy in which that same phenomenon of shared affirmation occurs. When we express a shared belief or conviction, when we affirm our faith together, when we bless the baptism of a new believer or welcome a new member, we powerfully knit our lives together with the thread of shared conviction, and we are bound to each other in these moments and beyond. Rituals of connection in worship remind us that we're here together for a reason, that we hold common beliefs and convictions, that there is a unique and special quality of our life together which draws us toward the divine and creates within them a powerful force of Gospel transformation.

Creating Liturgical Ties to Community in Corporate Worship

Singing "our song" is one important way our church makes and strengthens connections within our congregation, but a service thoughtfully planned with the intention of forging and nurturing ties of community will be infused in every movement with liturgy that draws people together and offers them meaningful spiritual engagement in a corporate setting. In every movement of worship, from the gathering, to the hearing of the word, to the sharing of communion, to the challenge of discipleship, there should be activities that pull people into shared holy space, liturgy that reminds them of the shared gift and responsibility of the community of faith. Some examples of rituals we use in constructing the liturgy at Calvary are discussed below.

Gathering Together

Gathering In

In the beginning of worship the community intentionally creates a space apart from the world outside its walls, to retreat, reflect, reevaluate and reconvene as the people of God. We can connect with each other in powerful ways during this time when we walk along the edge or traverse the verge of the new kind of living in community that is the church. In many services of worship we begin by some form of calling ourselves to worship, often a call-and-response format between a leader and the congregation. In that act of "talking to" each other in a formal way, we recognize each others' presence and establish connection as we come to worship, and we declare our intent to stand together.

It's common for the Passing of the Peace to have a prominent role in this first movement of worship. As we come in from the world outside we are always craving a peace we cannot find in the world. When we wish to each other, both corporately and individually, the peace of God, we are reminded even more profoundly that we come to a place that is different; we crave a reality that stands in contrast to the reality we often see around us. While calling ourselves to worship declares our purpose for gathering, we actually, tangibly bless each other by wishing each other the peace of God. This is a profoundly connecting action in which we invoke the Divine and voice our common need.

Another expression of worship that can connect us in the gathering in is the act of corporate singing. It's rare anyplace outside the church to find nonprofessional singers who regularly lift their voices to sing aloud. There is some element of vulnerability in this action, and along with it comes the recognition of the other: the voice that sings beside us and the lives that walk in tandem with our own. When we participate in these rituals of connection as we gather ourselves for worship, we more deeply and meaningfully designate a special time and place in which profoundly meaningful connections can happen.

Hearing the Word

Listening to the reading of Scripture together can be a worship ritual that connects us to each other. When we find and open our Bibles together, train our attention on the reader, or read a passage together, we are tapping into a deep well of history and tradition, the words of community that have been read and sung and recorded by people together for thousands of years. By pausing together to give the words attention and intention, we declare again that this is Holy Scripture, a powerful source of nourishment, sustenance, and inspiration, and this action draws us to each other as we undertake it. The corporate act of hearing a sermon or the declaration of the Word, by the same token, can become a powerful corporate act in which we form connections not only with the preacher but also with each other, as the declaration of the Word can be a powerful tie to connect those who declare it and those who receive it.

During this part of worship we often pray together or declare affirmations of faith as a group. The same power found in hearing ancient words of Scripture can be tapped in the corporate act of repeating the words of the Lord's Prayer in unison or reciting an affirmation of faith from the history and tradition of the larger Christian church. When we pray or affirm our faith together, we are building connections with each other and recalling connections with the larger arc of Christian faith and tradition. Anytime these connections are affirmed, they become stronger and more sustaining.

Another common ritual in the middle movement of worship is the celebration of communion, or the Lord's Supper. In so many of the same ways eating a meal together can tie us to one another, the celebrating, serving, and taking of this ritual meal can powerfully tie us to each other. The rituals that tie us together cannot be explored without a mention of this foundational ritual, begun by Jesus himself.

Becoming Disciples

In a final movement of worship we are blessed and sent into the world to take the power of the word we have heard, to allow it to transform our lives, and to live in such a way that the gospel begins to transform the whole world. Sometimes during this part of the worship experience we are challenged to give of our resources—money and time, or to more deeply commit ourselves to the practical expression of our faith. These rituals are often, again, tangible expressions of our connection to each other as we pass the offering plates hand to hand, and as we witness the sacrificial giving of those in our community of faith, we are tied to each other in ways that are deep and lasting.

There may also be rituals during this movement of worship that allow us to affirm decisions of faith and welcome new members. As we recognize, welcome, affirm new decisions, we are tied once again to each other. Finally, as we are blessed and commissioned to go and live our faith in the world, we are reminded yet again that we are not alone, that the ties that bind us lead us forward into the new world God imagines, as God's kingdom comes to be in new and wonderfully redemptive expressions.

These and many more rituals can tie us to each other as we yearn to be tied to God. Whatever these rituals may be in each different context, a worship experience must be planned to include numerous expressions of connectedness as together we live and practice the truth that we are always and ever connected to God.

4

Pastoral Prayers in Worship

SHARLANDE SLEDGE

EACH SUNDAY AS WE sing the processional hymn and I look out at the faces of people who have gathered to worship, I am struck by the needs of the people I see: the couple who has been trying to have a child, sitting behind the family of the baby we will dedicate that morning; the woman waiting for the results from the first round of medical tests; the nurse who worked the night shift at the hospital and still managed to get his children to Sunday School; the couple who were primed for retirement and suddenly find themselves raising two preschool grandchildren; the teenager who is trying desperately to fit in with the rest of the youth group; the couple whose daughter took her life by suicide just before Christmas; the young man, once a member of the youth group, now back from Afghanistan; the daughter who is struggling with the decision to move her mother to assisted living; the couple deeply mired in marital problems, trying to put on a brave face at church.

As I approach the pulpit to offer the invocation, I look around the sanctuary again and see faces of the faithful, who know that worship is where they are called to be this morning. They may not know the exact needs of the people sitting next to them, but through the grace of community they bear each other's burdens and taste the salt from each other's tears. I know that many of them read at least the front page of the paper or watch the Sunday morning news before they come to church. They know they are privileged people. They grieve the extreme poverty in our city and lament war and violence between nations. They worry about lands threatened by drought and storms as much as they do about the low wages paid to preschool teachers. Yet they realize that neither an inclusive community nor a generous life-style comes without a commitment to justice and hard work. Called beyond their comfort zone to be the hands and feet of Christ in this world, they still wonder if they will have the strength to face the tasks before them.

During the offertory, I look at the congregation once more, and this time I see grateful people. One sings each hymn with gusto, a testimony of her faith, though I know her life is, by many measures, an hour by hour struggle. I see a man who walks with the support of two crutches, yet is always the first in his chair for worship. I stand amazed by the presence of a courageous family who came to worship only two days after their daughter's death. I see a woman who receives a few days' worth of meals from our food pantry, who also volunteers in that same ministry as an act of gratitude. I notice as a man working two jobs drops his offering into the plate. I watch a twelve-year-old with wet hair slip into her place beside her parents after her baptism; her face, pure joy.

I see the people of our church bringing their whole selves to worship. Each person's week held its particular set of challenges, anxieties, and cares. Yet they lived out their common longing for healing in the context of a world where both suffering and the call to alleviate it are real. In gratitude for a compassionate, forgiving, and loving God and knowing that they sit in the "midst of many mercies,"[1] their presence in worship is one way they give thanks and praise.

These are the beloved people of God, whose needs for care, desires to serve, and expressions of gratitude are so vast that we can hardly take in even a glimpse of their lives. How, then, shall we pray for them?

Pastoral Understanding

The beginning point of prayer in the public worship setting is a pastoral understanding of the human condition and the common needs of all our souls. Since pastoral ministry has to do with the spiritual care of the congregation, the one who prays in worship needs a sense of the prayers on the hearts of the people. The task of the person offering the pastoral prayer is to gather the unspoken prayers of the people and give them voice. In the mystery of God, these prayers and sighs too deep for words seem to call out to be spoken aloud by someone who cares for the people.

Pastoral ministry is calling people into the presence of God. Focused attention to the pastoral prayer includes visualizing and praying for every person within the circle of the minister's spiritual care. I once ministered alongside a pastor who prepared for preaching by walking the circumference of the sanctuary each Sunday morning while reading his sermon aloud,

1. Brueggemann, *Prayers*, 97.

thereby gaining a connection with the people who would fill the space a few hours later. Now I often imagine the people sitting in chairs in the sanctuary and my thoughts inform my preparation of pastoral prayers.

An effective pastoral prayer may touch individual lives in ways beyond the planning, wisdom, or even hopes of the one who prays. The better the pastor knows the people and the culture of the congregation, the easier it is to frame and shape a prayer that speaks to everyone who hears it. Pastoral prayers are living words. Their text is written on the heart of the minister throughout the week. They take shape in the pastor's spirit during committee meetings, in the hallway outside a hospital room, while writing newsletter articles, in impromptu conversations in the church office, at the grocery store, and, yes, sometimes early on Sunday mornings.

Prayers of the People

The prayers offered in worship bear witness to the truth that we are all in this life together. As Walter Brueggemann writes, we pray with our brothers and sisters who share "a common mercy from God."[2] Our prayers affirm the solidarity of the Christian community by gathering all the praises and psalms, petitions and pains that people feel but may be hesitant or unable to express aloud. No matter its form, a prayer in corporate worship should be a prayer of the people, one to which each person who hears it can say "Amen."

Prayer in public worship, as so much of the Bible demonstrates, is a shared expression of faith. When we stumble to give voice to our prayers, the words of ancient scripture speak for us; generation after generation, the Psalms never fail to voice our longings, grief, and praise. How many times have we turned to Psalm 46 when words fail us in the face of death or destruction? "God is our refuge and strength, a very present help in trouble." Or when we cannot contain our wonder at the majesty of creation, Psalm 8 is exultant on our behalf: "O LORD our Sovereign, how majestic is your name in all the earth! You have set your glory above the heavens."

When Jesus' disciples asked him to teach them to pray, the opening word he taught them to use, "our," situated the prayer in the context of our common life. The Lord's Prayer is the prayer of God's people. How can we pray "Our Father" and not feel connected to all our brothers and sisters around the world? And how then can we not ask for daily bread for all of us? In feeding the hungry, granting forgiveness, and choosing to do good and not evil, we live out our prayers to help bring about God's kingdom. And so we pray, not only for our own sustenance and care, but also for the wisdom,

2. Ibid., xiv.

strength, and compassion to see and respond to the needs of one another, many of whom we may never see.

The emphasis in corporate prayer, like the teachings of the Lord's Prayer, should focus on the whole community's experiences before God rather than on a collection of individual and personal experiences. Certainly, the one who prays cannot name each individual concern within the context of worship, nor is that the purpose of the pastoral prayer. However, in praying the shared intercessions and petitions common to all of us, ministers create a space for individuals to fill in their own prayers and their own needs.

In its description of "the prayers of the people," the *Book of Common Worship* offers a helpful guide to these prayers of intercessions for worldwide and local concerns, including "the church universal, its ministry and those who minister . . . churches in other places, this congregation; the nations and those in authority; peace and justice in the world; the earth and a right use of its resources; the community and those who govern; the poor and the oppressed; the sick, the bereaved, the lonely, all who suffer in body, mind, or spirit; those with special needs. Those who have died are remembered with Thanksgiving."[3] The notes for these prayers suggest offering these intercessions in a manner that engages the people in prayer. Prepared by the one leading the prayer, they may be offered in a free style as a prayer for one voice or with pauses between petitions for silence, giving other people the chance to name their own prayers.[4]

Barbara Brown Taylor says the prayers of the people expand the concept of the pastoral prayer: "By praying not only for the universal church but also for the welfare of the whole world, the people of God discover that 'us' includes every created thing. We pray for those we have never met along with those we love. We pray for those who will not or cannot pray for themselves. We pray for the earth and its creatures; we pray for our enemies; we pray for the living and the dead. We become intercessors for the entire web of being to which we belong and in doing so we act like the priest we are, offering the whole world back to God in prayer."[5]

In the same way, she writes, we confess our sins: "We do not kneel as individuals, turning a private laundry list of sins over to God, but as the body of Christ, to confess the ways in which all humanity has missed the mark set for us, failing to love God with our whole hearts, failing to love our neighbors as ourselves.[6] Each time the community of faith confesses its complicity in excessive consumption, baptizes a new believer, approaches

3. *Book of Common Worship*, 97.

4. *Book of Common Prayer*, 97.

5. Taylor, *Preaching Life*, 72.

6. Ibid.

the table of bread and wine, sends a group on a mission trip, gathers in its grief, ordains new deacons, enters a weekend retreat, dedicates a garden, or blesses a meal it has the chance, through prayer, to approach God together and set the moment apart as a sacred.

Shaping Our Prayers

As we listen to the heartbeat of God and become attuned to the language of the Spirit within us, we gain strength and wisdom for praying on behalf of others. Generations of traditions—within the church universal and in the places where we worship—as well as our personal experiences, shape the way we pray. But, practically speaking, how *do* we shape our prayers? What preparation, language, forms, and rhythms are important to remember?

Preparation

In our Baptist tradition we place great value on extemporaneous prayers that are prompted by the movement of the Spirit. We are often called upon to "offer a quick prayer" before a meal, or we initiate prayer for God's strength and comfort with an anxious of suffering family. Other times we are prompted by God's Spirit to pray with others for discernment or, with eyes wide open, we kneel beside a child to give thanks for a dog's sloppy kisses or the first strawberry in the garden. These informal, spontaneous prayers keep us in tune with God's constant presence.

For those occasions when we are asked to offer public prayers, Ecclesiastes 4:2a offers a word of guidance: "Do not be quick with your mouth, do not be hasty in your heart to utter anything before God." In our "quick" and "hasty" world, giving thoughtful reflection to the words we prepare to offer in Christ's name and taking spacious time to remember those who need our prayers is a countercultural but necessary spiritual practice. If you are not used to speaking in public, read the prayer aloud several times to find the right cadence and expression. Sometimes, words that sound good on paper may be surprising tongue twisters when you speak them. If a microphone is available for you to use, use it. Practice.

Language

The purpose of pastoral prayers is not to encourage literary artistry but to offer prayers that are authentic, ordered, and fresh. Such prayers are natural and reverent, spoken slowly and loudly enough to be heard by everyone in the worship space. While rising out of the rich Christian heritage, pastoral prayers call for clear, incisive words that are mindful of the vocabulary of the people in the congregation today. They depend on the imagination of the minister, who uses the gift of empathy to translate the needs of the congregation into words that are meaningful to them.

To fill your reservoir of prayerful language, read poetry. Read more poetry. Read the psalms. Read them again. Listen to their themes. Focus on the images of God. Read through the hymnal, hymn by hymn, prayer by prayer, because that's what hymns are, after all: "All I have needed thy hand hath provided. Great is thy faithfulness, Lord, unto me." Or "O Love that will not let me go, I hide my weary self in thee." When you hear a prayer that speaks to you, ask the person who prayed it for a copy. Study its language, its form, its message and try to discern why it caught your ear and your heart. Collect books of classic prayers. Keep a notebook or computer file of words and prayer lines you like. Begin writing your own.

Form and Rhythms

Bringing a pastoral understanding to any prayer in the service—the invocation, the confession, the blessing of our gifts, the intercessions for the world—transforms any of these into a pastoral prayer. Yet when we speak of the pastoral prayer, we usually mean the longer, substantial prayer of intercession and petition. Most often, this is spoken as a prayer for one voice. However, the pastoral prayer is the most flexible form of public prayer. Since the Middle Ages it has empowered the congregation to contribute to the service. It calls for responses by members of the congregation after short petitions or "biddings" (requests) are spoken by the worship leader, such as "In your mercy . . . Lord, hear our prayer."

When different readers lead the responses, they contribute to the movement of the service through the variety of tones and pitches in their voices. The rhythms of the repeated responses also keep the congregation engaged in the prayer and not distracted by a long list of petitions. Be sure that the response the people say is something that they would actually feel and want to say. Now imagine the prayer without the insertion of responses. Once again it's an extensive prayer of intercession, a prayer for one voice. Though litanies or the petition/response format is most frequently for prayers of intercession, try using this form for prayers of adoration, confession, and thanksgiving. Composed in this way, the congregation will naturally express a rhythmic, united response.

Prayer in Context

Every prayer is set within a specific context. When a minister composes a prayer with the context in mind, the prayer's purpose is clear and its intention is authentic. It celebrates what needs to be celebrated, remembers the person who needs to be remembered, deepens the understanding of the day's lectionary text, situates the congregation within the liturgical year, acknowledges natural disasters, and places the church within the larger community and the world. Not to speak of any of these elements in worship lessens the effect of the prayer and waters down the authenticity of context.

The prayers below were created with attention to context—the theme of the day's service or the time in our common history. Each one contributed to the holistic nature of worship.

Lectionary Scripture
(Luke 10:25–37)

O God,
Balm to Our Wounds,
Great Physician to our Spirits,
we are all on the journey from
Jerusalem to Jericho –
going down the road,
going up the road,
or walking on a level place for a while.
We may be looking around the curve,
straining to see what is ahead of us,
or averting our eyes from the one we are approaching,
trying to decide whether to cross boundaries
or give aid to the person in our path or
to receive help ourselves.
O God, today we find ourselves in a familiar narrative,
of the one we call "good" and the man left beside the road
a story so compelling a child can tell it,
so familiar even those who haven't read the
gospel of Luke know the term "Good Samaritan,"
an encounter so significant to our life narratives
that it's real to us every day.
This morning touch us with your great compassion
as though for the first time.
Grant us a mercy so real that we remember
that you are present in our woundedness and through our
weakness,

made holy by you, we know your strength.
In our worship, here and throughout the week,
restore us to life for this road we travel,
for even with all its rocky places,
blind curves, and strangers,
this is the way to your welcome and wholeness
and the chance to help others in your name.

Amen.

Sharlande Sledge
Invocation, July 16, 2009
Lake Shore Baptist Church

Memorial Service

God of Great Compassion,
in the late afternoon shadows of deepest December,
we lean into your light . . .
for our spirits are spent with grief
and our hearts cannot take in all that confounds us.
With the psalmist, we lament:
"Oh, Lord, hear my cry! . . . Answer me."
With the prophet, we plead for you to comfort your people.
and with the magi we are already looking for a sign that
will lead us to your presence here in our midst.
In your mercy, O God, hallow these moments when
we remember your blessed creation, Deborah,
daughter of God, dearest one to Becca,
child of Boyce and Jane.

We come to thank you for Deb,
our fellow pilgrim on the road of life,
voice of beauty and justice,
who sang your song and
who longed for peace,
both in her own heart and for the world.
O God of Advent, who dares to go with us,
even to the deepest sources of our pain and suffering,
bring our restless spirits into the calming strength of your grace.
"Healer of our every ill,
light of each tomorrow,
give us peace beyond our fears,
and hope beyond our sorrows."

O Come, O Come, Emmanuel.
Come and dwell with us.

Amen.

Offered by Sharlande Sledge
memorial service for Deb Vardiman
Lake Shore Baptist Church
December 2011

Church Year
(season of Lent)

Oh, Lord, our God, during this season,
we find ourselves living in the middle of many things.
We find ourselves caught between
what has been and what will be.
We find ourselves living between
the joy of Christmas and the pain of the cross.
We find ourselves living between
the three kings and the crown of thorns.
We find ourselves caught between
a life of plenty and a life of poverty.
We find ourselves living.
We find ourselves caught.
We find ourselves when we listen to the words
of the man once born in the manger.
We free ourselves when we give of ourselves.
We live when we die to self and give to others.
Bless these gifts, O Lord, that we return to you.
They symbolize our gratitude for all you have given us.
They remind us of what you ask from us.
They free us to live in the hope of what will be.
They free us to live as those who love.

Amen.

Jim Nogalski
Blessing of our gifts.
Lake Shore Baptist Church
March 29, 2009

National Decision

O God, the election is upon us. As a nation it is decision time, and probably most of us don't know how to pray either as a community or as individuals. It's not cynicism so much, though no doubt some of us succumb to that. Forgive us.

But our dilemma is that as a community at worship we have so many different views. You know that. So how do we pray as a community?

Even as individuals it feels wrong to pray that our candidate will win, as if our prayer could cause you to determine who will be the next president or representative or judge. If anything seems clear in our world, O God, it is that you have left those decisions in our hands. And maybe that's why it's a frightening prospect, for so often we don't get it right—even when life and death are at stake.

What do you require of us, O God? Surely, that we act justly, that we love kindness, that we walk humbly with you. We know the words, but do we know the way? That's the problem—figuring out the way. So what can we pray for? Enlightened minds in the face of so many complications? O God, we do pray for that! For tender hearts in the midst of suffering that has national scope? O God, we do pray for such hearts! For faith that, despite the way things often appear, goodness is at the heart of reality, that you are at the heart of reality. O God, we do pray for that!

For by faith we believe that the future is open, that the future is your gift to us. Help us to seize it and to live it "finely aware and richly responsible." May the enlightenment, the tenderness and the faith we pray for guide us as individuals and as a nation in a time of great decision.

In the spirit of Christ whom we adore, Christ who is our model, in the spirit of Christ who redeems all the messes we make and gives us our future, we make our prayer.

Amen.

Offered by Robert Baird
Lake Shore Baptist Church
Sunday, October 31, 2004

Natural Disaster

God of Love,
stronger than the mountains,
deeper than the deepest fault-line
is your abiding love.

Though the land shivers with grief,
though familiar landmarks crumble
and are washed into the sea,
though exhaustion and fear encompass your children,
still and forever you are with us;
still and forever you love us.

Through the path of rubble and dust and ashes,
through gaping wounds in towns
and numbness in hearts and flesh that faints,
through unanswerable questions, in Japan
and here within our own community,
and within ourselves,
still and forever you are with us;
still and forever you love us.

Though we are small creatures on this
ever-changing, ever-shifting planet we call home
and are forever trying to find our way
through life that contains loss
and loss that contains life,
we are blessed because
still and forever you are with us;
still and forever you love us.

God of Healing and Mercy,
this is a day to call upon your compassion,
to be in one another's presence,
and in that presence to remind ourselves
of the enduring power of your love

. . . for we live in trust that we are loved, we are held,
and in that love and in that holding,
we find hope.

Our help is in the name of the Lord,
our refuge and our strength
and very present help in trouble.

On behalf of our fragile and broken world
and all our brothers and sisters in it and on behalf of ourselves,
we call upon your Compassionate and Merciful name,
for we are assured that

> still and forever you are with us,
> still and forever you love us.

Amen.

Offered by Sharlande Sledge
Lake Shore Baptist Church
Sunday, March 13, 2011

And all God's people said . . . "By the time we finish our prayers, we have yielded in gladness and become other than we were, carriers of hope that will not quit."[7] This is our prayer, O Lord. Amen.

7. Brueggemann, *Prayers*, xv.

5

Creeds and Freedom

Another Baptist Witness

Philip E. Thompson

A Modest Proposal

This chapter is admittedly different from the others in this volume. The other chapters address topics more common to Baptist churches. While there are differences in their understanding and practice, and while there may often be less reflection than we might hope, the worship of all Baptist churches includes in some form preaching, prayer, music, baptism, and observance of the Lord's Supper. And while most Baptist churches probably do not observe the church year or think of their worship precisely as "liturgy," such churches are not hard to find, particularly in urban areas. I know very few Baptist churches, however, that employ creeds in their worship. I must confess some surprise in finding any at all that do this through an informal survey of Baptist churches with a more formal approach to worship.[1]

---

1. Given limitations of space, I will address the three Ecumenical creeds, the Apostles,' the Niceno-Constantinopolitan (called Nicene), and the so-called Athanasian Creed. I use "creeds" to refer to these three; reference to "the creed" indicates the Apostles or Nicene. What I will say will apply to other confessions, such as the First and Second London Confessions, and to what are probably most "palatable" for Baptists, the "proto-creedal" elements in Scripture such as Rom 1:3–4; 1 Cor 15:3–7; Phil 2:6–11; or 1 Tim 3:16. My sense is that, if I can make a case for the Ecumenical Creeds, it will suffice for the others as well. These resources and more may be found in the appendix.

Beginning this project, my working assumption was that no Baptist churches

It is, in addition, not readily evident that what I am proposing is a good idea at all (though I would not write this chapter if I thought that!). There certainly are other elements of worship derived from the practices of the church catholic that are more comfortable for Baptists. Why should Baptists consider this one in particular when we might more comfortably embrace the rich biblical witness of the Lectionary, the instructive use of color and symbol from the church year, or more developed prayers at the pool and table? Are creeds not more about orthodoxy, right belief, than worship? Do they not risk making worship rather didactic, what Methodist liturgical theologian Don Saliers has called "flat EKG" worship?[2] These are important questions, ones requiring answers. One respondent to my informal survey commented, "We have enough 'catholic' elements to our service that I can envision the regular use of a creed putting a few over the top in their concern about our denominational identity!"

This Baptist pastor also named a second reservation this chapter might occasion. It may seem novel to suggest, for instance, Baptists think of their worship *as* "liturgy" rather than using that word merely to designate a more formal worship "style." Suggesting that Baptists use creeds, on the other hand, might well seem not just novel, but wrong, a positive violation

---

employed creeds in their worship. It occurred to me that I ought at least to attempt to test that, so I compiled a list of churches I know to be very reflective and intentional about worship and informally surveyed the pastors. These churches are all affiliated with the American Baptist Churches in the USA, The Cooperative Baptist Fellowship, or the Alliance of Baptists.

To my great surprise, of the twenty who responded, eight used some form of affirmation of faith, and five used one of the ecumenical creeds at least on occasion. The frequency with which creeds are included in worship varies among the churches that use them. I would like to express profound gratitude to the pastors who took the time to respond to my "knock at midnight," in alphabetical order without indication of response to my question: Brent Beasley (Broadway, Fort Worth, TX); Amy Butler (Calvary, Washington, DC); William Carrell (University Baptist, Baltimore, MD); Kyle Childress (Austin Heights, Nacogdoches, TX); Mike Clingenpeel (River Road, Richmond, VA); Jason Crosby (Crescent Hill, Louisville, KY); C. Welton Gaddy (Northminster, Monroe, LA); Jim Hopkins (Lakeshore, Oakland, CA); Andrea Jones (Millbrook, Raleigh, NC); Rodney Kennedy (First Baptist, Dayton, OH); James Lamkin (Northside Drive, Atlanta, GA); Mark McIntyre (University Baptist, College Park, MD); Tim Moore (Sardis, Charlotte, NC); Nancy Petty (Pullen Memorial, Raleigh, NC); Joe Phelps (Highland, Louisville, KY); Guy Sayles (First Baptist, Asheville, NC); Stephen Shoemaker (Myers Park, Charlotte, NC); Mitch Simpson (University Baptist, Chapel Hill, NC); Bill Slater (Wake Forest, Wake Forest, NC); and Scott Stearman (Kirkwood, St. Louis, MO).

Further inquiry led me to discover that the churches using creeds do not do so for aesthetic reasons, but rather have sensed and embraced creeds' wisdom.

2. Saliers, *Worship as Theology*, 28. Many people in our time might well be just as concerned that it produces "flat EEG" worship as well!

of historical Baptist convictions.[3] Historian Walter Shurden notes Baptists are "historically an anti-creedal people."[4] On the strength of this, he makes a normative claim, "Baptists are a non-creedal people!"[5] He is not alone; his claim reflecting a veritable cliché for generations of Baptists whose rejection of creeds is not arbitrary but a principled stance. It may be granted that Baptists guardedly accept confessions, yet these are carefully distinguished from creeds as being less binding and therefore less coercive.[6]

I have my work cut out for me. While the intent of this book is to assist theological reflection on the practice of worship and the various practices that comprise worship, most of the practices examined need no real justification since they are already practiced in some way, or can be imagined with little problem. Suggesting Baptists employ creeds in their worship might tax imagination. Thus, I must present a case for Baptists to recite creeds in worship, demonstrating that it is not incompatible with historic Baptist witness. My desire is for witness from Baptist history to guide and shape the theological reflection. Interrogation of the Baptist past will bring us to what I believe is a most important theological consideration, not only for Baptists, but for Protestants more generally in the early twenty-first century. This in turn will permit some gestures toward enriched practice in churches' worship life.

Baptists are not alone today in being suspicious of creeds. The attitude has become deeply ingrained in the West over the last two centuries, though antecedents stretch back farther still. While there are differences between the claims of more popular and more scholarly authors, creeds are defined as by nature oppressive and stifling of other spiritualities, even "other

---

3. For this reason the creed should not be thought of as one more "formal element" that a "liturgical style" may or may not include. I do not think it is helpful to think of liturgy in terms of formality. That kind of thinking, I believe, causes more problems than it solves. I intend this proposal for the consideration of all Baptist churches, regardless of the formality or informality of their worship.

4. Shurden, *The Baptist Identity*, 15. Weaver notes that there have been occasional aberrations in this pattern. See Weaver, "Baptists and Denominational Identity," 289.

5. Shurden, *The Baptist Identity*, 14; capitalization removed.

6. See McBeth, *The Baptist Heritage*, 686–87; Dunn, "No Freedom For the Soul With A Creed," 83; Cothen, "Truths or Truth," 92; Sherman, "Freedom of the Individual," 12; Halbrooks, "Why I am a Baptist," 5–7; Weaver, "Baptists and Denominational Identity," 289; Estep, "Baptists and Authority," 600–601; and Hinson, "Creeds and Christian Unity," 29–30.

Pelikan notes that there is overlap between the two terms, particularly in the ways they are employed. Two distinctions, however, seem most readily apparent. Confessions are more detailed than creeds, and for this reason are less suited for liturgical use. They rather serve as written guidelines for regulating the life of a community of faith. See Pelikan, *Credo*, 2.

Christianities" that have as much to commend them as does the oppressive "orthodoxy" that has no better claim to being "right" (the meaning of the prefix "ortho-") than being the religion of the successful.[7] Such is the opinion widespread and widely accepted in our day. According to Luke Timothy Johnson, however, "That's never been true."[8] Many are ready to believe it nonetheless. This fact sheds less light on the early church less than it does on about attitudes toward authority and religion in contemporary America.[9]

It requires, however, neither fictional conspiracy theory nor scholarly reconstruction of the emergence of orthodoxy to produce a dim view of creeds. The consciousness formed in the modern context is sufficient.[10] A mindset shaped by modernity prizes acceptance of truths only that one can understand. Anything less lacks integrity.[11] Assent to a statement not of one's own devising is mere "external conformity," and as such always a sign of bad faith.[12] The attitude has been developing for more than two centuries now, with the effect that "[t]here is something in the creed to offend virtually every contemporary sensitivity."[13] Leanne Van Dyk observes, "[t]he ecumenical creeds do not fare well in this cultural climate."[14]

Baptists emerged in the seventeenth century, and thus have from their beginning existed in and have been shaped to a degree by the sensitivities and sensibilities of modernity. Their numerous declamations against creeds have reflected these sensitivities and sensibilities, though Baptists have articulated them with their own particular inflection. We might well characterize this inflection above all with the word "freedom." By most contemporary accounts, freedom is the very *esse* (being) of Baptist Christianity.[15]

7. Dan Brown would be an example of the former, Elaine Pagels and Bart Ehrman of the latter. See Allen, "Do-It-Yourself"; and Burgess, "Going Creedless," 24–28.

I should note that, given the brevity of this essay and the size of my task, my references throughout are *per force* representative and not in any way exhaustive. Examples of similar thought may in most instances be multiplied a number of times. Cf. L. Johnson, *The Creed*, 4.

8. Cited in Allen, "Do-It-Yourself."

9. Burgess, "Going Creedless," 24.

10. Pelikan, *Credo*, 488.

11. Byars, "Creeds and Prayers," 86, and Van Dyk, "A Conversation with the Ecumenical Creeds," 17–18.

12. Webster, "Confession and Confessions," 126.

13. L. Johnson, *The Creed*, 7

14. Van Dyk, "A Conversation with the Ecumenical Creeds," 19. Hatch, *Democratization*, provides an excellent examination of the conditions that have enabled this phenomenon the various aspects of a cultural animus against creeds and other forms of traditional authority in the United States.

15. See Shurden, *The Baptist Identity*; and the essays in Neely, ed., *Being Baptist Means Freedom*.

This freedom has to do above all with the individual, and to this all other aspects of freedom are related.[16] Thus the *bene esse* (well being) of Baptists requires maximal human freedom. Creeds are said to usurp the place of authority that rightfully belongs to the Bible. Perhaps more accurately, they usurp the interpretive authority that belongs to the individual believer reading Scripture and articulating the meaning of Christian faith for herself.[17] They diminish faith by putting a premature end to the pursuit of truth.[18] The argument set forth most forcefully, however, by Baptist opponents of creeds is that they bind and coerce the conscience, thus assaulting the most precious element of human freedom.[19] It is little wonder, then, that "creedalism" signals for many Baptists the worst of all possible abuses of the religious rights of individuals.[20] One thus might well consider himself justified in assuming without question that Baptists' non-creedal or even anti-creedal stance "was in the beginning, is now, and ever shall be."[21]

Responding to Baptist Concerns Over Creeds

There are several arguments we might offer in response. For example, we might wonder if creedalism is not more of a "straw figure" in our context of institutional separation of church and state. Without the power of the state, how can a church "impose" creeds on people who are not coerced to remain

16. Dunn and Cothen, *Soul Freedom*.

17. Shurden, *The Baptist Identity*, 14; Weaver, "Baptists and Denominational Identity," 293–95. This view is not of recent vintage. See Gaustad, "Backus-Leland Tradition," 112.

18. Weaver, "Baptists and Denominational Identity," 290; and Cothen, "Truths or Truth," 92. Both quote John Leland, a Baptist leader in Revolutionary and early republican America. See Hatch, *Democratization*, 93–101 *et passim*.

19. Shurden, *The Baptist Identity*, 14; and Weaver, "Baptists and Denominational Identity," 291–99. Gaustad notes that Leland and his near contemporary Isaac Backus both resisted anything that encroached upon the "citadel" of conscience. See Gaustad, "Backus-Leland Tradition," 111–12.

20. The very language employed by Weaver, "Baptists and Denominational Identity," 291, conveys this as he speaks of "coerced creedal definition" of faith, implying as many Baptist writers do that if it is "creedal," it is necessarily "coerced." Cf. Dunn, "No Freedom for the Soul with a Creed," 83; Cothen, "Truths or Truth," 92–93; Shurden, *The Baptist Identity*, 14.

21. In my informal poll of Baptist pastors, this claim and slight variations of it were quite common. One summarized the standard response of the congregants she asked: "No. Never. We're Baptist. We don't use creeds." Others noted that their churches' non-creedal stances had to do with maintaining historic Baptist distinctiveness. There was acknowledgement of the mild irony of being non-creedal out of tradition, though not across the board among those with whom I corresponded.

there? Or we might also ask whether confessions, which Baptists accept in guarded fashion, are not more restrictive than creeds? They are, for instance, more developed on points of disputed doctrine not even addressed in the ecumenical creeds. Yet, they have served as bases for fellowship among Baptists in the past.[22] Would it be preferable in some ways for Baptists to claim they are "creedal, not confessional?" These are, I think, valid arguments, yet not the most useful paths along which to make a case for Baptists to employ creeds in worship. For that, we need to turn to Baptist history.

Examination of the sources shows approval of and agreement with creeds voiced throughout Baptist history.[23] We find among both General (Arminian) and Particular (Calvinist) Baptists of the seventeenth-century approval of creeds, and not in guarded fashion. For example, article XXXVIII of the General Baptists' "An Orthodox Creed," a confession from 1678, states:

> The three creeds, viz., Nicene creed, Athanasius's creed, and the Apostles creed, as they are commonly called, ought thoroughly to be received, and believed. For we believe, they may be proved, by most undoubted authority of holy scripture, and are necessary to be understood of all christians; . . . these creeds containing all things in brief manner, that are necessary to be known, fundamentally, in order to our salvation.[24]

The full text of these three creeds followed. In 1680, Particular Baptist pastor Hercules Collins published "An Orthodox Catechism: Being the Sum of Christian Religion, Contained in the Law and Gospel." In the Preface, he stated:

> I have proposed three Creeds to your consideration, which ought throughly to be believed and embraced by all those that would be accounted Christians, viz. the Nicene Creed, Athanasius his Creed, and the Creed commonly called the Apostles; the last of which contains the sum of the Gospel; . . . and I beseech you do not slight it because of its Form, nor Antiquity, nor because supposed to be composed by Men; neither because some that hold it, maintain some Errors, or whose Conversation may

22. Weaver, "Baptists and Denominational Identity," 289. Weaver's example was the use of the 1742 Philadelphia Confession as a basis for cooperation in colonial-era associational life. This confession is quite Calvinistic in orientation, and not all Baptists shared that perspective. Might there have been broader basis for unity in the Nicene Creed?

23. I must acknowledge from the start that though the early Baptists affirmed the creeds, as I will demonstrate, I have not located evidence that they used them in worship. I do not, however, believe that liturgical use of creeds is at any variance with the early Baptists' affirmation of them, and in fact is entirely consistent with that affirmation.

24. Lumpkin and Leonard, *Baptist Confessions of Faith*, 337.

not be correspondent to such fundamental Principles of Salvation; but take this for a perpetual Rule, That whatever is good in any, owned by any, whatever Error or Vice it may be mixed withal, the Good must not be rejected for the Error or vice sake, but owned, commended, and accepted.[25]

Collins likewise included the text of all three of the creeds throughout his catechism, along with the Ten Commandments and Lord's Prayer.

In 1687, General Baptist Bishop Thomas Grantham penned "St. Paul's Catechism." In it he included the text of the Nicene Creed.[26] It is presented in the part of the catechism teaching about the Trinity, and is introduced with the words:

> And that thou mayest know how this Great Mystery was understood by the Ancient Church, about 1400 years ago, I will here shew thee their Confession of Faith, published by a very great Council of the Christians in those days, wherein were 318 Pastors of the Church, who thus profess their Faith.[27]

The text of the Nicene Creed followed. The child's response at the conclusion of the creed is, "I must reverence this ancient Confession of Faith, for it's excellent Brevity, and especially for the solidity of the Matter."[28]

Grantham, one of the chief apologists for Baptists in their first century, was careful to show how Baptist teachings agreed with the creeds. In his most developed theological work, *Christianismus Primitivus*, he stated:

> As God hath delivered one Form of Doctrine to the Churches, so it's the duty of all Christians to hold and diligently to observe the same, and not to be *carried about with divers and strange Doctrines*, Heb. 13.9. And her Pastors are all warned, and accordingly to warn others, that they teach no other Doctrine, I *Tim* 1. for otherwise unity of Faith cannot be maintained; . . . [T]here hath been several Confessions of Faith published, among which that called the *Apostles Creed*, and the *Nicene* do seem to be of most venerable estimation, both for Antiquity, and the solidity of the matter, and for their excellent brevity, we do hereby declare to the world that we assent to the Contents

25. Collins, "An Orthodox Catechism," Preface, n.p.

26. Grantham, *St. Paul's Catechism*, 24–25. The General Baptists did have a more episcopal form of church governance in the seventeenth century, but that must be another story for another time.

27. Ibid., 24.

28. Ibid., 25.

thereof, . . . that all men may know that we are no devisers, or
favourers of Novelties or new Doctrines.[29]

There followed the Latin and English texts of the Nicene Creed. He then
presented the text of the 1663 version of the General Baptist Standard Confession, noting his desire, "to shew that though the composition of these
Articles be new, yet the Doctrine contained therein, is truly ancient, being
witnessed both by the Holy Scriptures, and later writers of Christianity."[30]

Roughly a century later, Andrew Fuller, one of the principal voices in
the emergence of "Evangelical Calvinism" in England that enabled the rise of
the modern Protestant missions movement, took up questions concerning
creeds in two letters penned to the Northampton Association churches.[31]
In "An Inquiry into the Right of Private Judgment on Matters of Religion,"
Fuller observes that the claim for the right of private judgment in matters
of faith and belief had been improperly extended. Rather than using the
principle solely to argue that Christians should not be subject to civil authorities in matters of belief religious practice, some were claiming persons
should not be bound by creeds or other formulas of faith of their churches.
Anything other than unfettered private judgment was taken to be a "species
of spiritual tyranny and repugnant to the liberty wherewith Christ has set us
free."[32] Fuller maintained to the contrary, this "supposed individual right"
is contrary to the founding principles of Christian churches. "A community
must entirely renounce the name of a Christian church before it can act
on this principle (of private judgment)," he stated bluntly.[33] "If this right
be paramount," he continued, "Christ came in vain."[34] These words from a
hero in the Baptist story must sound strange to many Baptists today. To this
we must soon return.

In "On Creeds and Subscriptions," Fuller took up directly the claim
that creeds are inconsistent with the liberty and rights of conscience. He
found it to be a shortsighted claim. Well-informed and consistent believers
need creeds, he asserted. Certainly, he granted that imposition of creeds by
civil authorities would be unwarrantable, "but if explicit agreement in what
may be deemed fundamental principles be judged essential to fellowship,

29. Grantham, *Christianismus Primitivus* 2.2.5.3 (59–60), emphasis original. Paren-
thetical insertion refers to the page numbers.

30. Ibid., 61. The "Standard Confession," along with "demonstrations" from Scripture and patristic commentators were then presented on pages 62–74.

31. He appears to include all confessions under this term.

32. Fuller, "Inquiry," 628.

33. Ibid., 629.

34. Ibid.

this is only requiring that a man appear to be a Christian before he can have a right to be treated as such."[35] While granting that creeds must be open to revision when perceived to be inconsistent with the will of Christ, and that they cannot replace God's Word as the ground of faith, this did not mean that creeds were not binding in some way.[36] No, he continued, creeds neither limit inquiry, nor bar weak faith.

Fuller introduced an analogy. Civil laws are expositions of the universal principle of equity, he observed. Yet no society says, "Let us agree to walk according to equity." They rather cast this conviction in the form of laws. So too it is with churches, creeds, and the Word of God, Fuller claimed. Creeds give distinct form to the Word of God.[37]

Admittedly, we do not find the same robustness in affirming creeds among Baptists as we move through the nineteenth or twentieth centuries. Baptists on both sides of the Atlantic were affected by various factors that led them to say less in this regard. While a thorough examination far exceeds the scope of this chapter, it is a very important matter. In particular we might note broadly that in the United States, the legacy of Great Awakening revivalism and the republicanism of the revolutionary and early national periods created an environment that was not friendly to creeds. This was so not just among Baptists.[38]

Yet we can still find acknowledgement of creeds and their function. I would note three examples from points along this time span. Admittedly there are fewer from which to draw, given the changes in Baptist thought. In the 1860s Ezekiel Gilman Robinson, professor of theology at Rochester Divinity School and one of the most influential of Baptist theologians of his time, gave a remarkable lecture on the relation of the church and the Bible.[39] He did not consider the position he articulated to be something new among Baptists. In a rather striking contrast from some of the declarations of historical Baptist practices and convictions we observed earlier in more recent writers, Robinson declared, "[T]he Baptists have always persisted in

---

35. Fuller, "On Creeds and Subscriptions," 629.

36. Ibid., 630.

37. Ibid., 631.

38. Again, see Hatch, *Democratization*. The dynamics of Baptist existence are varied and complex indeed, even more than Hatch is able to portray. I would recommend Leonard, *Baptist Ways*. In the United Kingdom, the rise of Oxford Movement "Anglo-Catholicism" led to reaction by Evangelicals generally, pressing them to downplay those aspects of ecclesial life high-church Anglicans emphasized.

39. Robinson, "The Relation of the Church and the Bible," 387–419.

a maintenance of the true use of creeds, and of the true relation of church prerogative to Scripture authority."[40]

When the Baptist World Congress met for the first time in 1905 in London, the first official act of the body was the recitation of the Apostles Creed. They were led in this by the venerable British Baptist, Alexander Maclaren. His prefatory remarks are instructive:

> I should like that there should be no misunderstanding on the part of the English public, or the American public either—before whom we are taking a prominent position, for a day at any rate—as to where we stand in the continuity of the historic Church. And I should like the first act of this Congress to be the audible and unanimous acknowledgement of our Faith. So I have suggested that, given your consent, it would be an impressive and a right thing, and would clear away a good many misunderstandings and stop the mouth of a good deal of slander—if we here and now, in the face of the world, not as a piece of coercion or discipline, but as a simple acknowledgement of where we stand and what we believe, would rise to our feet and, following the lead of your President, would repeat the Apostles' Creed. Will you?[41]

And the entire gathering rose and repeated the text of the creed. This act was repeated at the centenary Baptist World Congress in 2005.

Finally, I would note a 1986 article by then Southern Baptist historian E. Glenn Hinson.[42] It was written in the midst of the Southern Baptist Convention's theological and institutional upheaval that lasted from the late 1970s to the early 1990s. During this time full control of the Convention was shifting to conservatives, and these developments may be discerned in Hinson's argument. For instance, while admitting that his inclination was to say "never" to the use of creeds, Hinson averred that Baptists would do far better to orient themselves to one of the ecumenical creeds than to a list of points of doctrine characteristic of Protestant fundamentalism.[43]

More important for our purposes, however, are not Hinson's prescriptive proposals, but the historical claims he used to support his prescription. Quite striking is his assertion, "Baptists have never rejected and have frequently affirmed their agreement with the great ecumenical creeds, either

---

40. Ibid., 417.

41. Maclaren, "In the Name of Christ," 17.

42. Hinson, "Creeds and Christian Unity," 25–36.

43. Ibid., 30–33. Hinson favored the Niceno-Constantinopolitan Creed (381), commonly called the Nicene Creed.

explicitly or in repetition of content."[44] This certainly is not the same sort of historical assessment we noted earlier. Hinson's affirmation rests largely on his understanding of the close connection of Scripture and creed, in fact using the idea of canon as a partial justification for the legitimacy of the creed. The creed gives "canonical" interpretive guidance for the canonical writings.[45] He thus denies that creeds are a substitute for Scripture. They remain subservient to Scripture. "Creeds never acquired normative significance independent of Scripture, even during the fourth century when theological dispute was fiercest."[46]

Hinson granted that "confession" has a less authoritarian overtone than "creed," leading Baptists often to prefer that milder term.[47] Still, "Baptists have had a creed of some kind, that is, a common expression of belief, throughout their history."[48] Finally, both creeds and confessions have been put by Baptists to similar uses: 1) defense against slander; 2) to provide a basis of union; 3) distinguishing and identifying themselves in relation to other Protestant bodies; 4) instructing their constituencies in Baptist beliefs; 5) affirmation of ecumenical ties; and 6) to maintain a standard for determining orthodoxy.[49]

Differences in Convictions Concerning Creeds—
Theological Bases

We have before us quite an interesting state of affairs. While we have strong rejection of creeds by contemporary Baptists who champion freedom and claim the warrant of Baptist history, we find in Baptist history an equally strong affirmation of creeds and their value. What are we to make of this? Did the earlier Baptists care less about freedom than their more recent namesakes? Not at all. They did value freedom. Yet they gave a far different account of that freedom than more recent Baptists have tended to do. To state the matter simply, for earlier Baptists, freedom was found within structure (the church) and limits (the creeds and sacraments). These structures and limits were provided by God in God's own gracious freedom.

---

44. Ibid., 35.

45. Ibid., 26–27.

46. Ibid., 33.

47. Ibid., 29.

48. Ibid., 26.

49. Ibid., 30. We may see some of these reflected in the statements from the earlier Baptist centuries.

We have noted factors leading to significant changes in the period of the American Revolution and early republic.[50] It was a time, notes Hinson, during which there was a critical change in Baptist self-consciousness.[51] The most significant aspect of this change, I would argue, was the shift from emphasis from divine freedom with human freedom affirmed in a correlative manner to human freedom as primary.[52] With this shift in freedom's locus came critical changes in Baptist theology. One feature is particularly vital for our study: accompanying, and I believe resulting in, the growing animus toward creeds, Baptist ecclesiology (doctrine of the church) was weakened through subordination to the individual and the individual's prerogatives. The church has come to be understood as being logically and theologically subsequent to the free individual.

We will focus on a few prominent leaders of the nineteenth and early twentieth centuries as representative cases. Edwin S. Gaustad observed this in the thought of radical individualist and Baptist leader John Leland (1754–1841). Leland defined a church as, "any given number of pious saints, whose local situation, agreement of sentiment, and gracious affections, lead them to unite together."[53] He explained that Christ chooses individuals and brings them to faith. They are then "baptized into Christ," and on this basis received into the fellowship of the church. Thus, "The church is a fact after salvation . . . and not an agent of salvation."[54] This order became further entrenched in Francis Wayland, identified by Norman H. Maring as one of three principal shapers of "Baptist orthodoxy" in nineteenth-century America.[55] Wayland defined the church as a voluntary society of like-minded individuals, no different from any other voluntary society.[56] For both

50. To this point we have examined Baptists on both sides of the Atlantic. When Baptists emerged, both sides of the Ocean were British. Thus in broadly sketching the position in favor of creeds, it is not improper to keep both in view. The dynamics of the nineteenth century that led to significant changes, however, were different in England and the new United States. While the changes in both countries are important, given the scope and context of this project, we need to focus more on the American situation. Further we might note that where there are shared dynamics, we see characteristics of the American situation also in England rather than characteristics of the English situation present in America.

51. Hinson, "Baptist Experience," 217–21.

52. See Thompson, "Re-envisioning Baptist Identity," 287–302; and Thompson, "Sacraments and Religious Liberty," 36–54.

53. Leland, "Letter to Thomas Bingham," 643.

54. Gaustad, "Backus-Leland Tradition," 110–13. See also Hatch, *Democratization*, 93–101.

55. Maring, "Individualism of Francis Wayland," 135.

56. Ibid., 147–50. Wayland spells out his definition of the church in Wayland, *Notes on the Principles*, 179–80.

Leland and Wayland, uniting with a church was strictly optional for a saved individual.[57]

Baptist individualism came to its most mature expression in the enormously influential idea of "soul competency," first articulated by theologian Edgar Young Mullins.[58] Mullins said in his best-known work, *The Axioms of Religion*, "It is a species of spiritual tyranny for men to interpose the church itself, its ordinances, or ceremonies, or its formal creeds, between the human soul and Christ."[59] We can see in this statement that Mullins divided Christ and the church.[60] He defined freedom in religion as "exemption from State compulsion, social compulsion, ecclesiastical or priestly compulsion, creedal compulsion, or parental compulsion."[61] Clearly, the individual was in view as Mullins crafted this definition.

Early Baptist beliefs did not include anything that much resembled soul competency.[62] As a result, the church was of vital importance! "An Orthodox Creed" (1678), for example, not only made strong claims for the creeds. It made similarly strong statements about the church. Article XXX states:

57. Leland, "Backus-Leland Tradition," 643; and Maring, "Individualism of Francis Wayland," 148.

58. Space does not permit detailed discussion of how Mullins is variously interpreted. I do believe his intent was not to exalt the individual, but to keep the social aspects of religion in balance. My sense is that the ideas he developed ultimately served to undermine his best intentions. Further, few who have appropriated his thought have even tried to preserve the balance he sought.

59. Mullins, *Axioms*, 94. Mullins, "Baptist Conception," 59, declared in an international forum that the imposition of creeds on human conscience is quite simply "tyrannical."

60. See Mullins, *Axioms*, 54–55.

61. Ibid., 153–54.

62. I realize this statement is not in keeping with the "standard account" of Baptist historical identity. Mullins said that soul competency was the historical significance of Baptists, for example (ibid., 53). I have come to believe that such claims are more a retrojection of contemporary sensibilities into the distant past where it did not exist. Grantham is more representative of the early Baptists. In *Christianismus Primitivus* 2.2.1.1 (2) (pagination was not consistent, but began again with the second part of the second book), he observed:

> [W]here the form of Godliness is neglected, Religion will in a little time either vanish, or become an unknown conceit, every man being at liberty to follow (what he supposes to be) the motions of the Spirit of God, in which there is so great a probability of being mistaken as in nothing more; for Man's ignorance being very great, and Satan very subtile [sic], and the way of the Lord neglected, Men ly [sic] open to every fancy which pleaseth best.

The "form of Godliness" in this case means the outward means of grace, the church with its creeds and sacraments; in other words, the very things that Baptists of the last century have tended to reject on the basis of soul competency.

[W]e believe the visible church of Christ on earth, is made up of several distinct congregations, which make up that one catholick church, or mystical body of Christ. And the marks by which she is known to be the true spouse of Christ, are these, viz. Where the word of God is rightly preached, and the sacraments truly administered, according to Christ's institution, . . . that is a true constituted church; *to which church, and not elsewhere, all persons that seek for eternal life, should gladly join themselves.*[63]

The church had an unsubstitutable role in matters of faith and salvation. There is ample evidence to which we may turn for confirmation of this. When Baptists began the practice of hymn singing in the seventeenth century, one of their earliest hymn texts declared, "O follow them that follow Me, And thy Foot ne'er shall slide!"[64] Likewise, in a remarkable passage from Particular Baptist John Bunyan's *The Pilgrim's Progress*, Christian comes to the Interpreter's House. Before he is shown sin, Law, Gospel and grace, he is shown a picture of a person who "can beget children, travail in birth with children, and nurse them himself once they are born." Why is Christian shown this prior to all else? The Interpreter explains that it was because the one pictured was the only one "whom the Lord of the place whither thou art going hath authorized to be thy guide, in all difficult places thou mayest meet with in the way."[65] We see here an understanding of the church distinctly different from more recent versions, not as a voluntary association of the saved, but as a pilgrim people through which salvation is mediated. It is, however, the predominant way earlier Baptists understood the church, and indeed it existed in the hymnody of Baptists well into the nineteenth century before being gradually displaced by the "subsequentialist" understanding.[66]

Why did the earlier Baptists so closely connect salvation to the church? Again, to put matters most simply, it is because they, far more than Baptists of the last over two hundred years, began with God's freedom. They concluded from Scripture and the testimony of the church through history that

---

63. Lumpkin and Leonard, *Baptist Confessions of Faith*, 327–28. Italics added. See also Grantham, *Christianismus Primitivus*, Book II part 1, chapter 1, section ii, page 36, where he asserts, "The regular way to claim the Priviledges [*sic*] contained in God's Oracles, is, for Men to be imbodied [*sic*] as His Church and Family, by the just observation of his Ordinances."

64. Keach, *A Feast of Fat Things*, #85.

65. Bunyan, *Pilgrim's Progress*, 98. There are contemporary interpreters of Baptist life who take this to be a symbol of the church. See Hinson, "Baptists and Spirituality," 657.

66. See Thompson, "Memorial Dimensions of Baptism," 304–24; and Thompson "Re-envisioning Baptist Identity."

God had freely connected the church intimately to Christ, indeed to the divine life of the Holy Trinity.[67] Thus they believed that true freedom, which is in and not apart from Christ, is known only in and through the church and her life, not apart from it. "Christ dwells in his Church by the Holy Spirit," stated Grantham, and thus is the "habitation of God."[68] Baptists were enjoined to seek salvation in the true church because there they encountered Christ. Early Baptists could even call the church "mother."[69] "Here you *received* your first spiritual Breath, or Life," declared Keach; in the church "many Souls are daily Born to Christ."[70] Baptists sang of the church, "And all her Members joyned be To thee in sacred bonds, And influence they have from thee, In thee her glory stands."[71]

The Baptist forebears believed Christ would lead his people into all truth in the church. This conviction alone makes sense of the earlier Baptists' affirmation of creeds, which represent the mind of the church. We may see this throughout Baptist existence. It is present in "St. Paul's Catechism." "I pray now inform me concerning . . . the true Christian Religion according to the Gospel; Lest . . . we be found to neglect our own Salvation. And first, I desire to be instructed, whether the Holy Spirit, or the Holy Scripture, or the Holy Church must be our guide in these soul-concernments?" The answer began, "There is no doubt but that these three agree in one Testimony: for the Scriptures are the Testimony of the other two."[72] While certainly not being identical, it seems a similar understanding lay behind Fuller's comment, which we saw earlier, that if a kind of thoroughgoing individualism be paramount, then Christ came in vain. Earlier Baptists did not believe one could be with Christ yet be apart from the church.

We see the same logic enduring into the nineteenth century. Ezekiel Gilman Robinson explained, "[O]ne clearly marked and divinely appointed office of the church is to stand side by side with the Bible, *as the visible body of the invisible Christ, as the manifest dwelling-place on earth of the saving power of the living God*."[73] It was, however, over the course of that same century that a strong concept of the church was eroded almost entirely in the name of human freedom.

67. We may see a separation of Christ and the church in the statements from Leland, Wayland, and Mullins noted earlier.

68. Grantham, *Christianismus Primitivus* 2.1.3.11 (74–76).

69. See Grantham, *Hear the Church*.

70. Keach, *The Glory of a True Church*, 66, italics added. See ibid., 62–68

71. Keach, *Spiritual Melody*, #121. This was the first English Baptist hymnal. See McElrath, "Turning Points," 4.

72. Grantham, *St. Paul's Catechism*, 12–13.

73. Robinson, "The Relation of the Church and the Bible," 388, emphasis added.

With full development of the individualistic impulse the church receded in theological importance for Baptists.[74] It is little surprise. Since later Baptists divided Christ and the church, the church was bound to become superfluous. If the soul was free to seek Christ for salvation without mediation, seeking the church was a diversion from true faith. If the church was merely a diversion, the creeds, along with the sacraments, could only be a violation of individual soul's prerogative in her relation to Christ. Indeed, the kind of individualism that entered Baptist thought renders the use of creeds literally unthinkable. For example, because the individual was primary for Wayland, there could never be a confession of faith of any sort for Baptists since no single statement could comprehend all religious opinions in a given church.[75] We are not surprised, then, to find Charles Deweese insist in recent years that creeds historically have no value for Baptists. By extension, he argues on the grounds of individualism against any claim that the church may have an authoritative witness.[76]

Sad irony abounds. This weakening of the church stands in contradiction to what many Baptists believe of themselves. Walter Shurden has commented, "[O]ne may accurately say that what Baptists have given to the world is an ecclesiology, not a theology."[77] We might say more accurately still that Baptists largely lost the richness of their own ecclesiology, having now essentially very little to give anyone. Indeed, Maring noted over a half century ago that in the nineteenth century, Baptists lost a sense of the holy, catholic church.[78]

---

74. This phenomenon is examined in thorough detail by Priestly, "From Theological Polemic." See also Thompson, "Re-envisioning Baptist Identity."

75. Maring, "Individualism of Francis Wayland," 151.

76. Deweese, *Defining Baptist Convictions*, 21–23. One wonders how far back "history" goes for him.

77. Shurden, "The Baptist Identity and the Baptist Manifesto," 325. The very distinction of ecclesiology from theology demonstrates the separation of the church from the rest of doctrine.

78. Maring, "Individualism of Francis Wayland," 136. Along with this, he continued, "earlier adherence to confessional statement gave way to the myth that Baptists have no creed but the New Testament."
We would expect historians to be aware of these alterations, whether they interpret them as losses or not. We might wonder, then, why historian C. Douglas Weaver, in an essay rejecting creedalism, relates Wayland's comment that denominations with creeds had schisms, but for Baptist the Bible alone was permitted to be pure truth. Baptists, Weaver relates Wayland claiming, were different because they relied only on the New Testament. See Weaver, "Baptists and Denominational Identity," 291. Weaver failed to note, however, that Wayland quite openly admitted that he "pretend(ed) to no learning in ecclesiastical history" (Wayland, *Notes on the Principles*, 16).

Turning Again to the Church—and to the Creeds

The burden of this chapter is not simply to persuade Baptists to use the creeds in their worship. It is to urge Baptists to be aware of the need for us to examine how we have thought about freedom, and to strengthen our ecclesiology. Indeed, apart from this deeper theological concern, questions concerning the elements of worship and how they are engaged remain quite superficial.

I believe the theological changes associated with a shift from divine to human freedom that entered Baptist life in the eighteenth century and came to mature form through the nineteenth and into the twentieth were not changes for the better. They were the result, not of careful reflection, but of forgetfulness of the past and from being shaped by the culture and politics of the American republic.[79] We would do well to understand these matters, especially our ecclesiology, in ways more like the Baptist forebears than their later namesakes. Of course, as I have noted, something like that is necessary for the practice of reciting creeds to be intelligible. Yet I urge this not for pragmatic reasons (so my proposal will make sense). Nor do I urge it for antiquarian reasons, as though mere chronology constitutes a strong reason to favor Baptist views of earlier times.

Rather, I urge this more robust ecclesiology for three reasons. First, I urge it on theological grounds. If our theology has coherence, we cannot separate the various doctrines and indeed must show a consistency among them. If we for whatever reason weaken our ecclesiology, we very likely will weaken our christology.[80] Conversely, if we profess a robust christology we need to profess as well an equally robust ecclesiology.[81] I also urge it on historical grounds. While we should not make their witness normative in every matter, I believe we should listen carefully to the witness of those who first were Baptists. We need to discern carefully their genius and learn from them. Finally, I urge it on the grounds that we should have better reasons than amnesia and unperceived cultural influence to justify theological shifts such as we have seen in the last two centuries.[82]

How, then, ought we think about and employ creeds in light of this ecclesiology? While it may at first seem off target, I suggest that we think

79. Thompson, "Dimensions of Memory, 46–66.

80. I believe we can indeed demonstrate just such an attenuation of christology during the same period as the changes we have traced in this chapter.

81. I would also include pneumatology (the doctrine of the Holy Spirit) here, though it exceeds the scope of this chapter.

82. No deep Baptist convictions are dependent upon the ideas that have come to characterize Baptist life during this time: missions, evangelism, the personal dimensions of discipleship, nor religious liberty.

of the creeds primarily as political declarations. This claim, I know, might seem to some only to confirm their greatest reservations. I do not intend by this to imply creeds are instruments by which Christians are brought into mindless conformity and "lock step" on doctrinal positions with no regard for personal questions, reservations, and doubts. What I mean by saying the church and creeds are "political" is that they embody and gesture toward the vision of what God intends human life to be. In its most basic sense, politics is an argument about what the goal of human life is and how life together should be structured for the embodiment of this goal. This is, in brief, the "gospel," the Good News of God in and for the world that brings human life to its goal, its salvation.[83]

This is, I believe, faithful to the genius of our early Baptists. The reason they believed the church was essential to salvation was because they believed that the church was where God in divine freedom intended this goal, revealed in the teachings and ministry of Jesus Christ, to be most fully visible. This Good News of God's goal for human life had been corrupted by state usurpation of the church, since all earthly states aim at goals at variance in some way with the gospel. The corruption had been remedied in the other Dissenting churches, though only partially. Significantly, all of these other churches employed creeds. Yet the Baptists did not simply decide that the creeds were the problem and abandon them. Why? They seem to have understood that was risky, and not a helpful solution. More radical groups had discarded creeds and sacraments. The Baptists appear to have believed these radicals had discarded essentials of the gospel in the process.[84] The Baptists' response was to keep the creeds (and sacraments) and to struggle to bring their life together into conformity with the vision set forth in them, and to continue to interpret them in the context of their ongoing attempts to live faithfully.

We who live and struggle for faithfulness to the gospel in the late modern West, particularly the United States, do not face precisely the same issues as did our forebears living under an established and persecuting Church

---

83. It is for this reason that L. Johnson, *The Creed*, 10, rejects the idea that the creed is a late imposition on the gospel but a natural development of what began as a variation of the *Sh'ma Yisrael* (Deut 6:4). See also McKnight, *King Jesus Gospel*. Johnson notes that the boundaries established by the creeds are not for the sake of making Christians think and act alike one hundred percent, but so that the church may speak a prophetic word to the world. See Johnson, *The Creed*, 302.

84. We should note that the Baptists did tend at times to lose members to these more radical groups, which made the Baptists more insistent on their interpretation of the Christian faith. I have examined aspects of this in Thompson, "Seventeenth-Century Baptist Confessions," 335–48.

of England.[85] Yet our challenges remain. Timothy Johnson has noted that nihilism is the *modus operandi* of the marketplace:

> [t]he most widely used language in the world today is commerce, the most practiced form of politics is war, the best vision the world offers—evolution, through competition—has no apparent goal or point, and certainly no concern for the weak and vulnerable who will lose out in any such competition.[86]

He states further that Christianity that leaves individuals free to seek their own vision leaves them vulnerable to capture by these lesser visions of human life. But the creed, he continues, tells the world a truth about itself that it does not know.[87] So has it ever been, that God has declared another way through a "peculiar people." Baptist historian Glenn Hinson concurs, noting that "The creeds are, as it were, the covenant story *in nucleo*." The creeds are thus a means by which the church and its members declare loyalty to the cause of the God of Israel and of Jesus Christ. In reciting the creed, persons are connected with the people of this One God through the ages from the call of Abraham to the consummation of all things.[88]

---

85. We do well to note that only as Baptists came to be "at ease" in and with the new American republic did they move wholesale to abandon their creedal and sacramental inheritance.

86. L. Johnson, *The Creed*, 303.

87. Ibid., 300–304.

88. See Pelikan, *Credo*, 217–24; and Chan, *Liturgical Theology*, 110–11. Pelikan cites George Huntston Williams's observation that it was the Arian party, against which the Nicene Creed was formulated, that was more ready to attribute a divine epiphany in the emperor rather than the Nicenes who are painted in such unfavorable light today. It is possible that the concerns about forced conformity remain. Certainly, there is some degree of unity that will be set by the creed's boundaries. Yet no church tolerates an utterly unbounded openness. The creed has the advantage of at least setting these boundaries explicitly. Yet within these boundaries there is greater room than many people today realize for exploration. See L. Johnson, *The Creed*, 315: "The creed consistently affirms *what* without trying to specify *how*, and thus . . . the minds of believers are free to examine and investigate, without constraint, the gaps left within by the creed's propositions, and their minds are not imprisoned by extraneous and possibly unworthy explanations or elaborations," emphasis original. Jennings Jr., *Loyalty to God*, 14–18, notes that the words of the creed are not assertions of greater or lesser probability, but a rich description of the God to whom Christians pledge loyalty. Jennings's exposition of the creed demonstrates that the realities toward which the creeds gesture are inexhaustibly deep mysteries. We might consider that the creed provides "space" for a more truly diverse unity than is often the case in many Baptist churches today where the mechanisms by which differences are negotiated and accommodated are woefully lacking. Thus Van Dyk, "A Conversation with the Ecumenical Creeds," 31, borrows counsel from the poet Rilke, "I want to beg you, as much as I can . . . to be patient towards all that is unsolved in your heart, and try to love the questions themselves."

With this in mind, how should Baptists employ the creeds in their worship? While we might name other ways, it seems to me the one that most powerfully connects with Baptist practice historically is to employ the creed at the time of the baptism of believers.[89] The Apostles' Creed emerged from the church's baptismal practice in its early centuries.[90] In particular, it developed from what is known as the "interrogation." This sounds somewhat combative, and in a sense it is. It recognizes that baptism marks a radical exchange of loyalty from, to use the biblical term, "no-god" to the one, true and living God. Thus, each candidate for baptism is herself the site of a contest between the triune God, signified in the three articles of the creed affirmed one at a time, and the fallen powers of the world, signified in the liturgical forms as "the devil, all his pomp, and his vain promises." Upon this renunciation of that which leads to death and embrace of the One who is Life, the candidate was baptized.

I will leave reflections and recommendations concerning the larger liturgical patterns of baptism to other writers and will focus instead on the changes in baptismal understanding this sort of practice necessitates. Probably the most widely attested understanding of baptism among Baptists in recent decades is that it places focus on the believing individual. Indeed, the very act of baptism is interpreted as symbolizing the faith of the one who is baptized. According to C. Welton Gaddy, for example, "Baptism is a post-conversion dramatization of conversion."[91] Employment of the creed brings the focus more fully to what John Donne called the "three Personed God" and also to the community that professes to listen to the voice of this God and not a stranger.

During my time as the pastor of a local congregation, we employed the articles of the creed as a means by which the one baptized could declare her/his loyalty to God and the church. The congregation in which that person would "seek for eternal life," likewise reaffirmed their loyalty to God through affirmation of same articles in a renewal of their own baptismal vows.[92] This sort of practice requires quite a different view of the baptismal rite. It is, however, more faithful to the practice and understanding of those

89. The other two are in response to the reading and proclamation of Scripture and as part of the celebration of Communion. Granted, as we see, use of the creed will bring Baptists to think again about these liturgical practices. I believe, though, this is a good thing.

90. See Ferguson, *Baptism in the Early Church*, 351–53.

91. Gaddy, *The Gift of Worship*, 141–42.

92. This approach also enables the cultivation of a sense of stability of place and community, which the monastic tradition teaches creates the conditions for an authentic freedom in Christ.

who were called "Baptist" many generations before our own. In a baptismal chant, Baptists intoned in the mid-nineteenth century:

> And walking in Thy Name in the communion of Thy people,
> In the joy of our faith we will thankfully obey Thee.
> As in the likeness of Thy resurrection we are raised with Thee,
> So in union with Thy life may we live with Thee.[93]

This joyful life, life in union with the Lord, and with the Lord's free people, not only finds representation, but is fostered in and through the word of the creed.

93. Turney, *Baptismal Hymns*, 72.

6

Reclaiming the Liturgical Heart of Preaching

RODNEY WALLACE KENNEDY

TAKE A CHURCH ANYWHERE in the world on a Sunday morning and with the inner eyes of the heart we see a congregation with every space filled. The air filled with angels, the great cloud of witnesses, the Trinity, the congregation. "But you have come to Mount Zion and to the city of the living God, the heavenly Jerusalem, and to innumerable angels in festal gathering, and to the assembly of the firstborn who are enrolled in heaven, and to God the judge of all, and to the spirits of the righteous made perfect, and to Jesus, the mediator of a new covenant, and to the sprinkled blood that speaks a better word than the blood of Abel" (Heb 12:22–25). The pastor/author of Hebrews describes, in figurative language, the church gathered for worship and the place is packed as surely as the angels seen by William Blake. In 1765 at the age of 8, William Blake saw his first vision while walking on Peckham Rye. 'A tree filled with angels, bright angelic wings bespangling every bough like stars.'

I hope that the reader will sense that preaching, divorced from its liturgical body, and treated as a solo act has diminished impact no matter how sincere, entertaining, or powerful the preacher. Sermons have context and part of that context is the community of faith and its worship, and this includes the audience of the biblical community from Genesis to Revelation, and the witness of all the saints down to the present.

Preaching, apart from an organic relationship with the worship of the church, like Cain, has wandered the earth in different rhetorical guises, trying to be all things to all peoples. When obsessed with being interesting, preaching has resorted to bowing before the gods of entertainment. With prejudice,

I suspect that the preponderance of PowerPoint in contemporary pulpits has at least something to do with a feeling of powerlessness. I have suffered through so-called sermons about the preacher's most recent vacation, the latest self-help book the preacher has read, and imitations of David Letterman mixed with Dr. Phil. How has it come to pass that sermons can be so glib, so damn interesting in prosperous times and so lacking when a word of judgment, hope, forgiveness, or rebuke needs to be spoken? Sermons riddled with stories about the preacher seem to glorify the preacher rather than the God of the preacher. Isn't such self-glorification more an act of idolatry than a way of praising and thanking God? A sermon should be about the God who raised Jesus from the dead and empowered a church through the Holy Spirit to continue his ministry. Gardner Taylor says, "The preacher ought to try to bring the people before the presence of God and within sight of the heart of Christ. No sermon can do more. None should want to do less."[1]

When self-conscious and lacking ego-integrity, preaching has fretted over the loss of confidence in language and cowered before the arrogant claims of postmodernity that there are no meta-narratives, only individual stories lacking in meaning and reality. In these and other less flattering guises, preaching has become a vagabond upon the face of the earth.

The sermon exists within a liturgical galaxy of prayers, hymns, confessions, and Scripture. To treat the first half of worship as the "opening act" and the preacher as the "star attraction" is a cultural accommodation that has little in common with the worship of the church across the centuries. Any sermon that can breathe on its own, apart from allegiance to worship is a mere echo of the authentic Word. Sending forth a sermon divorced from its worship context would be like sending our astronauts into space naked. The accommodated nature of the church may stem partly from the failure of "the clergy to help those they serve know how to speak Christian"[2]

The Word Essential to Preaching

Theologically, the text and the sermon connect the people to God. Sermons divorced from the steady reading of Scripture from the Old Testament and New Testament epistles and Gospels are the rhetorical equivalent of a tree falling in a forest. Preaching is a necessary practice for biblical reading. John Wright, in *Telling God's Story*, says that preaching too often takes as its task to find "applications" for the text when its "task should be to turn

1. Quoted in Bond, *Contemporary African American Preaching*, 54.
2. Hauerwas, *Working with Words*, 87.

a congregation away from one narrative world into another."[3] Our worship depends on our feeding on the Word from the Pulpit and the Table.

For Baptists, it should at least be ironic that a people claiming to be a people of the Book, often find so little time during Sunday worship to read the Bible orally. Isn't there something odd about a worship that can only make room for two or three verses of Scripture? This puts the worship of the people of God in a double divorce: sermon divorced from the rest of worship and worship divorced from the Word of God.

Baptists originally reacted against the Bible being the property of elite clerical experts. People wanted the right to read the Bible for themselves, read the Bible in private. Much that has formed Baptist faith rises from this insistence on the individual's right to read the Bible. This has been a mixed blessing. Rowan Williams claims, "What badly needs to be recovered now is the sense that the Bible is to be read *in company*."[4]

Part of the task of faithfully reading Scripture is to covenant together to sit beneath the authority of the word within the church. The pastor is called to be the primary interpreter (not infallible, not inerrant, not authoritarian) of Scripture and the church is to read Scripture together with the pastor and others who are recognized as having the gift of teacher.

For example, when is the last time a Baptist church studied the 6th chapter of John to test our insistence that communion is only an act of remembering and not a sacrament? Or listened to the reading of the Last Supper to hear the voice of Jesus tell us to have the meal every time we gather? Or the story of the disciples in Luke 24 who didn't know Jesus in the reading of the word but in the breaking of bread? Or the story of Philip and the Ethiopian eunuch's baptism? Luke has rhetorically created two stories that emphasize the church's worship around the sacraments of preaching, communion, and baptism. Are we listening to our anti-Catholic prejudice or the text?

The reading of the lessons of Scripture provides a bridge to the sermon and the other acts of worship. If there is to be a word from the Lord on Sunday, the odds are better if the congregation has engaged in the oral reading of the lessons of Scripture. This is a primary reason for suggesting the use

3. Wright, *Telling God's Story*. See also Stanley Hauerwas: "I would contend—a contention well developed by John Wright in his book *Telling God's Story*—that preaching is the appropriate practice for biblical readings. Wright argues that contemporary preaching too often takes as its task to find 'applications' for the text when its task should be to turn a congregation away from one narrative world into another" (*Working with Words*, 99). I contend that our preoccupation with "application" as the mainstay of preaching is a method of accommodation to the world, i.e., the medium has become the message.

4. Williams, *Tokens of Trust*, 124, emphasis original.

of the common lectionary in Sunday worship. In addition, a preacher can maintain an ongoing sermon dialogue by participating in lectionary reading groups with members of the congregations. For five years I have been part of a Monday night lectionary group that reads and discusses the upcoming lessons for the next Sunday. The group consists of university professors, business persons, a piano teacher, a retired engineer, a teacher's aide, and a theology doctoral student from a nearby university. In the context of Evening Prayer worship, I have reaped such benefit for the Sunday worship and sermon. On Thursday mornings, I meet with a second group of my church members, for reading and discussing the lectionary lessons. This is a group of ten persons and includes a cross section of our congregation. Monday evening and Thursday morning readings connect to Sunday worship and preaching in ways I had not anticipated. Members of the two groups often hear their points of view quoted in the sermon, with full credit, of course.

In other words, pastors and congregations who hang out together with Scripture have a way of sticking together through good times and bad. At First Baptist Dayton we swap biblical and personal stories and offer up interpretations for the community's critique. The magisterium of a Baptist church is the place designated for the variant readings that we give to Scripture. Whether or not such a polity works in a faith community seduced by liberal democracy and hyper-individualism, I don't yet know. I am struggling with the idea. So far the ride has been worth the price of admission—the giving up of some individualism and notions about pastoral authority.

My experience in these reading groups leads me to recommend not only the lectionary but the preaching of sermons from the lessons of the lectionary. This doesn't mean that all four readings have to be part of the sermon every week. There are weeks when how the readings actually relate is a "mystery." It means that the entire witness of Scripture needs to have a place in the pulpit. The stories of the Hebrew scripture, the amazing diversity of human lives and challenges found there, make for riveting drama. As Ellen Davis reminds us, "Christian biblical interpretation is dangerous when it is pursued in ignorance or disregard of the long history of Jewish interpretation, and also Jewish martyrdom."[5] Davis then recommends Jews and Christians read and study Scripture together. As she says, "The ordinary ranks of faithful Jews and Christians have an opportunity to grow in their faith as they read and learn together. Perhaps we are standing at a new juncture in the history of the two households that call themselves Israel."[6]

5. Davis, "Teaching the Bible," 23.
6. Ibid., 26.

If anyone knows drama, it should be the preacher. A steady stream of nothing but gospel readings from the pulpit not only produces a seriously limiting canon for the preacher, it also produces a polluted stream variously known in Christian history as one or the other form of Gnosticism. Preach the whole witness of Scripture. Connect biblical stories with the many stories floating out there in our post-modern culture. Engage the multiple voices that impinge upon your listeners during the week.

"Scripture, of course, is the source as well as the paradigm of Christian speech."[7] In a world where preachers are the last generalists standing, the preacher is still required to be a specialist in Scripture. This is not to suggest that the preacher fills the sermon with an array of Scripture quoted here and there with no apparent connection to the sermon. The preacher is not an eleven-year-old Sunday School student taking part in Bible memory drill.

The Congregation Essential to Preaching

As Chaim Perelman and L. Olbrechts-Tyteca taught us a speaker must pay attention to the audience, considering both the audience at hand and the universal audience.[8] An audience is "the ensemble of those whom the speaker wishes to influence by his argumentation. Every speaker thinks, more or less consciously, of those he is seeking to persuade; these people form the audience to whom his speech is addressed."[9] For our purposes the audience is the congregation; the speaker is the preacher; the sermon is the argument.

The essential consideration of the preacher is the construction of the audience which should be adequate to the occasion. The preacher forms a concept of the anticipated audience in his or her mind as close as possible to reality. "Knowledge of those one wishes to win over is a condition preliminary to all effectual argumentation."[10] In this sense, the sermon rises out of the act/s of love for the people by the preacher. Carlyle Marney always said the preacher must love people and couch everything said in the gospels. "A great orator is one who possesses the art of taking into consideration . . . the composite nature of his audience."[11] The preacher who communicates truth claims seems animated by his audience. This is not the case for the ardent

---

7. Hauerwas, *Working with Words*, 88.

8. Perelman and Olbrechts-Tyteca, *The New Rhetoric*, 30–35. This is an essential text for students of preaching.

9. Ibid., 19.

10. Ibid., 20.

11. Ibid., 22.

enthusiast who is absorbed with what he himself considers important and who preaches as if there were no audience that needs persuading.

The preacher "swayed by passion argues without taking sufficiently into account the audience he is addressing: carried away by his enthusiasm, imagines his audience to be susceptible to the same arguments that persuaded him."[12] "The making of a preacher," said Bossuet, "rests with his audience."[13] "It is indeed the audience which has the major role in determining the quality of argument and the behavior of orators." As a experienced preacher once told me, "Tell your congregation that if they want better preaching, they should demand it and then be prepared for the demands of such preaching." The advice is as ancient as the chief of Greek orators, Demosthenes: "Your orators never make you either bad men or good, but you make them whichever you choose; for it is not your that aim at what they wish for, but they who aim at whatever you think they desire. You therefore must start with a noble ambition and all will be well, for then no orator will give you base counsel, or else he will gain nothing by it, having no one to take aim at his word."[14]

Preachers are always tempted by the sirens of bad sophistry to make of the sermon a cute idea, a knack for the well-turned phrase, the kowtowing to the prejudices of the audiences, and the emotional claims that please and "tickle the ears." As Paul warns Timothy, "For the time is coming when people will not put up with sound doctrine, but having itching ears, they will accumulate for themselves teachers to suit their own desires, and will turn away from listening to the truth and wander away to myths" (2 Tim 4:3–4).

As Plato insists, our preaching can be a mere technique like cooking: "The generic name which I should give to it is pandering; it has many subdivisions, one of which is cookery, an occupation which masquerades as an art but in my opinion is no more than a knack acquired by routine."[15] Following Plato's analogy, anyone wishing to prepare barbecue shrimp can go to the Cooking Channel web site and find the recipe and follow the directions. Using the same technique for preaching fails.

"For we do not proclaim ourselves; we proclaim Jesus Christ as Lord and ourselves as your slaves for Jesus' sake" (2 Cor 4:5). Here are two paradigms for all preachers. One, we do not preach ourselves. This word alone should make us wary of sermons stacked with biographical stories, especially those that make fun of our own faults (My wife says: "Don't brag on

---

12. Ibid., 25.
13. Quoted in ibid., 33.
14. Ibid., 24.
15. Plato, *Gorgias*, 38.

your sins.") Two, we preach Jesus Christ as Lord. We do proclaim Jesus as a community immersed in the life of Jesus, a congregation dead and buried with Jesus, and raised from the dead with Jesus. We preach means that preaching is never an individual effort. Preaching has an organic relationship to worship. "The sermon is action; the sermon is what the preacher speaks joined with what the rest of the congregation hears."[16]

Daily worship and immersion in the language of worship—hymns, prayers, and litanies—will impart a rhythm to our preaching as well as a deeply genuine piety and devotion. Reading through and singing the hymns of various hymnals will strengthen your preaching. Reading through the various denominational books of worship is a good start. Daily morning and evening prayer from The *Book of Common Prayer* will sustain and empower preaching. Moreover, as non-Catholics we are often unfamiliar with the harmonics of the Mass. Yet, Pat Conroy says:

> Because I was raised Roman Catholic, I never feared taking any unchaperoned walks through the fields of language. Words lifted me up and filled me with pleasure. I've never met a word I was afraid of, just ones that left me indifferent or that I knew I wouldn't ever put to use. When reading a book, I'll encounter words that please me, goad me into action, make me want to sing a song. I dislike pretentious words, those highfaluting ones with a trust fund and an Ivy League education. Often they were stillborn in the minds of academics, critics, scientists. They have a tendency to flash their warning lights in the middle of a good sentence."[17]

Preaching As Sacrament

David Buttrick argues that Luke's story of the disciples on the Road to Emmaus in Luke 24 is a reconstruction of Christian worship in the first century.[18] What we get is a service based on the preaching of the Word and the breaking of bread. The disciples knew Jesus in the breaking of bread. This doesn't mean the teaching of Jesus, the explaining of the meaning of Scripture

16. Long, *The Witness of Preaching*, 16.

17. Conroy, *My Reading Life*, 86.

18. Buttrick, *Homiletics*, 400. Buttrick says, "Though the account moves along like a story, in v. 27 we have formula words associated with preaching, and in v. 30 we have formula words associated with Eucharist—a pattern of Word and Sacrament in the life of the church. In addition, we have credal material in v. 19 and v. 30, creeds used by early Christians." Buttrick argues that we are encountering a structure in which the living reality of Christ risen is known.

from Moses through all the prophets, was irrelevant. The Word combined with the breaking of bread made possible the opening of eyes. Paul, after all, tells us "For it is the God who said, 'Let light shine out of darkness,' who has shone in our hearts to give the light of the knowledge of the glory of God in the face of Jesus Christ" (2 Corinthians 4:6). In Rom 10:14, Paul boldly asks, "And how are they to hear without someone to proclaim him?"

Those Anglicans who started the Baptist church were steeped in the *Book of Common Prayer*. Did they throw away their prayer books immediately upon their baptism? Even if they did, the prayers, the words, the forms of worship were in their hearts and minds and on their lips. They were in the habit of practicing worship of Word and Table.

Even when they prayed spontaneous instead of written prayers, the words of the prayer book found their way into Baptist worship. My childhood was spent playing baseball and memorizing vast portions of the King James Version of the Holy Bible. While I rarely use the KJV anymore and never read from it in the pulpit, when I quote Scripture, I unconsciously bring out and forth the language of the KJV. Gratefully, we never recover from the faith that gave us birth and nurtured our hearts and minds.

Even when Baptists claim aversion to written prayers, our spontaneous, "from the heart" prayers are often filled with repetitive phrases and favorite words. This is not an accusation but an affirmation. Repetition is, after all, another word for worship.[19] My father, sixty years a Baptist deacon from the hills of North Louisiana, prays with the intimacy of a man who has been talking to God all those years. His prayers are filled with familiar phrases: "As we come to your throne of grace," "in the precious name of Jesus," and "we offer ourselves to your service, O Lord."

The Word read in worship, proclaimed by preacher and congregation ("We preach Christ"), the invoking of the Holy Spirit to transform the sermon into the transforming power of salvation—all these elements suggest sacrament. The sermon can be conceived as the third sacrament of the church. The Collect for Purity in the *Book of Common Prayer* rightly precedes the reading of the Scripture lessons and the sermons. The words of this prayer are suggestive of the sacramental possibilities for the sermon: "Almighty God, to you all hearts are open, all desires known, and from you no secrets are hid: Cleanse the thoughts of our hearts by the inspiration of

---

19. Hauerwas, *Working with Words*, 87. Hauerwas says, "To speak well, to talk right, requires that our bodies be habituated by the language of the faith. To be so habituated requires constant repetition. Without repetition, and repetition is but another word for the worship of God, we are in danger of losing the grammar of the faith. At least part of your task as those called to the ministry is to help us, as good teachers do, acquire the habits of speech through the right worship of God."

your Holy Spirit, that we may perfectly love you, and worthily magnify your holy Name, through Christ our Lord." Through the action of the Holy Spirit there can be outward signs of an inward grace. The Prayer for Illumination in the *United Methodist Book of Worship* invokes the same Holy Spirit: "Lord, open our hearts and minds by the power of your Holy Spirit, that, as the Scriptures are read and your Word proclaimed, we may hear with joy what you say to us today. Amen." A Baptist evangelist kneeling for prayer just before he preaches is the same idea and invokes the same Holy Spirit. While less formal and not offered by the entire congregation, the purpose is the same. The words of the priest during the Great Thanksgiving of Holy Communion asks for the same result in the sharing of the bread and cup as the Baptist preacher sharing his sermon: "Pour out your Holy Spirit on us gathered here, and on these gifts of bread and wine."

The Holy Eucharist is called the "sacrament of sacraments" in the Orthodox tradition. It is also called the "sacrament of the Church." The eucharist is the center of the Church's life. Everything in the Church leads to the eucharist, and all things flow from it. It is the completion of all of the Church's sacraments—the source and the goal of all of the Church's doctrines and institutions. The same may be said of the sermon in Baptist practice. What I'm attempting here is the balance of Word and Table—coequal partners in the work of the Holy Spirit.

Preaching, when the Holy Spirit overshadows it, is the word made flesh. This at least gains the sermon a nomination as the third sacrament. St. Augustine called preaching an audible sacrament. Preaching has the potential to take its place with baptism and communion as the third sacrament for Baptists.

In his lectures on preaching, given at the Confessing Church seminary at Finkenwalde (1935–1937), Dietrich Bonhoeffer rooted his homiletic in the incarnation of the Word. Furthermore, he emphasized the real presence of that same Word in the ordinary words of the preacher. In his own words: "The proclaimed word is the incarnate Christ himself. The preached Christ is both the Historical One and the Present One . . . Therefore the proclaimed word is not a medium of expression for something else, something which lies behind it, but rather it is the Christ himself walking through his congregation as the Word."[20] Bonhoeffer speaks of the sermon as the *sacramentum verbi*—the sacrament of the word.

20. Bonhoeffer, *Worldly Preaching*, 126.

Conclusion

Preaching, then together, preacher, congregation, the cloud of witnesses, we are never left alone. Instead we preach the Word and we use words because they are the essential elements of the preaching craft. The Bible is the church's book and aside from the church has no other conceivable usage. The words of the preacher are the byproduct of the preachers' habits and practices of reading, observing, and gathering in the midst of a local congregation where preacher and people do the work of love. Above all, we preach Jesus Christ, crucified, dead, and raised from the dead.

Using words with all the creativity we possess, the preacher makes metaphors, symbols, analogies, images, speech acts, and arguments dance with the Lord of the Dance and makes known the story of God—Father, Son, and Holy Spirit. Preaching, when the Holy Spirit overshadows it, becomes the word made flesh. It becomes Jesus talking again to his church as he did in the Sermon on the Mount and the parables. Stay focused my brothers and sisters! We, all of us, preach the story of Jesus, whom God raised from the dead, by the power of the Holy Spirit. Those who worship well are more likely to preach well!

7

Communing Together

Baptists Worshiping in the Eucharist[1]

Scott W. Bullard

Introduction

It might seem peculiar to some that an essay on the Lord's Supper would appear in a book about Baptists worshipping together. Many Baptist groups[2] long ago jettisoned the Supper from their weekly worship.[3] In so doing, they are not unlike many other groups who would classify themselves as "Protestant evangelicals."[4] Such groups, by and large, decided

---

1. The author would like to thank Amber Inscore Essick, co-pastor of Port Royal Baptist Church in Port Royal, KY, for reading and offering comments on an earlier version of this essay.

2. The author recognizes that there is validity in the old claim that "there is no Baptist Church, only Baptist churches." Thus, since this article does not claim to speak of all congregations or various Baptist denominations specifically, but rather of Baptists more generally, the author will focus upon trends in Baptist life rather than make an attempt to accurately depict all congregations.

3. Baptist life is still centered in the American South. The Southern Baptist Convention, headquartered in Nashville, claims just under 16 million members, while the Cooperative Baptist Fellowship, headquartered in Atlanta, claims partnership with 1,900 churches. The National Baptist Convention, which is also headquartered in Nashville and claims to be the largest predominantly African-American Christian group in the United States, claims 10 million members. Interestingly, National Baptists participate in the Lord's Supper monthly, not quarterly. One National Baptist employee of my institution, Judson College in Marion, Alabama, refers to the Supper as "the sacrament."

4. James W. McClendon Jr. called these groups "*baptists*." Though long conflated with Protestants, according to McClendon "baptists" have their roots in "'sixteenth-century

long ago to observe the Supper on a "quarterly basis"—having the meal of fellowship every three months or, more precisely, whenever a month happens to have five Sundays, Baptists typically observe the Supper on the fifth Sunday of the month.[5]

Moreover, when Baptists *do* gather for the meal, they have sometimes tended to emphasize what the meal is not. "This is *not*" a sacrament; this bread is *not* Christ's body, and this cup is *not* Christ's blood. This emphasis is rooted in both the claims of their spiritual ancestors and in the theology of some of their most esteemed and valued theologians (who were, of course, also seminary professors for thousands upon thousands of future Baptist pastors). Augustus H. Strong, for example, one of the most influential Baptist theologians—when he could be prompted to speak of the Supper at all—seems in his major works to bring up the Supper in his systematic works only to explain what it is *not*—namely, to point out that the Catholic position is erroneous because it holds that "by a physical partaking of the elements that the communicant receives saving grace from God."[6] Edgar Young Mullins, seen by many as the single most influential theologian in Baptist history, rarely raised the issue of the Supper in his theological writing and similarly affirms a purely symbolic view of the meal.[7]

In light of these trends in Baptist theology and history, this essay seeks to ask, and even answer, the following questions: Do Baptists need to revise their understanding of the Lord's Supper? Is the 'purely/merely symbolic' understanding of the Supper one which is faithful to the biblical narrative, and is the popularity of this view one reason that Baptists practice the Supper less frequently than other Christian groups? Finally, and most importantly,

---

Christian radicals' and represent a third type of Christian community, a third understanding of 'church.' It is local, Spirit-filled, mission-oriented, its discipleship always shaped by a practice of discernment" (McClendon, *Doctrine*, 45, 343). According to McClendon, among the many contemporary groups with baptist roots are "Disciples of Christ and Churches of Christ, Mennonites, Plymouth Brethren, Adventists, Russian Evangelicals, perhaps Quakers, certainly Black Baptists (who often go by other names), the (Anderson, Indiana) Church of God, Southern and British and European and American Baptists, the Church of the Brethren, perhaps some Methodists, Assemblies of God, assorted intentional communities . . . missionary affiliates of all of the above" (McClendon, *Ethics*, 34–35).

5. There are many reasons for this occurrence—some of them very good reasons—and various of them will be mentioned in the pages that follow. For now, we will be content to add here that Baptists also often participate in the Supper on Christmas Eve, and more rarely even on "Maundy Thursday." Again, National Baptists typically participate in the Supper on a monthly basis.

6. Strong, *Systematic Theology*, 543.

7. Mullins, *Axioms*, 41.

in what ways can a new, yet biblical, vision of the Lord's Supper contribute to the building up of the Body of Christ and the kingdom of God?

Eucharist and Baptists' "Simple Biblicism"

Baptists are, in some sense, a Reformation people. That is, on some level, Baptists owe their existence in part to the Protestant Reformation, begun by Martin Luther's attempted reform of—and eventual opposition to—the Catholic Church in the early-to-mid-1500s. Of course, part of the legacy of the reformers was their opposition to Catholicism's understanding of the Supper, of baptism, and of Scripture. Though this essay focuses on the former, a few words must be stated about the relationship between Scripture and the way in which the Supper has been interpreted down through the centuries.

Many have argued that the Reformers worried that many positions occupied by the Church could be attributed to "mere tradition" and not to sound interpretation of Scripture. This is one reason for Luther's desire that Scripture be available to all Christians. That said, Christian groups who observe the Supper on a weekly basis, do so in part because they believe that the Bible calls for them to do so. This is important to recognize because (even if Baptists disagree with this interpretation of Scripture) part of Baptists' legacy as Reformation people means that for them Scripture is uniquely authoritative, that it is (in the words of McClendon) "uniquely fit to be the doctrinal handbook of the teaching church."[8]

Groups who take the Supper on a weekly basis have historically claimed that the book of Acts implies that the early Jerusalem church took the Supper every time they gathered for worship when it notes that, after the arrival of the Holy Spirit, "they devoted themselves to the apostles' teaching and fellowship, to the breaking of bread and the prayers" (Acts 2:42). A few sentences later, Luke adds that "day by day, as they spent much time together in the temple, they broke bread at home [or "from house to house"] and ate their food with glad and generous hearts, praising God and having the goodwill of the people" (Acts 2:46–47a). Of course, this is a matter of interpretation, an interpretation which requires that one believe that from this the phrase "breaking bread" evokes the words of the Last Supper, that in such breaking of bread early Christians re-enacted and on some level experienced the meal that Jesus shared with his disciples on the night before he was crucified, that they did so as an act of worship, and that this practice was characteristic not only of Christians in Jerusalem but of other churches as well.

8. McClendon, *Doctrine*, 25.

Such interpretations also take seriously that Paul tells the troubled church at Corinth in 1 Corinthians 11 that when they come together, it is not to eat the Lord's Supper, and in telling them this he implies that eating the Lord's Supper is precisely what they were *supposed* to be doing when they gathered. Moreover, Paul insists that the eucharist, when taken properly, should unify them as the body of Christ—"we who are many are one body, for we all partake of the one bread" (1 Cor 10:17). These final emphases, recalled and interpreted down through the centuries, have caused Christian churches of different stripes to say that this act, practiced weekly and even as "the heart of the church,"[9] pulls members of the church "godward" but also together as the body of Christ.[10]

It is important to note that Baptists are a Reformation people for another reason: the early reformers changed much doctrinally, but at the same time retained much of the Catholics' order of worship. This included the continuation of practices such as baptizing infants and weekly observance of the Eucharist.[11] Continuation of pre-Reformation practices may even be evident in the phrase, coined by Calvin and repeated by Luther, that the church is "wherever the Gospel is rightly preached and the sacraments duly administered."[12]

Baptists, however, owe their existence in part to another group of reformers, reformers who thought that Luther, Calvin, and others did not carry their reforms far enough, and indeed they often came to oppose those reformers. Most often mentioned by contemporary Baptists is the fact that the Anabaptists of the 1520s, and later "Baptist" groups who encountered their Anabaptist conversation partners in Holland in 1609, believed that Luther and Calvin, had they taken their understandings of Scripture and salvation to their logical conclusions, would have more strongly protested the practice of infant baptism.[13] Indeed, the very reason Baptists have

9. De Lubac, *Splendour*, 74.

10. Irenaeus, *Against the Heresies* 5.2.3 (PG 7:1125–27); Augustine, *On Christian Teaching* 3.9; idem, *Commentary*; Aquinas, *Summa Theologiae* III, q. 75, art. 1–5; Luther, *Large Catechism*, 92; Luther, "Pagan Servitude," 256–57; Calvin, *Institutes*, 4.17.14; 4.17.33; Schmemann, *Eucharist*, 28–29, 194.

11. That infant baptism might have been theologically problematic, however, did occasionally trouble an elderly Luther. See Althaus, *Theology of Martin Luther*, 369–70.

12. Calvin, *Institutes*, 4.27.44.

13. Anabaptist figures are indeed arguing for believer's baptism in the early 1520s, and by 1527 the Schleitheim Confession argues for believer's baptism. One way in which Catholics, Lutherans, Presbyterians, and others say that infant baptism is biblical is through pointing to instances in Scripture wherein "entire households" of persons are baptized by early Christian missionaries such as Paul (see 1 Cor 1:16, for example). The question has persisted: "What does Scripture mean by 'entire households'?"

their name is because of the practice of believer's baptism, given to them by Dutch Mennonites (an Anabaptist group) and taken back to England by these separatists who were at odds with the Church of England.

Not quite as famous in popular culture, however, is the Anabaptist, and later Baptist, protest lodged against Rome's understanding of the Lord's Supper. It is less clear when, and why, weekly eucharist (or better, weekly observance of the Supper) disappeared from Baptist churches, but most believe that Baptists and other reformation groups would have been disturbed by language like this:

> Christ . . . who is at the right hand of God . . . is present in many ways to his Church . . . But he is present . . . most especially in the Eucharistic species. The mode of Christ's presence under the Eucharistic species is unique. It raises the Eucharist above all the sacraments . . . This presence is called "real"—by which is not intended to exclude the other types of presence as if they could not be "real" too, but because it is presence in the fullest sense: that is to say, it is a *substantial* presence by which Christ, God and man, makes himself wholly and entirely present.[14]

That the substances bread and wine become the substances "body" and "blood" is known in theological circles today as the doctrine of transubstantiation. Early on in the historical literature we hear from Anabaptist martyrs who, when asked to affirm that the substances "bread" and "wine" change to become Jesus' body and blood, respectively, answered "I know nothing of your baked God."[15] Another Anabaptist martyr, when asked just prior to her execution about the nature of Christ's presence in the Supper, responded "What God would you give me? One that is perishable and sold for a farthing?"[16] She also told a priest that morning that if the bread truly was Christ's body, then he daily crucified Christ in consuming the bread.[17]

It is a certainty that arguments over transubstantiation have for centuries divided Christians about what "happens" to the elements of bread and wine in the Supper. Anabaptists initially, and Baptists later, have said by and large that little, if anything, "happens." Grace is not conveyed through the elements, as in the sacramental understanding of the rite. Rather, the bread and wine (or, more often, grape juice) are "mere symbols" of Jesus' body and blood.[18] Elizabeth Newman claims that because of this "sub-Zwinglian"

14. *Catechism of the Catholic Church*, 1373–74.

15. George, "The Spirituality of the Radical Reformation," 348.

16. Ibid.

17. Ibid.

18. Curtis Freeman has called the "merely symbolic" position the "sub-Zwinglian"

view, because "symbol became emphasized over against reality, the practice itself atrophied. Thus many Baptists and other communions came to celebrate the Lord's Supper only a few times each year."[19] Along the same lines, the novelist Flannery O'Connor, after her peer Mary McCarthy said she admired O'Connor's Catholicism and asked if she didn't think the eucharist was a "pretty good" symbol, said of the eucharist that "if it's just a symbol, then to hell with it!"[20]

Is the view of the eucharist as "just a symbol" related to what some consider to be its relative disappearance? Are there other reasons—perhaps good reasons—that this rite is practiced less frequently? Baptist theologian James McClendon lamented in the 1980s that the primary meaning of the meal is "lost to sight in ecclesiastical struggles over what happens to bread and wine when certain words are said over them."[21] Similarly, Laurence Paul Hemming has recently pointed out that while worrying so much about what happens to the bread and the wine at Communion, Christians have often neglected to think about what happens—or ought to happen—to themselves! Thus, Hemming adopts the term "transubstantiation," so long associated with the essential change of the bread and wine, and employs the term to describe the change that also occurs in the ecclesial body during the eucharist. We ought to focus our attention, he notes, on "transubstantiating our selves."[22]

---

position (Freeman, "'To Feed Upon,'" 210). Coined by C.W. Dugmore, in using this term Freeman claims to distinguish between Zwingli's *actual* sacramental theology on the one hand and the symbolism most have *attributed* to him on the other hand. Theologically speaking, Freeman believes it is important to note that even in his most polemical writings, "Zwingli did not exclude the presence of Christ in the Supper, but preferred to speak of God's omnipresence through the Spirit" (Freeman, "To Feed Upon By Faith," 208). Elsewhere, he uses "sub-Zwinglian" to describe theologians and pastors who have such a thin conception of symbol that they can find little reason to observe the Supper more than two or three times a year, since they believe that any practice that is observed too often leads inevitably to a lack of appreciation of that practice (Freeman, "Where Two or Three," 264).

19. Newman, "The Lord's Supper," 217.

20. For this O'Connor quote, see her letter to "A," dated December 16, 1955, in O'Connor, *The Habit of Being*, 125.

21. McClendon, *Witness*, 379, quoting Yoder, "The New Humanity," 44.

22. Hemming, "Transubstantiating Our Selves," 418–39.

A Brief History of the Eucharist
As Generator of Ecclesial Unity

"Transubstantiating our selves"? Into what? One thing Hemming's quip assumes is that in participating in the Lord's Supper, we migrate from seeing ourselves simply as individuals to seeing ourselves as members of a body. Indeed, Hemming would say that we are transformed into a body, the body of Christ. Hemming's quip is provocative, to be sure, but is it theologically correct?

It may surprise some readers to learn that Hemming's claims about the fellowship meal are not new, even among Baptists, and that those who promote such a mindset believe it is ultimately rooted in Scripture. In addition to telling the divided Corinthian church that "we who are many are one body, for we all partake of the one bread" (1 Cor 10:17), Paul tells some of the earliest Christians not that they are "individuals" (for such a word would not come along for many centuries), but that "they are members of one another" if they have been baptized.

Along these lines, the *Didache*—a first- or second-century liturgical handbook which may indeed predate some books within the New Testament canon and claims to be the teaching of the apostles—includes the prayer "as this piece of bread was scattered over the hills and then was brought together and made one, so let your church be brought together from the ends of the earth into your kingdom."

The Fathers who followed Paul reinforced these ideas of Christians' oneness with one another. As Anglican historian Dom Gregory Dix—speaking about the earliest interpretations of 1 Corinthians 10:17—has argued, in patristic literature

> there is a curious "reversibility" about this idea as it appears in the Fathers. Sometimes . . . the sacrament becomes the Body of Christ *because* it is offered by the church which is the Body of Christ. Sometimes, as in St. Augustine, the church is the Body of Christ *because* it receives the sacrament which is His Body.[23]

Dix goes on to say that both ideas can be true, and both go back to Paul in 1 Corinthians for their starting-point.[24] Another twentieth-century theologian, the French Jesuit theologian Henri de Lubac, similarly states that the early literature was concerned with the Supper being a generator of unity. He shows that the Supper has always been about believers' unity—unity

---

23. Dix, *The Shape of the Liturgy*, 251.
24. Ibid.

with God and with other Christians.[25] Even after the Nicene controversies, he says, we hear Augustine say in a sermon on John 6 that Christ says "I am your food, but instead of my being changed into you, it is you who shall be transformed into me," they unhesitatingly understood that by their reception of the Eucharist they would be incorporated the more into the Church."[26] Later we hear from William of St. Thierry, who said that "to eat the body of Christ is to become the body of Christ,"[27] and also (with an emphasis on the church community) Gerhoh: "by eating the body of Christ they became the body of Christ."[28]

Thus in his book *Corpus Mysticum* de Lubac makes an extended argument that "the mindset of the Church in the first millennium through much of the eleventh, twelfth, and thirteenth centuries" was such that the church would have been unintelligible without weekly observance of the eucharist, that the church was *not* the church, did not become the body of Christ, without the Supper.[29] Indeed, de Lubac notes, as do McClendon and Hemming, that the eleventh-century transubstantiation controversies inspired by Berengar's views on the substantial nature of the communion elements created a major distraction—not only for those arguing that the bread and wine were "truly" and "substantially" Christ's body and blood, respectively, but also for those maintaining that they were "mere symbols."[30] Berengar, a bishop in France, made waves in making the claim that in the eucharist Christ was "mystically, not truly" present ("*mystice, non vere*").[31]

This portion of the story, of course, has been well-documented and routinely taught even in Protestant and Baptist seminaries. However, de Lubac's account of what followed is only now becoming well-known. Doctrinally speaking, the Christian church, countered Berengar's claims with

25. Lubac, *Catholicism*, 89.

26. Ibid., 99. Lubac does not say where Augustine says this, but the quote is an allusion to *Confessions* 7.10.16, and actually Augustine says there that Jesus says "I am the food of strong men, grow and you shall feed upon me; nor shall you convert me, like to food of your flesh, into you, but you shall be converted into me."

27. William of St. Thierry, *De natura et dignitate amoris* (PL 184:403). Cf. Lubac, *Corpus Mysticum*, 82.

28. Gerhoh, *In Psalmum* 9 (PL 193:780d). Cf. Lubac, *Corpus Mysticum*, 82.

29. Lubac, *Corpus Mysticum*, 88. *Corpus Mysticum*'s writing also preceded the destructive and utterly divisive Second World War by only a few months, though its publication was delayed until 1944 because of the difficult conditions in France during the war. Thus was the theme of unity very important to de Lubac. See Lubac, *Corpus Mysticum*, ix.

30. Lubac, *Corpus Mysticum*, 114.

31. McCue, "Doctrine of Transubstantiation," 386. Cf. Knowles, *Evolution of Medieval Thought*, 88–89.

the statement that in the elements Christ was "truly" present, and further that Christ was therefore not "mystically" present. The latter portion of this claim constitutes a mistake, de Lubac says, for when the church claims to be the *corpus mysticum* (the mystical body) and that the eucharist is the *corpus verum* (the true body), the church overshadows herself as the real or "true" body of Christ—a claim which she can Scripturally and therefore legitimately make. In other words, by emphasizing that the "true body" is located (solely) in the eucharistic elements,[32] she marginalizes Paul's emphatic message to the church that "you are the body of Christ!" (1 Cor 12:27)

Perhaps to the chagrin of Baptists, de Lubac is not concerned to deny Christ's "real presence" in the eucharist in pointing this out. However, he carefully makes the case that while there are two mysteries in those works of the ancients which focus upon the eucharist, "the first of them, the Real Presence, stands out less boldly" than the mystery of the church which is generated by the eucharist's power.[33] In spite of this, de Lubac claims, in the later stages of the medieval era "eucharistic theology became more and more a form of apologetic and organized itself increasingly round a defence of the 'real presence.' Apology for dogma succeeded the understanding of faith."[34] This constituted a mistake in emphasis in de Lubac's eyes, for since the medieval teachers were "fixated on the truth of presence," they forgot that the eucharist's link to the unity of the church is central.[35]

McClendon and de Lubac both want to emphasize, then, that in the eucharist it is not only the elements employed in the rite which are changed (if they are changed at all for McClendon), but those persons who participate in the rite. Persons become members of one another through baptism for Paul, but also—somehow—become one body through partaking of the one loaf. Thus does McClendon call these "re-membering signs." Thus does de Lubac claim that "the eucharist makes the Church."[36]

Why Is Eucharistic Unity Important?

To contemporary Christians, it can be easy to forget why Church unity is and has been crucial. The recipients of Paul's letters were persecuted by the likes of Emperor Nero. Augustine witnessed the fall of a Roman Empire and wrote *The City of God* when the church was threatened with new forms of

32. Lubac, *Corpus Mysticum*, 162, 167, 248–51.

33. Lubac, *Catholicism*, 100.

34. Lubac, *Corpus Mysticum*, 220.

35. Ibid., 221.

36. Ibid., 88.

persecution. Standing up to such forces requires that one not "go it alone," but in solidarity with others. Contemporary Baptists—indeed all Christians—would do well to recall that the earliest Baptists were also acutely aware of the possibility of persecution and, therefore, of their need for one another. They fled the State and the Church as English Separatists around 1600, encountered Anabaptists in 1609, and returned to be labeled "Baptists" because—contrary to the practice of most everyone else of the era—they taught and practiced believer's baptism and baptism by immersion. Just as ancient Christians had to explain their beliefs to Roman emperors, these early Baptists penned letters to the King of England, explaining their doctrines and practices.

Might this be a reason, then, that in seventeenth-century England, long after their return to England, General Baptists did not sing the song of "mere symbol" in full-throated unison as we might assume they did? Their "Orthodox Creed" (1678) states that just as Israel "had the manna to nourish them in the wilderness to Canaan, so we have the sacraments, to nourish us in the church and in our wilderness-condition."[37] In General Baptist Thomas Grantham's *Christianismus Primitivus*, the Supper is instituted by Christ "to keep himself in the remembrance of his chosen disciples,"[38] but also so that his body and blood can be "fed upon by faith."[39] Moreover, in significant sections in his work, Grantham maintains that a portion of the grace conveyed in the Supper lies in the unity of the church. It is the Supper in which "Christ gathers his people together at his own Table as one family."[40] Thus is the Supper a vital basis of church unity for Grantham, not "inferior to any doctrine in the gospel tending to preserve the unity of the Church of God. Hence it is expressly called the communion of the body and blood of Christ."[41]

Scholars have taken note of Grantham's connection between the Supper and the unity of the church, noting that while anti-sacramentalism swirled around him, the practice of the eucharist—still offered on a weekly basis for Baptists in his era—was one which, according to Grantham, strengthened and unified the body of Christ. It is this last part from which Baptists can glean going forward. The Supper is not only given to the church by Christ in order that they may be drawn into God; it is also given to the church that they may be drawn into one another. This is quite necessary in

37. "The Orthodox Creed," art. 19.
38. Grantham, "Christianismus Primitivus," 93.
39. Ibid., 94.
40. Ibid., 95.
41. Ibid., 94.

the contemporary context, I believe, and for two reasons: first, because some would argue that as we make our way deeper and deeper into the twenty-first century, Christians, especially in the West, must come to grips with the fact that they reside in the *post-Christian* West, and in simply naming themselves "Christian," Christians swim against a very swift current. In order to swim against a swift current, Christians must be unified, must retain some sense that they are a "body."

Secondly, the challenges facing churches and their pastors may be more subtle than ever, and at the same time as powerful as earlier challenges. Of course, there is nothing—or very little—that is new under the sun. Are the problems of violence, a skewed understanding of sexuality, and classism still a problem in twenty-first-century North America, just as they reared their ugly heads in first-century Rome and Corinth (or even in pre-exilic Judah)? Certainly, mind-blowing statistics such as "more humans were killed by violent means in the twentieth century than all other centuries combined," and "91% of Americans will have sexual intercourse before they are married" continue to keep pastors and Christian leaders awake at night. Statistics, however, also show that westerners are working more than ever, and when they do have moments away from work, they are investing their time (and dollars) in things other than the church.

A "T.G.I.F." culture has engrained in us the idea that "our" time away from work is just that—ours, and not the Church's or anyone else's. And it is not hard to understand why this is the case. Evangelicals in North America are some of the busiest people in the world. During the week, even after going to work, many shuttle their children all over town—and, increasingly, they are not rushing to youth choir or Wednesday night Bible studies. Rather, in an effort to encourage "achievement," Christian parents find themselves picking up their children from school, getting them to rehearsals or to athletic practices. Pressed for time, often Christian families are tempted to neglect other, important practices: nightly Bible reading, prayers, and—since this is an essay on the Supper—eating together.

Many scholars believe that these challenges are at an all-time high, prompting *Christianity Today*'s Shirl James Hoffman to wonder if investing so much time and money in youth sports or other ventures necessarily means "spending our leisure moments comparing talents, plotting self-advancing agendas, and . . . stifling feelings of sympathy might foster mindsets that negatively frame our thinking in other endeavors."[42] Thirty years ago *Sports Illustrated*'s Frank Deford prophetically spoke about a phenomenon

---

42. Hoffman, "Sports Fanatics," Christianity Today, online: http://www.christianity-today.com/ct/2010/february/3.20.html?start=1.

he called "Sportianity," but did he see this coming? As I know all too well, even the children of many clergy spend four-five times as many hours per week in athletics than they do at churches, engaging in what Hoffman calls "a triumphal evangelism blended with competitive zeal."[43]

Re-Membering the Body

Such trends have prompted Barry Harvey to suggest that the body of Christ spends much of its time being "dismembered" throughout most weeks. Indeed, playing on an idea put forward a decade earlier by Catholic theologian William Cavanaugh—who noted that the communist government "dismembered" the church in Chile throughout the 1970s and 1980s—Harvey notes that one does not have to live under the reign of an oppressive government in order to be divided. While at work, for example:

> People's time must either be used to the full or switched off when it is no longer needed, that is, they must be flexible or laid off . . . human beings are therefore dismembered, stripped of any residual identity and reduced to a series of functions that are exercised solely in accordance with the demands of the market. They must not be tied to a place, but prepared to move to follow employment. They must not be tied by time, but be prepared to work all hours and days of the week, especially Sundays.[44]

When I was a seminarian and young Youth Minister serving under a wonderful mentor, Bob Albritton, pastor of Millbrook Baptist Church in Raleigh, NC, Albritton once said to me, "you have to be so utterly welcoming when a family arrives at church on Sunday morning, because you never know what they've had to go through simply to get to church." Surely, when our work and even our play seem to dismember us, worship is direly needed for our healing, for our re-membering.

But what kind of worship? As noted above, in most free-church worship, since the Supper is practiced annually at worst and most often quarterly, the sermon and its preacher have taken on a more central role in modern and contemporary worship services. For the earliest churches the eucharist, held at least weekly, was almost always "preceded by a service of the word, with readings, preaching and intercessory prayer, concluded by the exchange of a holy kiss, as a 'seal' of their prayers and an expression of unity."[45] Thus has

43. Ibid.

44. Harvey, "Re-Membering the Body," 109.

45. Bradshaw, *New Westminster Dictionary*, 172.

proclamation of the word through preaching, along with the eucharist, been an important feature in Christian worship services since the inception of the faith. Many would argue, however, that the sermon has replaced the eucharist as the "heart" of most free churches' worship services. On Sunday mornings, after the singing of two or three hymns and saying or (more often) listening to two or three fervent prayers, the sermon occupies most of the last half of the worship service. This is an emphasis taken to lengths which, according to Anglican theologian David Broughton (D.B.) Knox, is foreign to Christianity from the Apostle Paul until well after Martin Luther.[46]

McClendon, who calls preaching one of the three "remembering signs" in his Systematic Theology, has called members of the body of Christ to a more frequent celebration of another of these remembering signs—the Supper—even as a remedy for disunity in a "troubled" Baptist church which he served as pastor in California.[47] By making this move in a Baptist church in North America constituted primarily of Caucasian members,[48] McClendon could be called a "radical."[49]

Of course, it has often been pointed out that the increasing centrality of the sermon in Protestant and Free Church worship was part of a long overdue corrective to the alleged mentality that participation in the eucharist was a mechanical, human work in which the believer could attain a purely spiritual salvation.[50] Indeed, as early as the fourth century preachers

46. Knox, "The Nature of Worship." Knox is an Anglican priest, theology teacher, and has been principal of Moore College in Australia for twenty-eight years. Critics of his statement here may cite Acts 20:7–11, where a man named Eutyches falls out of a third-story window and dies because he fell asleep during one of Paul's very lengthy teaching sessions. It is disputed, however, whether Paul is preaching or even teaching within the context of a worship service. Moreover, this passage does not indicate that this was a normal practice for the apostle.

47. McClendon, *Making Gospel Sense*, xix. We are reminded that in *Doctrine*, the Supper is a "sign of salvation" over against sin, which McClendon defines as "refusal" of Jesus' "way," as "reversion" to the old, inferior way of life, but finally as "rupture"– rupture of the relationship between God and humans and rupture of the relationships within the church, the body of Christ (McClendon, *Doctrine*, 132).

48. Again, National Baptists have largely retained the practice of observing the Lord's Supper on a monthly basis.

49. Again, McClendon calls himself a radical Christian in *Biography as Theology*, saying, "I am a *radical* Christian. 'Christian'—that pays tribute to Augustine and Edwards, to Schleiermacher and Barth, and to all who challenge pat solutions, proximate loyalties, as idolatrous. 'Radical'—that affirms my solidarity with experience-saturated believers: with Anabaptists so little known, with revivalists and pietists, with Pentecostalists and communal celebrants of many sorts" (McClendon, *Biography as Theology*, 69–70). Of course, as one of my primary teachers Ralph C. Wood often points out in class, radical comes from the word Latin *radix*, which means "root."

50. For a balanced reading of this reaction, see Haymes, "Towards a Sacramental

complained that churchgoers came only for the eucharist and resisted any preaching having to do with moral reformation.[51] Moreover, one might argue that though most Protestants and members of free churches are not gathering around the eucharistic elements on a weekly basis, the hearing of most sermons is an act done primarily in community.[52]

On the other hand, not being explicitly reminded of the church's unity—or better, not being "re-membered" to one another—on a weekly basis in the practice of the Supper generates another vacuum which Robert Jenson takes note of: the privatization of Christianity coupled with believers' inability to articulate reasons for, or even affirm, the unity of the church. Without this specifically Christian rite in which Christians are pulled both godward and made one with one another the church is but a human society of which one can "volunteer" to be a member of one minute and then "unvolunteer" the next, just as one could volunteer or unvolunteer were she or he a member of the local chamber of commerce or country club.

This privatization is dangerous on many levels, according to Jenson, who believes that if we get our beliefs wrong "we cannot help but get our lives wrong."[53] Thus, when Jenson affirms that since the dawn of Christianity "freedom is not escape from the body, but the resurrection of the body,"[54] he is claiming that when one's faith becomes an essentially private and voluntary affair, it is not simply a very thin conception of the church which results, but rather nothing less than a mentality which could result in Christians marginalizing other people. For example, he claims that when "religion becomes a private affair, we no longer pray 'O Lord, succor the poor'; we pray instead 'O Lord, make us feel better toward the poor.'"[55] His point: the church has allowed a foreign understanding of freedom—namely the Western and relatively new notion that freedom is primarily a private individual's right to "life, liberty and the pursuit of happiness"—to influence

---

Understanding of Preaching," 262–63. Also, see Knox, where he balances this claim with the point that "to put trust for salvation in rites which had no other support than church tradition was idolatry, and the depriving of the true God of His due honour. Yet medieval worship consisted in almost nothing else than this. For this reason, the reading of the Bible and its exposition in the sermon are essential and central elements in public worship. For unless the people hear the Scriptures in their own language and understand the meaning, their faith cannot be rightly directed to the true promises of God" (see Knox, "The Nature of Worship").

51. Bradshaw, *New Westminster Dictionary*, 173.

52. With the advent of televangelism, this claim might be difficult to uphold.

53. Hauerwas, "Only Theology Overcomes Ethics," 255. Hauerwas is the one who says Jenson "believes" this.

54. Jenson, "Kingdom of America's God," 64.

55. Ibid.

the uniquely Christian understanding of freedom: "being able to drink from one cup with the rich and the poor, the healthy and the alarmingly diseased . . ., having to forgive and be forgiven."[56] In order to be freed to serve others, then, it is crucial that the ecclesial body regularly and intentionally gather around the eucharistic body.

Contemporary Concerns

As interim pastor of a divided Baptist church in California, McClendon once urged his congregation to move from a quarterly observance of the rite to a monthly observance.[57] This essay has endeavored to demonstrate that—bickering or not—all churches are divided, are at once the body of Christ and dismembered humanity. This essay has also attempted to demonstrate, however, that Baptist pastors, theologians, professors, campus ministers, and others would do well to remember that God makes us a body, "members of one another" through the Lord's Supper.

Other practices dubbed "re-membering signs" by McClendon, such as preaching and baptism, will always be especially important in Baptist circles—and yet preaching on "Communion Sundays" ought to be more specific about the Church's historical reliance on the meal (in both good and bad ways) and the need for a thicker Eucharistic theology, occasionally pushing in the direction of connecting the practice of sharing the meal to the life of the congregation and to the individual lives of the members of the congregation.

Similarly, preaching, Sunday School lessons, and/or mid-week congregational studies might focus upon the history of the practice, or perhaps the long-forgotten symbolism embedded in our worship. Do our church members know why members of other communions take the eucharist every week, or, in some ecclesial groups, every day? Is it because they are overly reliant upon "tradition," or is it because of their ecclesial group's interpretation of a passage such as Acts 2, where it is said that the members of the Jerusalem church, "day by day, as they spent much time in the temple, broke bread from house to house and ate their food with glad and generous hearts, praising God and having the goodwill of all the people" (Acts 2:46–47)?

It is also a sound practice to ask congregations to think about the significance of having members pass the Communion plates and cups to one another. Is this an embodiment of their theological claim that "every member is a minister"? Could we, as some churches have encouraged, ask

56. Jenson, *On Thinking the Human*, 44.
57. See McClendon, *Making Gospel Sense*, xix.

our members to say "the bread of life," or "the cup of our salvation," or other traditional phrases as they pass the plate and cup to one another?

Finally, could Baptist churches occasionally have members come forward to take the elements from a common cup? Given our emphasis on congregational autonomy, the answer is certainly "yes!" This practice would stretch some church members, to be sure, but it would also aid them as they attempt to think about the Supper as a communal practice rather than a purely inward experience.

Again, as Hemming has noted, "what happens to us in the eucharist?" is as important a question to ask as the more traditional questions "what happens to the bread?" or "what happens to me?" We have stated previously the benefits of re-visiting the Acts passages, but one thing we have not yet touched on is that the radical "communalism" of Acts extended far beyond sharing meals together on a daily basis. As many have noted, Acts states that the members of this, the very earliest of churches, held all things in common. Is there a connection between a more regular practice of the eucharist and an openness to sharing our "possessions"? Could the stories of persons like Dorothy Day or Teresa of Calcutta help our congregations make those connections? Finally, what is the relationship between the eucharist and church stewardship?

A more intentional use of the eucharist in the church's liturgy can push a congregation in radical and positive directions. Moreover, as Baptists continue to see themselves as characters in the continually unfolding narrative that began in creation, continued through Israel, Jesus of Nazareth, and the early church, a more intentional—and perhaps more frequent—practice of the eucharist makes sense as a continuation of biblical and historic Christianity.

8

Baptism

The Substance and the Sign

Elizabeth Newman

Our name notwithstanding, it is often observed that baptism has held a diminished place in Baptist life and thought. Anthony Cross, for example, argues that a Baptist theology of baptism has been subordinated to "evangelistic enthusiasms." He adds that outside of their heated debates with paedobaptists, we have "made little of the rite."[1] In practice, this subordination has often resulted in baptism being understood as a spectator phenomenon (i.e., the congregation passively watches what happens to the candidate) and as *merely* symbolic (i.e., only a representation of a prior, real experience). The purpose of this essay is to demonstrate the errors about the ordinance into which the Baptist mind has sometimes fallen and to suggest correctives. At the same time, I will argue that the Baptist mode of baptism most fully displays the gospel witness.

---

1. Cross, *Baptism and the Baptists*, 454–55. The full quotation reads: "[Baptists'] theology of baptism is subordinated to their evangelistic enthusiasms, for they emphasize the importance of conversion but not the act of initiation into the church." Cross adds that that the "overwhelming majority of Baptists writing on baptism have done so within the ecumenical context," which suggests they hold an "ambivalent attitude toward baptism." They defend believer's baptism, on the one hand, but on the other, pay little attention to the rite (ibid.).

Baptism: "Merely Symbolic"?

The philosopher Ludwig Wittgenstein has said that "the meaning of a word is its use." He meant to call attention to the various ways that context shapes the meaning of the words we use. Nowhere is this more evident that when we use the word "symbol" in a religious, or more specifically Christian context. At times, symbol, like sign, can indicate a present reality. For example, a red-orange glow in an early morning sky is a sign of the presence of a rising sun. Or, a red octagon is a symbol for "stop," such that the symbol-word brings into being a new reality: the stopping of a car. In both of these examples, there is an intimate and inextricable connection between the sign and the signified.

One might, however, say that something is merely symbolic, by which she typically means that the symbol can easily be separated from the signified. In this sense, "we think of signs as pointers to something that is *absent* (as in 'Las Vegas: 450 mi.')."[2] It is this latter usage of symbol that has dominated much Baptist thinking about baptism. In part, this emphasis on "merely" comes from a Baptist suspicion of a sacramental understanding that seems to confer magical powers to baptism.[3] Such usage is also shaped by a strong modern distinction between real/symbol or literal/figurative, in which the real and literal constitute the objective world, while the symbol/figurative is an added level of personal meaning to a prior reality.[4] Whether it is a suspicion of sacramentalism or the priority of the real over the merely symbolic, the result for contemporary Baptists has been an impoverished theology of baptism. Yet what is the alternative? Surely those early Baptists who argued against a "superstitious" practice of baptism in which "infants dying in infancy, without baptism, go to purgatory or *limbus infantum*" were correct to regard this as erroneous.[5] At the same time, as I will show more fully, describing baptism as "merely" or "only" symbolic diminishes the reality of baptism as a grace-filled sign.

2. Bauerschmidt, *Holy Teaching*, 255, emphasis added.

3. According to the *Encyclopedia of Southern Baptists*, for example, the word "sacrament" was avoided by Baptists "because of the magical implications of the word." Originally, however, "sacrament" was a secular word indicating a pledge of allegiance to the Roman army. The author adds, "If 'sacrament' were used in the way it was originally used, it would be a good word to specify both baptism and the Lord's Supper" (T. Smith, "Baptism," 106). I return to a discussion of "magical thinking" later in this essay.

4. For a particularly insightful critique of these dichotomies, see Poteat, *A Philosophical Daybook*. Poteat notes, for example, about the modern imagination: "What is literal and direct is what is serious and real; all the rest of our talk is, however pleasing and even irresistible, secondary or tertiary" (ibid., 10).

5. "The Orthodox Creed," art. 28.

"The Baptism With Which I Am Baptized, You Will Be Baptized"

To begin to see how baptism is a grace-filled sign, I begin with Jesus' baptism.[6] It is typical in many Baptist churches to have an image of Jesus' baptism by John in the river Jordan above the baptismal pool, a tradition that can be traced back to the early church.[7] This juxtaposition of Jesus above the baptismal pool rightly suggests that the baptism of Jesus is intimately related to our own.

Jesus, of course, received the baptism of repentance. In this baptism, John is calling the Israel of his day to prepare for the coming of the Messiah by repenting for her sins, being cleansed and awaiting God's longed-for kingdom. As Susan K. Wood states, "John's baptism had as its purpose the gathering of a messianic people who would be prepared for the coming Messiah."[8] Eschatology, or expecting the fullness of time to arrive, is thus key to understanding the baptism of repentance. Yet, as many have wondered, why does Jesus, the promised Messiah and one without sin, need this baptism? John himself objects saying, "I need to be baptized by you, and do you come to me?" (Matt 3:14).

We can respond by turning to the church's understanding of Jesus as the figure of the suffering servant in Isaiah. The ecumenical treatise, *One Lord, One Baptism*, for example, relates the divine declaration at Jesus' baptism—"This is my Son, the Beloved, with whom I am well pleased," (Matt 3:17)—to Isaiah's first servant song, "Here is my servant, whom I uphold, my chosen, in whom my soul delights; I have put my spirit upon him; he

---

6. My own analysis of baptism begins with the baptism of Jesus for the reasons that I indicate. One may, however, begin by turning to images of water in the natural world and show how God in baptism transforms these. For an excellent example of the latter, see discussion of birth, cleansing, and refreshment in Fiddes, "Baptism and Creation," 47–67. Robin Jensen notes that the early church itself incorporated "pre-Christian sensibilities about the relationship of bathing to initiation and cleaning [which] was underscored by the use of bath-like architecture and elements (e.g., stripping, anointing, and plunging into water)" (Jensen, *Living Water*, 280). These various approaches to baptism are best understood as complementary and overlapping.

7. See, for example, the dome mosaic of the Orthodox Baptistery in Ravenna, Italy (fifth-century).

8. Wood, *One Baptism*, 4. Wood is relying upon an earlier ecumenical document of The Commission of Faith and Order from the World Council of Churches, *One Lord, One Baptism*. I am grateful to Wood for bringing this document to my attention. In regards to John the Baptist, the commission states, "Both his preaching and his baptism were conditioned by the unique situation in which they took place: the eschatological situation, the drawing near of the messianic kingdom" (World Council of Churches, *One Lord, One Baptism*, 50).

will bring forth justice to the nations" (Isa 42:1).[9] The similar pattern in these verses invites the reader to see the beginning of the messianic age in Jesus and to interpret it "through the lens of the suffering servant in such a way that what is said of the suffering servant applies to Christ."[10] Thus Jesus, the suffering servant of the Lord, enters vicariously into "the sin of many" (Isa 53:12), to bear this sin as his own so that all might participate in his righteousness.[11] Jesus' baptism is not a baptism of repentance for himself. Rather, Jesus enters into solidarity with sinners in order to make them righteous. "The messianic kingdom was established only through the fact that he, 'the righteous one, my servant,' makes many righteous by bearing their iniquities (Isa 53:11)."[12] Whereas the baptism of repentance points to the imminent arrival of the messianic kingdom, the baptism of Jesus indicates that the messianic kingdom *has come in the person of the suffering servant.* Jesus' baptism thus foreshadows his death (see Mark 10:39), while also anticipating his resurrection.

At the same time that Jesus in baptism enters into solidarity with all, his own identity as Son through the Spirit is disclosed. Jesus is already the Son, but in baptism, his identity as Son of the Father through the Spirit is publically displayed. The baptism of Jesus is thus integral to his life and mission: confirming the promises to the people Israel, prefiguring his own death and resurrection, and initiating the kingdom of God in his own person as the one who will heal us from sin and death.

I want to emphasize that while the Lord's baptism points beyond itself, it is more than merely symbolic. Jesus' baptism is not a sign that can be separated from an independent reality. It is rather participation in God's covenant and in God's renewal of all creation. Stated more fully, as we have seen, Jesus' baptism: 1) both fulfills and transforms the baptism of John, 2) is an act of solidarity with all sinners, 3) prefigures or points toward Jesus' own suffering, death and resurrection and 4) and is an act through which Jesus establishes the messianic kingdom by fulfilling all righteousness (Matt 3:15). Jesus' baptism, in other words, is a "charged," grace-filled event in which the same Spirit is present who will raise Jesus from the dead (Rom 8:11). It is not merely symbolic but is the way in which God in Christ enters into the realities of our time and place in order to fulfill divine promises and make present the reality of God's kingdom, whether with John the Baptist

9. World Council of Churches, *One Lord, One Baptism,* 53.

10. Wood, *One Baptism,* 6.

11. This is also Paul's interpretation in 2 Cor 5:21, "For our sake he made him to be sin who knew no sin, so that in him we might become the righteousness of God."

12. World Council of Churches, *One Lord, One Baptism,* 53.

in the river Jordan, or with those gathered around the baptistry at Pleasant View Baptist in Richmond, Virginia.

While acknowledging the richness and depth of Jesus' baptism—solidarity with sinners, etc.—we might still be tempted to argue that *our* baptism is purely representational. After all, it seems implausible that our baptism is necessary to "fulfill all righteousness" (Matt 3:15). And yet, in Mark's Gospel, Jesus says, "[T]he baptism with which I am baptized, *you will be baptized*" (10:39). In baptism, we too enter into solidarity with all sinners, not of course as One without sin, but as those forgiven of the sin we share with all humanity. While our sin is uniquely our own, it is also true that "all have sinned and fall short of the glory of God" (Rom 3:23). In baptism we acknowledge not only this commonality in sin, but even more, our common death to sin which is a death in Christ. Just as baptism pointed Jesus toward his own death and resurrection, so also is our baptism an indication—or even more—a shared participation in Christ's own death and resurrection. Yet, how can we participate in an event which the Christian church has lifted up as unique and unrepeatable? It is *because* Jesus' life, death and resurrection are unique—the culmination of God's healing of our sin and death—that we are able to die and rise with Christ. To be baptized with Jesus' baptism is to participate in God's way of healing and saving the world. In this sense, our baptism fulfills all righteousness as we are made participants in Christ's solidarity with sinners, his suffering and new life, and God's kingdom now present on earth.

Baptism and How God Saves

But, one might respond, immersion in water is symbolic of this reality, not the real thing. As noted, Baptists have often reacted against a view of baptism that makes the practice seem "magical" or superstitious, as if water saves rather than God. They have been "concerned about what they see as the danger of ritual to claim for human action what should be wholly subject to the sovereignty of God."[13] The worry, which is often associated with a misunderstanding of *ex opere operato*,[14] is that baptism comes to function

13. Ellis, *Gathering*, 211.

14. *Ex opere operato* was a teaching that developed in response to the Donatist controversy in the fourth century. The Donatists believed that priests who had denied the faith under persecution should not be allowed to remain as priests due to their impurity, and that the baptisms performed by them were invalid. They wanted a pure church. Augustine, however, argued that the grace of baptism is efficacious despite the sin or impurity of particular clergy. As stated in the Catholic Catechism, this teaching means that "the sacrament is not wrought by the righteousness of either the celebrant

mechanistically, apart from faith. To refer to the earlier example, baptizing dying infants to ensure their entrance into heaven will seem to most Baptists a serious misunderstanding of baptismal practice.[15] In response to this mechanistic understanding, Baptists have typically rejected the idea that "water saves," stressing instead the sovereignty of God, the baptism of believers and the necessity of faith.

Such concerns rightly raise questions about *how* God saves. Is baptism necessary for salvation? For many Baptists, the response would be "no," as they will claim that God can surely save children and adults who have not been baptized. Yet, if baptism is not necessary for salvation, why baptize? Perhaps the most common response is that baptism is an act of obedience (i.e., Jesus commands to go and baptize) and that it is a testimony to the congregation of an individual's faith. Baptism is also typically understood by Baptists as connected to church membership.[16] The emphasis falls on the conviction that one is saved through faith; to suggest that baptism is directly connected to salvation is to fall into the "magic" thinking trap discussed above.

Surely faith, understood as both the good news of salvation through Christ and our trust in God, is essential.[17] When baptism, however, is merely

---

or the recipient, but by the power of God," cited in Wood, *One Baptism*, 69. Its intent was not to underwrite a "magical" view of the sacraments, but to uphold the conviction that "Christ and the Spirit are the principal actor (principal cause) in the sacrament through the agency of the sacrament (instrumental cause)" (Wood, *One Baptism*, 69). Rightly understood, *ex opere operato* does not deny the necessity of faith but indicates that the object of faith is Christ and the Spirit rather than the purity or perfection of the minister or laity.

15. Historically, this view has been taught, by Augustine, for example. More recently, however, The International Theological Commission of the Roman Catholic Church states, that "the Catechism [1992] teaches that infants who die without baptism are entrusted by the Church to the mercy of God, as is shown in the specific funeral rite for such children." This conviction, they state, should not be used to negate the necessity of baptism or to delay it. See International Theological Commission, "The Hope of Salvation for Infants who Die without Being Baptised."

16. These three understandings of baptism (obedience, testimony, and church membership) are in the *Baptist Faith and Message*, both the 1963 and 2000 edition: "Christian baptism is the immersion of a believer in water in the name of the Father, the Son, and the Holy Spirit. It is an act of obedience symbolizing the believer's faith in a crucified, buried, and risen Saviour, the believer's death to sin, the burial of the old life, and the resurrection to walk in newness of life in Christ Jesus. It is a testimony to his faith in the final resurrection of the dead. Being a church ordinance, it is prerequisite to the privileges of church membership and to the Lord's Supper" (Southern Baptist Convention, "1963 Baptist Faith and Message," VII; and Southern Baptist Convention, "The Baptist Faith and Message [2000]," VII). See also Brackney, "Doing Baptism Baptist Style."

17. Jaroslav Pelikan describes this distinction as "the faith *which* one believes [*fides quae creditur*]" and "the faith *with* which one believes [*fides qua creditur*]" (the objective

symbolic of a prior faith, the conclusion—often drawn—is that baptism is separate from salvation. Yet, I want to argue that baptism is crucial to salvation. Of course, in writing this, I hasten to add that "salvation" means more than "getting into heaven." Salvation, related to the word *salve* or healing, describes the ways that the Triune God seeks to heal and restore all of creation. Adam is a "type of the one who was to come" (Rom 5:14) and points to the reality that God's salvation in Christ "re-capitulates" all of creation. Christ, as fully divine and fully human, fulfills for creation what Adam could not.[18] In order to engage the relation between salvation, new creation and baptism more fully, I turn first to a debate in the early church over the question of how God saves.

In the second century, a group of Christians argued that it was "pointless to lead to water."[19] They meant by this that baptism was not only unnecessary but superfluous. Why? Irenaeus of Lyons describes their rationale: "the mystery of the ineffable and invisible Power should not be performed through created things, visible and perishable, nor that of unthinkable and bodiless realities through sensible and corporeal things." In short, they believed that God does not use created things for salvific purposes. Rather, "perfect redemption is simply the Gnosis of the inexpressible Greatness . . . by Gnosis the whole state of ignorance will be dissolved, so that Gnosis is the redemption of the inner man."[20] The reader will no doubt recognize this as a form of gnosticism. Gnostics believed that an inner, typically secret knowledge (gnosis) is what saves us rather than God's mighty deeds in history. For gnostics, the world is not created good by God. Rather God saves humans *from* their bodies and *from* the created world. Since water is a created substance, gnostics believed that God would not use it to save; salvation is rather an inward, spiritual reality. The gnostic rejection of baptism is thus a firm statement on their part that salvation involves the inner self and not the material world. They concluded that God's salvation did not entail the renewal of creation.

---

and subjective aspects, respectively, or knowledge/assent and trust), in Pelikan, *Credo*, 49; brackets original.

18. Irenaeus of Lyons engaged this notion of "recapitulation" in his refutation of the gnostics. Joel Kurz nicely summarizes recapitulation: "Christ submitted himself to Adam's circumstances and achieved the reversal of the events which led to death and the sullying of creation. Creation and redemption coexist within the divine economy, so Christ's restoration of creation and humanity occurs within the matrix of movement toward the eschatological fulfillment and consummation. By assuming Adam's flesh and successfully retracing his events, Christ was initiating and executing the process of recapitulation" (Kurz, "Gifts of Creation," 122).

19. Grant, *Irenaeus of Lyons*, 86.

20. Ibid.

In contrast to a gnostic understanding, orthodox Christianity affirms that in the cosmic drama between God and humanity, God desires to restore all of creation: "He [Christ Jesus] is the image of the invisible God, the firstborn of all creation; . . . all things have been created through him and for him" (Colossians 1:15, 16). In the saga of salvation stretching back to Abraham, therefore, God engages a people in order to restore all of creation and to bring it into communion with Himself. If we look specifically at water, numerous places in Scripture recount God shaping, sending or pouring forth water in order to save His people. A familiar passage from Exodus reads, "Then Moses stretched out his hand over the sea; and the LORD drove the sea back by a strong east wind all night, and turned the sea into dry land; and the waters were divided. The Israelites went into the sea on dry ground, the waters forming a wall for them on their right and on their left" (14:21–22). In the Exodus event, God saves a people, Israel, by transforming the water into a way of salvation. It is not the water that saves—God does—but the Creator works within creation, so that the Israelites might walk through the waters unscathed. God is saving them not with a secret knowledge, but with His own mighty, miraculous and visible deeds within the created world. God's saving deeds culminate in Jesus Christ, who stands at the center of renewed creation. Such renewal makes possible a reversal of the fall and of a departure from the Garden of Eden. Irenaeus states that church is itself "the first-fruits of a restored humanity."[21] As Joel Kurz notes, "The church is the context in which humanity receives the divine nourishment of a restored creation; it is . . . 'a wellspring in creation (in which abides) a giver who pours out gifts to the world.'"[22] In God's renewed creation, water is no longer a threat or a source of death, but instead becomes a means of new life in and through Christ, a reality concentrated in the practice of baptism.

In the catacombs, the early church often visually related the different stories of water in God's salvation. In the Catacomb of Peter and Marcellinus (Cubiculum 62, dated AD 330), for example, a scene of Jesus' baptism is placed across from the figure of Moses.[23] Moses is striking the rock in the hopes of receiving the promised water, as narrated: "Then Moses lifted up his hand and struck the rock twice with his staff; water came out abundantly, and the congregation and their livestock drank" (Num 20:11). The fresco in the center of the catacomb cubicle depicts seven guests, a servant on the left,

21. Cited in Kurz, "Gifts of Creation," 123.

22. Ibid. Kurz is citing Gustaf Wingren.

23. Jensen, *Living Water*, 22, notes that Wilpert and De Bruyne both identify this character as Moses, though Zimmermann and Fausone identify him as Balaam.

117

and on the right, six large jugs. A figure of Jesus is set to transform the water into wine at the Cana wedding. The juxtaposition of these scenes connects baptism to other ways that God transforms water in order to bring about a new creation.

Other early baptisteries depict the woman at the well; "Jesus asks her for ordinary water, but he offers something better: the water of eternal life."[24] One can also find in early baptisteries, among other images, the three women coming to the tomb (reinforcing "the Easter aspects of baptism"[25]); deer coming to the water (relating Psalm 42 to baptism and to the "longing for the fountain that remits sins in the same way that the deer longs for the spring of water"[26]); and Noah's Ark ("linking the flood with baptismal cleansing and the dove with descent of the Holy Spirit and a sign of peace").[27] Such images reveal how the early church saw baptism in relation to other Scriptural stories involving water; in each of these, water is not just water, but a way that God cleanses, heals and provides for a people.

The conviction that God heals (*salve*) through the baptismal waters can be seen in some Baptist prayers as well. For example, Virginia Baptist minister Eleazer Clay (1744–1836), in his *Hymns and Spiritual Songs*, published the following: "Eternal Spirit, heavenly Dove, / On these baptismal waters move; / That we through energy divine, / May have the substance with the sign."[28] The Spirit hovering over baptism calls to mind the Spirit hovering over creation, making new creation possible. In praying for "the substance with the sign," these early Baptists were praying that true death and resurrection may coincide with being "buried" in the water and rising again. "On these baptismal waters *move*" is a prayer for the Spirit to be present in the water so that all those gathered may be transformed.

We see here the conviction that baptism both signals and makes real a dying and rising with Christ. Similarly, the authors of the 1644 London Confession, in defending "plunging the whole body under water," maintained that the sign must "answer the signified." The signified is identified with "washing the whole soule in the bloud of Christ," the "interest the Saints have in the death, burial, and resurrection," and, thirdly, "together with a confirmation of our faith, that as certainly as the body is buried under water, and riseth again, so certainly shall the bodies of the Saints be raised by the

24. Jensen, *Living Water*, 277.

25. Ibid., 278.

26. Ibid., 252.

27. Ibid., 268. As Jensen notes, this is Tertullian's interpretation.

28. Clay, *Hymns and Spiritual Songs*, cited in Thompson, "Re-envisioning Baptist Identity," 291–92.

power of Christ in the day of the resurrection, to reign with Christ."[29] In "answering the thing signified," this early Baptist confession implies that the signified is a present reality, the gift of new life to be brought to complete fruition in the day of resurrection.

In the eighteenth century, Baptist pastor and theologian Morgan Edwards records the following baptismal prayer:

> Thou that didst come from Galilee to Jordan come now also from heaven to ____ and meet us on the banks of this river . . . We know that thou art present every where, but ah! Let it not be here as at first on the banks of the Jordan when thou didst stand among the croud, and they knew it not! O let us find the messiah here! Thou that comest by water and art witnessed to of the water come by this water, . . . and afford us communion with thee in thy baptism; for in the water and in the floods thy presence is promised![30]

"Thou that comest by water . . . for in the water and in the floods thy presence is promised." We see in this prayer the conviction that God promises to be with a people in and through the water: meet *us* on the banks of the river, let *us* find the Messiah here!, afford *us* communion. It thus offers a vivid contrast, referred to earlier, to "the congregation as predominantly spectators of that which the candidate is doing."[31] Edwards's recorded prayer is rather an ecclesial prayer of participation. Participants will not drown (floods) but rather, in baptism, will find "communion with thee," that is, a communion with the Triune God who alone provides our salvation.

To return, then, to the question of the relation between salvation and baptism, these various sources, and I would emphasize more broadly the whole trajectory of God's ways in the world, emphasize that salvation

---

29. "London Confession," art. 40.

30. Morgan Edwards, *The Customs of Primitive Churches*, cited by Thompson, "Re-envisioning Baptist Identity," 291–92. Luther's well-known "Flood Prayer" relates similar themes: "We pray through the same thy groundless mercy that thou wilt graciously behold this N. and bless him with true faith in the spirit so that by means of this saving flood all that has been born in him from Adam and which he himself has added thereto may be drowned in him and engulfed, and that he may be sundered from the number of the unbelieving, preserved dry and secure in the holy ark . . . Amen" (cited in Wood, *One Baptism*, 126).

31. Cross, *Baptism and the Baptists*, 457. The full context reads: "The emphasis placed on baptism continues to centre on the candidate . . . This individualism has meant Baptists have continued to find difficulty in expressing the provenience of God's grace the and corporate dimension of the rite . . . The corporate dimension [of baptism] continues to revolve around the congregation as predominantly spectators of that which the candidate is doing."

involves our being made part of something larger than ourselves: God's communion with a people (Israel/church) and a new creation in Christ. We are now no longer our own. We belong to Christ and thus are also "members one of another." This is not about mere conformity, but about allowing ourselves to become "abundant life," a wellspring of faith, hope and love for the world. Seen in this light, the command to baptize (Matt 28:19) is not random, but related to patterns of salvation already established in the Old Testament. Just as Israel flees captivity through the waters of the Red Sea in order to go to the promised land, so also in baptism do God's people leave behind all that binds them so that they might enter into the freedom of communion with one another in and with the Triune God. This is not only a human action, but a possibility given through the grace of God. Just as Jesus, when he was baptized in the Jordan, saw the Spirit descend and heard a voice from heaven, "You are my Son, the Beloved; with you I am well pleased" (Mark 1:11), so also does Christ say to us, "you are my beloved sons; you are my beloved daughters, with you I am well pleased." In baptism, the church enacts the conviction that what Jesus is by nature—the Son of God—we are, by adoption, the sons and daughters of God (Rom 8:15).[32] So understood, baptism is a grace-filled event for the whole church, not a mere symbol in which nothing happens (some Baptists), nor an insurance policy against one's fears of damnation (some Catholics, United Methodists and others).[33]

To summarize, in my view a rich theology of baptism will describe baptism as an ordinance with sacramental significance.[34] That is, baptism

32. Thus Baptists can sing, "Baptized in water, Sealed by the Spirit, Marked with the sign of Christ, our King; Born of one Father, We are His children, Joyfully now God's praise we sing" ("Baptized in Water," *The Baptist Hymnal*, #362).

33. An emphasis on Christ's desire for all to come to the baptismal waters is intended to highlight the way of salvation as described in patterns of Scripture: Christ in baptism recapitulates and brings to fulfillment Israel passing through the Red Sea. What of those inside the church who refuse to be baptized? If baptism is a gift, then one is rejecting God's gift and thus cutting him or herself off from the *fullness* of God's saving love.

34. I gleaned this language from Neville Callam, "Caribbean Baptists sometimes put it like this—'Something happens to us whenever we partake of the Lord's Supper' . . . they experience the gracious hand of God upon their lives, forgiving their sins, offering them nourishment for the pilgrimage of the Christian life, and drawing them into ever deeper communion with the Trinity . . . ordinance is understood to have sacramental significance"(quoted in Anglican Communion Office and Baptist World Alliance, *Report*, 58).

I find this phrasing also quite rich: "The water signifies new birth. The sacraments are the signs which indicate symbolically Jesus' presence (that is, the Holy Spirit, grace)" (*A New Catechism*, 255). The richness, in my view, lies in the fact that sacrament, sign, and symbol are interrelated in a way that opens up the potential abundance of each

is indeed an ordinance (a command). Yet, at the same time, it is a gift of communion with Christ and the body of Christ, making possible our new creation together. To describe baptism as a gift of communion is but another way of highlighting the presence of God's grace in our baptism. Rightly understood, the grace present in baptism is not mechanically conferred, as if grace were a quantifiable substance. Rather, grace names a "relationship of communion"[35] through the power of the Spirit. Christ is really present in baptism as the *"principal actor,"*[36] *the One who through the ministrations of the church baptizes us into his own life, death and resurrection. God in Christ through the Spirit uses the waters of baptism to cleanse, heal and unite so that* "in the one Spirit we were all baptized into one body—Jews or Greeks, slaves or free—and we were all made to drink of one Spirit" (1 Cor 12:13).

Such a position does not negate the need for personal faith. It does, however, enlarge our understanding of the objective dimension of faith in that it more fully situates "Jesus is Lord" in the saga of God's salvation of the cosmos. This position also does not negate the presence of God's grace in bringing to conversion those who are not baptized. To the contrary, just as the Hebrew people responded to God in order to move toward freedom through the Red Sea, so also does God's grace always go before human response. At the same time, I would emphasize that just as God desired the Hebrews to go through the waters to freedom, so also does Christ desire the baptism of all, with the extraordinary offer that our baptism is a participation in His baptism, which is also a participation in his life, death and resurrection.

The Mode of Practice

While I have been critical of a strong current in Baptist life that sees baptism as "just" symbolic,[37] I also want to argue that the Baptist mode of baptism— the immersion of a believer in water—most fully represents the Gospel witness. For most Baptists, no doubt, this will hardly need arguing. There seems to be scant Scriptural evidence for the baptism of infants. Those churches that practice infant baptism will typically point to passages where entire households were baptized, assuming that this would have included

category.

35. Wood, *One Baptism*, 42.

36. Ibid., 166.

37. Others who have made wonderful contributions to this debate include, but are not limited to, Fowler, *More Than a Symbol*; Ellis, *Gathering*; Ellis, "Believer's Baptism," 23–45; McClendon, "Baptism as a Performative Sign," 403–16. For an excellent description and engagement with some of the debate surrounding baptism as symbol or sacrament, see Cross, *Baptism and the Baptists*.

babies or young children as well. Most Scriptural descriptions of baptism, however, are about adult believers: the well-known Ethiopian eunuch, the various converts in the Book of Acts, and, not least of all, whole groups who responded to the Gospel and were baptized.[38]

There is a sense in which this aspect of the baptism debate appears to have "won the day," so to speak. The well-known *Baptism, Eucharist and Ministry* document of the World Council of Churches states: "While the possibility that infant baptism was also practised in the apostolic age cannot be excluded, baptism upon personal profession of faith is the most clearly attested pattern in the New Testament documents."[39] A Catholic Catechism states, "Though we have taken the example of the baptism of adults, because the meaning is clearest there, infant baptism is far and away the most common."[40] In a similar vein, Catholic theologian Susan K. Wood states, "Since the restoration of the catechumenate after Vatican II and with the promulgation of the Rite of Christian Initiation of Adults, adult baptism is normative for Roman Catholic understanding of the sacrament even though statistically more infants may be baptized than adults. Adult baptism is normative because of the faith engaged and also because the rite involves a conversion of life not experienced by the infant."[41] One may rightly wonder what exactly it means to describe believers' baptism as normative, while still maintaining infant baptism as the typical mode of baptism. One response, common in those churches that practice infant baptism, is to say that faith is indeed present and real, but it is "faith by proxy, the faith of parents, godparents, and the Christian community."[42] Such differences in faith requirements notwithstanding, one sees in these other ecclesial bodies a willingness to acknowledge believer's baptism as the sign that most fully embodies the signified: burial and new life; washing and cleansing from sin; and imitation of Jesus' baptism.

While Baptists can welcome these acknowledgements of believer's baptism as in some sense normative, we are still faced with the question of whether or not to acknowledge the baptism of infants as a real baptism. If baptism is only a symbol of a prior faith or conversion experience, then it will most likely follow that infant baptism is not a genuine baptism because the infant or young child has no such conversion. To see baptism as a

---

38. For an interesting engagement of these passages in a sacramental light, see Porter, "Baptism in Acts," 117–28.

39. *Baptism, Eucharist and Ministry*, 3

40. *A New Catechism*, 250.

41. Wood, *One Baptism*, 174.

42. Ibid.

grace-filled sign (an ordinance with sacramental significance), however, as I have been arguing, opens up some different doors and presents other challenges. First, it calls into question a rationalism that has sometimes shaped Baptist understandings of baptism. For example, some justify believer's baptism by saying, "He (or she) knew what he was doing."[43] If human reason becomes the ground for baptism, however, then not only does this exclude those who seem to lack reason (the mentally handicapped, for example), but it assumes that reason alone provides sufficient ground for the life of faith. Such a view is problematic in that it fails to fully register the mystery of God's providential grace. Secondly, baptism as a grace-filled sign opens up possibilities to see infant baptisms as genuine, albeit not as fully Scripturally performed as believer's baptism. Such a view can acknowledge that God's grace and promises are present in infant baptism (along with the pledge of the family and church to bring the child up in the faith), while at the same time maintaining the witness of believer's baptism as normative. Finally, baptism as a grace-filled sign provides theological space to see baptism not only as a single event, but as a way of life that we live by the grace of God. In other words, baptism is a lifelong process: "baptism takes effect according as we die daily with Christ, die to sin, and as we daily rise with him, being daily renewed in the new life in Christ."[44] In baptism, we die to our old selves with their false desires, sins and distorted allegiances, and rise to new life in Christ who has made possible a new kingdom in the world. As Paul emphasizes, "Therefore we have been buried with him by baptism into death, so that, just as Christ was raised from the dead by the glory of the Father, so we too might walk in newness of life" (Rom 6:4). Baptism is a grace-filled sign that we are to live into across the course of our lives.

Yet, one might object, baptism does not necessarily lead to new life. Many are baptized, after all, and continue their same old patterns of life. As Michael Budde puts it,

> The bonds of baptism are spiritualized and sidelined in favor of the blood-and-iron ties of patriotism and ethnonational solidarity, the dollars-and-cents sinews of capitalism, and the idolatry of modern and postmodern selves. In such a world it is unremarkable that Christian Hutus can slaughter Christian Tutsis the week after Easter; that Christian interrogators can torture Christian prisoners with impunity; that a Catholic military chaplain can bless the atomic bomb that destroyed the largest

43. McClendon, "Baptism as a Performative Sign," 413.
44. World Council of Churches, *One Lord, One Baptism*, 57.

concentration of Catholics in Japan, including seven orders of nuns.[45]

Budde's comments are a tragic reminder of how easy it is for Christians to forget their baptism. Dietrich Bonhoeffer has stated that "every member serves the whole body, contributing either to its health or to its ruin, for we are members of one body not only when we want to be, but in our whole existence."[46] If our baptism does not define our daily lives as members one of another in Christ, then other false identities will. Baptists, of all Christians, ought to remember this as we greet one another as fellow *Baptists* in the name of Christ.

45. Budde, *The Borders of Baptism*, 10.
46. Bonhoeffer, *Life Together / Prayerbook of the Bible*, 92.

9

Music as Liturgy

C. RANDALL BRADLEY

MUSIC IS AT THE heart of all good liturgy. Within the liturgy, music enables, facilitates, inspires, leads, enriches, serves, and embodies. Music can function in any capacity within a liturgical framework—it can proclaim, pray, praise, confess, and send. With the vivacity to personify the boldest praise and the tenderness to embody the most contrite confession, music speaks beyond words; and when combined with text, it fits us with a liturgical instrument that outstrips the power of any other.

The song of the church always springs from love—from the love God's people have for God. Because true love is always in search of expression, a church deeply in love with God will sing. Much like a person in love with another, love will lead us to take risks, let down our guard, lose our inhibitions, and chance being misunderstood and misperceived. Just as the toughest father will exhibit tenderness for his daughter whom he loves, and the most aloof mother will rejoice over the return of her son whom she loves, people in love with the God of the universe will find ways to express their devotion. According to Myles Connolly in his novel *Mr. Blue*, "If one loves anything, truth, beauty, woman, life, one will speak out. Genuine love cannot endure silence. Genuine love breaks into speech. And when it is great love, it breaks out into song."[1] While our efforts to encourage people to sing sometimes involve cajoling and guilt, the real impetus for singing in church is love itself. When we love deeply, we are moved to express our love, and we are willing to sing in spite of our skill level, our training, or our dislike of the form we use. Our love breaks forth because we cannot

1. Connolly, *Mr. Blue*, 74.

restrain our love expression even if we might appear foolish to others. Such self-abandoning love is at the root of the church and its vigorous singing.

Music's Place Within the Liturgy

Historically, music in many free churches was viewed as a commodity whose purpose was to serve preaching. Finding its roots in evangelistic meetings, music was used to draw in the crowd, and it was a means to prepare people to receive the sermon. Through singing lively songs with lilting melodies, people were able to forget their problems, and their defenses were lowered through the trust and communal spirit that music engendered. As the sermon approached, the congregation was treated to "special music" which might be a solo rendition of a popular gospel melody or a rousing choral performance. Following an extended sermon, the lively music of the pre-sermon session was replaced with pleading melodies extolling the saving power of Christ. Punctuated with emotive words from the preacher, stanza after stanza was sung while music's power wore down the crowd's resistance, and they moved down the aisles to trust God more fully.

While the scene has shifted and the prominence of evangelistic meetings has diminished, the bipartite form of singing and preaching has remained. In traditional Free Church worship, music can still be viewed as "preliminaries"—as preparation for the sermon. Even within the praise and worship movement in which music's role has been elevated, the bipartite form is still firmly fixed, i.e., a song set of twenty or so minutes followed by an extended sermon. Furthermore, in most traditional Free Church worship, the "sung service" may have little connection or direct interaction with the "preaching service." Ironically, while the Free Church has the freedom to explore new forms, it has sustained a pattern that, while functional, lacks full liturgical integration and imagination. Even while boasting its license for flexibility, this pattern often fails to integrate extended scripture reading, substantive prayer for the individual, and corporate body and the world; furthermore this tradition often relegates communion to quarterly observances.

Could it be that fully integrating music, word, and prayer could reignite the church's worship and bring about congregational renewal? The Free Church has the ecclesial suppleness to explore worship models involving seamless integration of worship elements while using time-tested liturgical forms and outlines as guides. By integrating sung refrains to punctuate Scripture, fragments of songs to add meaning to prayers, preaching that uses song for illustration and application, and by involving music meaningfully into communion, we could move past "singing only" and "word only" models—word, prayer, and Scripture could be integrated into a liturgical tapestry. Sermons can be divided in smaller segments enhanced by musical affirmation and reflection. Songs of different styles can be connected with meaningful readings, individual worship elements can be connected by carefully conceived transitions, and prayer and testimony can be woven with music—the disparate line up of individual worship elements that characterizes our worshipping past could be fully-integrated.

For much of our history, we have failed to think about music intentionally. While in the past we have invested heavily in musical training for our ministers, we have largely ignored liturgical preparation and worship studies. At the same time, our penchant for success has overruled our ability to discern and reflect. Once we discover a form that works, even if for a church in another region of the country, we have been quick to adopt and slow to evaluate. Much like our early missionaries who imposed Western songs and worship practices on indigenous cultures, we have continued to rely on our liturgical and musical fallbacks rather than re-imagining worship for an ever-changing cultural landscape and changing spiritual context. Both within the Free Church's traditional, evangelical, and contemporary leaning worship constituencies, we have argued about music and critiqued it for its style and likeability; however, we have failed to ask whether songs are singable, whether they have theological depth, whether they are contextually appropriate, and how they might be liturgically incorporated. Given music's immense power, failing to consider music intentionally is dangerous. By allowing the music and the texts we sing to go largely unchecked, we have committed a decades-long error, and the church could be many years in righting itself. By relying on commerce and culture for our liturgical playlist, by relying solely on tried and true historical repertoire, by singing lesser texts and tunes believing that the short term good mattered most, by theologians ignoring the important task of writing the songs of the church, and by failing to acknowledge music's power, our work for the future is immense. While many churches have been obsessed with growth and pragmatism, and others have held rigidly to worn traditions, the spiritual formation implicit in liturgy has been neglected, and generations of worshipers have lacked the liturgical experiences that could have formed us more fully.

Considering Words

Liturgical leaders have long-recognized the inadequacy of words to convey desired meaning and embody nuance. However, even in some recently published books on worship, writers are still propping up the legend that words are true, that words are reliable, and that words accurately hold the gospel message. If it were true that words can accurately hold truth and communicate in a clear and precise manner, why do we spend inordinate amounts of time using words to explain our words? Why are e-mails and electronic communication frequently misunderstood? Why do advertisers, who spend the most to communicate their messages, use fewer and fewer words? While some within the church are moving forward in their understanding that words are limited, worship in many churches is more word dominate than any other gathering in our culture. Since words carry multiple meanings and are dependent on context, they can be easily misperceived. While speakers are fully aware of their intended meaning, listeners who perceive words from their own contexts may assign completely different meanings. Words, like other liturgical tools, are symbols. Their meaning is dependent on experiences, context, education, and social standing. As symbols, words must be interpreted, and the listener determines their interpretations. Words are always open for multiple interpretations, and the speaker has no more control over their meaning than he or she has for any other auditory, visual, or enacted symbol. However, words embody more nuance when they are used in combination with auditory and visual stimuli.

Why Music Is Needed

Music moves beyond words by adding dimension to text—it flavors, gives depth, offers nuance, and provides a glimpse into deeper ways of understanding. The listener interprets truth, and truth comes to us in many forms. We intuit truth, we sense truth, we touch truth, we feel it in our bodies as we sing, and we smell it and taste it as we interact with others in community. We know truth to be present when we hear our individual melodies joining with our neighbors to create music that we recognize as beyond our own finity. We find ourselves in a place that we could never have imagined or created—a place where God comes to us in new ways. God can become real to us in these musical acts of worship. God can reveal God's self in moments lacking cognitive content, lacking logical liturgical progression, lacking clearly articulated liturgical goals, and lacking measurable learning outcomes. God uses our meager liturgical efforts to accomplish God's desires in worship. God meets us in worship and God transforms us into God's new creation. Through our encounter with God, God restores our soul, replenishes our emptiness, recalibrates our priorities, refurbishes our desires, and reinstates our desire for God's self.

Music As Dialogue

Music within a liturgical framework always functions as dialogue. As music assumes the voice of God, the congregation responds to God's initiative. Similarly, as music expresses the needs of the people and informs God of our condition, God responds with grace. The ongoing dialogue that is prominent in Scripture and within the church's liturgical history corresponds to the musical conversation in which music speaks for both God and the people as the conversation of worship ensues. While conversation occurs among the people themselves, such as greetings or the passing of the peace, worship at its core is about the dialogical interaction between God and God's people.

Music and Liturgy

Music serving faith is at its best when it functions within a liturgical framework. While religious music can be present in the concert hall, on the performance stage, and in other places, liturgical music functions best when it is contextualized within the liturgy itself. According to Nicholas P. Wolterstorff, liturgy calls for music. While liturgy can function without music, and it does not inherently need music, "the testimony of history is that the liturgy cries out for, calls out for, music. The church has always felt that, in ways too mysterious to describe, music profoundly enhances its liturgy. The way to put the point is perhaps this: in its assemblies the church has always found itself *breaking out* into music, especially into song."[2] Furthermore, liturgy is enhanced by music. All acts of worship can be furthered by the addition of music. Since music helps us to express what we are sometimes not able to verbalize, music serves word, prayer, Eucharist, and other liturgical actions.

Lastly, music must fit the liturgical action that it serves. The mood and spirit of the music must be in line with the liturgical action—music expressing confession must be intimate and personal; music praising the God of the cosmos must be grounded and fitting to honor the God of all times and generations. However, some music may not be fitting for certain liturgical actions within particular contexts, for whenever the music itself conflicts with the message of the text, the strength of the music will usually upstage the text. For instance, if we were to sing a message of God's forgiveness to a musical setting that emanates anger and frustration, the message of forgiveness would be lost and misunderstood due to music's ability to overpower textual meaning. Fittingness does not allow for all forms of music to fit with

2. Wolterstorff, "Thinking about Church Music," 11.

all texts. When the marriage of text and tune is incongruent, inherently the power of music will override the meaning of the text; consequently, any attempt at liturgical function will be lost.[3]

Music Connects Liturgy With Life

Music is a catalyst for connecting our everyday lives with God. The liturgy through which we encounter God gives voice to God's daily interactions among us. According to Don Saliers, "Whether around campfires or in recital halls, on the playground, or in the synagogue, and church, the act of singing has brought together a kind of acoustical gathering of life."[4] Music connects to the holiness of God whether directly within the liturgy or within our lives outside the presence of the gathered community. All of life is holy, and when we experience God in all of life, our worship gatherings take on new and deeper meaning.

Music gives voice to our grief, offers resonance to our lament, and utterance to our doxology. Music is fully capable of holding all the emotion that our lives can muster. The total depth and breadth of the fully-lived life can be held within the confines of song. Where emotion is experienced, song lives and thrives. Saliers summarizes, "Let our music, then, and our language not be a luxury but something like breathing, like heartbeat, like manna in the desert. Let it not be so much a public status symbol, not so much an aesthetic treat, but an instrument whereby our loves, our hopes, our anguish, our delights, yes even our untruths may be, as it were refined."[5]

Levels of Music Participation

The initial stage of musical participation is always the simple act of doing it, i.e., singing and making music in the gathered assembly. The first step is always participating in the phenomena—the actual singing, reading, and dramatic action of the liturgy itself.[6] Levels of participation and the type of participation varies from one context to another; therefore, the church's music should consciously explore all the ways in which we respond to the liturgical action around us—aurally, kinesthetically, visually, and tactilely.

3. Selected ideas above are drawn loosely from Wolterstorff's essay "Thinking about Church Music."

4. Saliers, "Sounding the Symbols of Faith," 19.

5. Ibid., 21.

6. Ibid., 23.

Similarly, music emboldens our participation and our action. Through singing we become aware of the voices of others around us, and we come to understand that we are not alone with our need to worship God. We join together in solidarity with others who also give their gifts to God in worship. By combining our song with others around us, our song becomes confident—we express it from deeper places within our soul, and our spirit proclaims God bravely and with courage. Consequently, the solidarity of the communal song sends us forth to be more daring in our Christian living, and the light of Christ shines more brightly within us and to others.

Lastly, music allows us to engage with God. When we sing in worship, we engage with God through the ongoing dialogue of liturgy. In essence, our singing and making music is akin to a dance in which we interact with God in both a grand ballet spectacle and in intimate personal confession.[7]

Exploring Music's Power

Music holds immense power. Individuals define themselves according to the music that they listen to, countries choose songs to symbolize their cultural and ethnic identity, movements create songs to represent their goals and aspirations, and advertisers use music to sell their products and create brand loyalty. The church uses music to inspire the faithful, further its beliefs, form its people into Christ's image, and portray a hopeful face to the world. Every significant spiritual movement throughout history has utilized music to further its message, and a body of new song has spawned from noteworthy movements. Music has the power to incite anger, calm frayed nerves, solidify political candidates, hawk products, and rally patriotic fervor. All the while, throughout history God has given music's power to the church, and God has drawn some of the world's finest and most capable musicians to write and lead the church's music. Particularly significant is the combination of words with music. Frank Burch Brown highlights this important relationship when he states, "When we want our words to reach out as far as possible, and so to be transmitted and translated to the world at large, we turn to song—that is, to words and music together . . . Singing takes hold of the body and the imagination, of the heart as well as the head."[8] Yet music's power also has an underbelly. Just as its influence can be used for intellectual and spiritual enhancement, it has the ability to be used in

---

7. The concepts above were drawn loosely from Saliers, "Sounding the Symbols of Faith."

8. Brown, *Inclusive yet Discerning*, 55.

manipulative and coercive ways both within the broader culture and within the church.

What Music Is

Music is communal. With its ability to draw people together, to create a common voice, and rally us toward a central message, music is most effectively practiced within a community. When effective community is established, music will result, and when music is present, community is most often present. The two work together, and discerning which engenders which is often impossible.

Music is hospitable. Music is welcoming, breaks down barriers, and is easily exchanged. Nothing is more effective in welcoming the stranger than music. Likewise, since effective hospitality in worship always involves mutual gift giving, songs are easily exchanged within a communal setting. Much like people in Africa who always offer you a song once you have sung to them, congregations who use music as an agent of hospitality, receive songs to add to their community's storehouse of congregational song.

Music is missional. Music is not contained in a location. No good song ever stays in one place. In earlier days, songs were transmitted through travel; i.e., when someone traveled to another place they invariably took their songs with them. In today's world technology assures that songs are disseminated at an unprecedented level. Music may well be the next important frontier of the church as it naturally moves the church from the safety of sanctuary to go beyond the walls of the church building and join God in the work that God is doing among those God is gathering outside the traditional church. Music will likely serve as catalyst and facilitator.

Music is multilingual and multi-musical. Music speaks all linguistic languages, and it also speaks all musical languages. Music of the church can be found in any musical language available on the planet, and it travels well cross-culturally. As we face the future, the church will begin to sing all languages—both linguistically and musically. This shift will require the church's leaders to learn new ways of guiding others to new places.[9]

Music is contextual. All effective liturgy is contextual. It always functions within a given time and place—it can never be fully duplicated. While we duplicate the worship gathering using the same liturgy and music, utilizing a different setting with new people will alter the worship and its outcome. Music should be carefully chosen to fit the particular context in which it is

9. For a further discussion of the church's music as community, hospitality, missional, and multi-musical, see Bradley, *From Memory to Imagination*.

expected to serve. For instance, music meant for a small rural congregation may not be equally effective in an affluent urban setting. Likewise, music from a Baptist church in Hong Kong may not function as effectively within the context of a Baptist congregation in Nairobi. Of all art forms, music moves from location to location with ease; it nevertheless needs the constraints of context to define and give it fuller meaning.

Singing As Worship Embodiment

The process of singing itself offers much to the discussion of the church's music. Singing is both an intellectual and a physical activity—the mind and the body are both fully engaged. Singing is required to enliven the liturgy because, according to Kathleen Harmon, "The answer lies in two actualities of song; the effect of the physical activity of singing on the body present and self awareness, and the deeper engagement of will and intention involved in the choice to sing."[10]

Singing as liturgical action is a mutual activity occurring in community. It is the only activity that engages large numbers of people in simultaneous breathing, exhaling, phonating, and articulating. When we sing, the air in the room shifts simultaneously, and over time even our heart rate and our blood pressure may start to synchronize. David Burrows points out, "The singers themselves have the sensation of expanding, in attenuated form, into surrounding space and filling it."[11] Harmon continues, "When we sing, we know that we are here, that we are alive, that we are connected, and that we are powerful . . . Singing induces this consciousness because it generates an awareness of physicality that is simultaneously a groundedness in self and a giving of that self away."[12]

When we sing, we embody liturgy. The words and the notes that we sing are re-created within ourselves in a way that helps us to engage with them in ways deeper than listening to others, reciting words alone, or in movement. When we sing and our intellect and our bodies are fully engaged, we reach a different—a third state—of engagement and awareness. All the while, our singing moves us beyond the state of visible presence within the community to a state of audible presence as well. By our singing, we announce to God and to others that we are doubly present—visually and audibly.[13] This fully active presence announces our intentions to others and it serves as

10. Harmon, *The Mystery We Celebrate, the Song We Sing*, 43.

11. Burrows, *Sound, Speech and Music*, 20.

12. Harmon, *The Mystery We Celebrate, the Song We Sing*, 44.

13. This section is loosely dependent on the work of Kathleen Harmon.

The Missional Shape of Liturgy

CAMERON JORGENSON

FOR ALL THE MIND-BOGGLING diversity in Baptist life, one of the most common convictions we share is the sense of calling to serve the purposes of God in the world. Embedded in the Baptist genetic code is a deep and abiding commitment to mission. This impulse expresses itself differently in each group. The Southern Baptist Convention's approach to missions that emphasizes "decisions for Christ" looks a bit different than the missional approach of the Cooperative Baptist Fellowship that emphasizes social justice and work among the poor. Whatever the flavor of the endeavor—whether the work resembles that of Billy Graham or Walter Rauschenbusch—Baptists are a people on mission.

The fact that Baptists are hard-wired for mission poses an interesting challenge for a book like the one you hold in your hands. To some readers, this much attention given to a theology of worship may seem like fussing over window dressing, neglecting the central matters of kingdom work for the sake of pleasantries. These are fair objections; after all, the connection between mission and liturgy is not obvious.

So, how do liturgy and mission relate? More to the point: does this conversation advance the Kingdom of God, or have these essays been an elaborate intellectual evasion of the *real* call of Christ?

This chapter offers a straightforward, if unexpected, answer. To put the matter succinctly: we can, and we must, think theologically about liturgy (i.e., the shape of our worship) because worship lies at the very heart of God's mission in the world. It is essential that we grasp both the nature of

God's mission and the nature of *our worship*, for when we do, we'll see how inseparable these two realities are.

The *Missio Dei*

What exactly is the mission of God? A lot rides on this question. Our answer says a lot about our picture of God, the work of God in Christ, the state of the world, the role of the church, and how we conceive of the "apostolic" task that has been given to all Christians. So, for all who take their faith seriously, defining the nature of this task is of vital importance. And, for obvious reasons, missiologists are especially keen to answer the question.

In the eighteenth century, the modern missions movement was born. For two hundred years this movement experienced explosive growth and was, in several respects, a "success story." In retrospect, however, we can see that the results were mixed. Evangelistic good intentions were intertwined with more sinister elements like cultural condescension and political exploitation by Western imperial aspirants. As this awareness began to dawn on the missiologists of the twentieth century, a period of reflection about the nature of mission began.[1]

Missiologists began to wrestle with the definition of "mission."[2] They wondered, is mission simply a task given to the church that enables its growth and expands its reach? Or, is mission something more than a task, something essential to the church's very being? Deeper still, they wondered whether mission was somehow connected to the very work, and therefore, to the very being of God. Their debate led them coin a phrase that helped to summarize their convictions about the nature and role of God's mission in the world: *missio Dei*.

According to *missio Dei* theology, "the missionary act is grounded in, and flows from, the very nature of the triune God."[3] A host of principles are generated by this basic insight, and several have become unofficial slogans for the contemporary "missional" mindset, including: "'God is a missionary God,' 'the church is missionary by her very nature,' and 'the church participates in God's mission.'"[4]

---

1. For a deep engagement with modern developments in the theology of missiology, and a critical engagement with the Trinitarian deficiencies in much "missio Dei" theology, see Flett, *The Witness of God*.

2. The most pivotal meeting for the development of the *missio Dei* theme was the International Missionary Council at Willingen in 1952.

3. Flett, *The Witness of God*, 35.

4. Ibid.

Since these slogans have become so commonly used, one could easily miss how radical these convictions actually are. The claim that God is on mission is, in fact, a stunning statement about the very character of God. The unsettling claim is that God does not simply give marching orders to the church; rather, God is on mission. It is the grace of God, then, that invites the church to participate in the work of God. Yet, this invitation is not extrinsic (i.e., an external "add-on") to the nature of the church. Rather, just as the "body of Christ," is conformed to the image of the Son who was sent by the Father, so we too are sent. To take the image one necessary step further: if we are created in the image of this triune God, then it is natural to see the "sending/sent" nature of the Trinity expressed in the essence of the church. As Andrew Kirk suggests, "The Church is by nature missionary to the extent that, if it ceases to be missionary, it has not just failed in one of its tasks, it has ceased being Church."[5]

When we realize that mission is not simply what the church does, but who it is, when we finally grasp that mission is a participation in the nature of God and a co-laboring in God's own works, the gravity of the task becomes clear. We are standing on holy ground.

This sobering realization frees us from Pelagian illusions of human-generated, technique-driven "revival," as if God's missionary task were simply the product of the right combination of prayer, slickly produced worship services, and marketing savvy. Simultaneously, a proper understanding of the *missio Dei* frees us from hyper-Calvinist assumptions that would leave the task of mission entirely to the mysterious workings of Providence. Correct understanding of God's mission inevitably redirects the bad habit of thinking about mission as *ours* to pursue (or not to pursue) however we please. Nothing could be further from the truth. The missionary mandate is a call to participate in the very nature and work of God. It makes us who we are called to be: co-workers with Christ and participants in the divine nature (2 Pet 1:3–4).

Worship As Participation

It is only when we have peered deeply into the nature of mission that the connection between mission and worship becomes clear. The elusive link between the two is not to be found where many seek it, that is, in a subordinate relationship where worship serves mission instrumentally, using gathered worship as the primary "tool" for the church's outreach. Rather,

---

5. Kirk, *What is Mission?*, 30.

the link between worship and mission is to be found in their nearly identical connection with the character and nature of God.

As we have seen, mission is not an extrinsic task given to the church, instead, it is the expression of the "sending" nature of the Father, the "sent" nature of the Son, and the corresponding "sent" nature of the body of Christ, the church, which is gathered, empowered, and indwelt, by the Spirit. The logic of the *missio Dei*, then, is based on a logic of participation; similarly, there is a participatory logic that drives a proper understanding of worship. Worship, in the fullest sense, is the seamless garment of praise offered by the whole of God's creation. What is more, just as mission is ultimately rooted in the nature of the God who sends, so too is worship an outgrowth of the character and nature of the God who is love.

The Epistle to the Hebrews opens new horizons for our understanding of worship, primarily by way of its picture of Jesus Christ as the ultimate high priest. It reminds us that Jesus was tempted and tried, and therefore, he can sympathize with the plight faced by all mortals (4:15). Furthermore, it pursues at length—especially in chapter 5 and chapters 7 through 10—the claim that Jesus was uniquely capable of offering himself as a perfect, complete, and eternally reconciling sacrifice. These are the quintessential claims of classic evangelical Christology, emphasizing the deity and lordship of Jesus Christ and his atoning work. While true and helpful, this standard account overlooks some crucial aspects of Christ's high priestly ministry described in Hebrews, and lost with them are insights about the nature of Christian worship.

While Hebrews does emphasize the complete, "once-and-for-all," nature of the sacrificial work of Christ on the cross, the cross is not its chief preoccupation. No, the emphasis is the ongoing work of Christ who lives and reigns as our great high priest, an undeniably liturgical image. We are instructed to "approach the throne of grace with boldness," precisely because we "have a great high priest who has *ascended* into heaven,"[6] (4:14) and who "*serves* in the sanctuary, the true tabernacle set up by the Lord" (8:2). This bold claim suggests that the ongoing work of Christ is his priestly mediation in the context of the heavenly tabernacle, the reality toward which the earthly sanctuary in the Old Covenant pointed as a "copy and shadow" (8:5). Previously, humankind worshipped through types and figures of the heavenly reality, but Christ, the fulfillment of that anticipation, established perfect worship and intercession in heaven, utterly transforming the nature of worship.

---

6. Literally, "passed through the heavens." All biblical citations in this essay will come from the New International Version.

This transfigured worship explains why, having established a deeper understanding of the sacrifice of Christ and his ongoing high priestly role, Hebrews exhorts us to "draw near to God with a sincere heart and with the full assurance that faith brings," having a cleansed conscience and a body washed with "pure water"[7] (10:22), and not to give up "meeting together, as some are in the habit of doing" (10:25). Given the new reality ushered in by Christ's work on the cross and his ongoing high priestly role, the act of Christian worship takes on a new significance—not as an *anticipation* of a future fulfillment, but as a *participation* in a heavenly reality.[8]

When we are gathered together for worship, it is the Spirit who speaks through the scriptures (10:15); it is Christ himself who speaks and offers words of warning (1:2, 12:25). When we worship together we are surrounded by a mighty cloud of witnesses whose examples enable us to "throw off everything that hinders," as we run the race (12:1). What is more, when we worship,

> [we] have come to Mount Zion, to the city of the living God, the heavenly Jerusalem. [We] have come to thousands upon thousands of angels in joyful assembly, to the church of the firstborn, whose names are written in heaven. [We] have come to God, the Judge of all, to the spirits of the righteous made perfect, to Jesus the mediator of a new covenant, and to the sprinkled blood that speaks a better word than the blood of Abel. (12:22–24).

It is tempting to think of this as a rhetorical flourish, this idea of being surrounded by a cloud of witnesses, or of worshipping alongside "thousands of angels" in the "church of the firstborn." But to dismiss this participatory language as a mere literary device would be to miss Hebrews' insistence that Christ is serving as our high priest, leading the worship of heaven, and mediating on our behalf.

Hebrews is not our only source for this transformed vision of worship. In fact, despite the many puzzling aspects of the Book of Revelation, its portrayal of heavenly worship in chapter 5 corresponds beautifully to what we have already explored. In this vision we witness a crisis in heaven: a sealed scroll needs to be opened and no one is found worthy for the task. But then the "Lion of the Tribe of Judah" arrives, appearing in the form of a Lamb that was slain. At his entrance, the twenty-four elders and the "four living creatures,"[9] bow down and sing a song of praise to the Lamb. Suddenly,

7. Presumably, this "pure water" is the water of baptism.

8. For an important introduction to the historical, philosophical and theological issues surrounding this theme of "participation," see Boersma, *Heavenly Participation*.

9. The identity of the twenty-four elders and the four living creatures is not entirely clear. For a helpful survey of the interpretive options, see Aune, *Revelation 1–5*, 287–92, 297–307.

innumerable angels surround the elders and offer a song of praise of their own. Finally, another cast of characters joins the chorus. John, the witness of these things, hears "every creature in heaven and on earth and under the earth and on the sea, and all that is in them, saying: 'To him who sits on the throne and to the Lamb / be praise and honor and glory and power, for ever and ever!'" (5:13)

In the final moment of that scene we see the whole of creation, humans together with the entire cosmos, whether in heaven or on earth, joining in the worship of God and the Lamb. Consistent with the conviction that the heavens declare the glory of the Lord (Ps 19:1), the rocks desire to cry out (Luke 19:40), and the whole creation groans as it awaits the redemption of humanity (Rom 8:18–21), the fifth chapter of Revelation depicts the universal praise of the cosmos. This passage, then, is a holy window into the hidden reality of worship; through it we discover that when we worship, it is with saints and angels that we sing.

Revelation's vision of the cosmos at worship and Hebrews' portrayal of Christ as the ascended high priest are complimentary images that help us understand the nature of Christian worship. Together they enable us to see that the worship in heaven is not a distant, eschatological reality that can only be realized at the end of time—this is the worship that commenced at the triumph of the Lamb who was slain. In other words, the picture of cosmic worship in Revelation is indeed eschatological, but "the end" began when the ascended Christ took his seat at the right hand of the Father to serve as a priest forever in the line of Melchizedek.[10]

Already we can see the stunning structural parallel between worship and mission. The real significance of mission for the church is that it is a participation in something prior, and something bigger, than us; it is a participation in what God is already doing in the world. In the same way, worship is beyond us, a reality ancient in origin and cosmic in scope. So, when we worship we do not simply engage in a defining activity, we are united with brothers and sisters throughout the ages in the act that is highest and best. In the spirit of Andrew Kirk's observations about mission, we could say rightly that the church is by nature a communion of worship to the extent that, if it ceases to worship, it has not just failed in one of its tasks, it has ceased being church.

However, can one go a step further to claim that worship, like mission, is a participation in the very nature of God? On the face of things, this is a tall order. After all, if God worships, and to worship anything other than

---

10. To explore further the apocalyptic nature of Hebrews, see Moffitt, *Atonement and the Logic of Resurrection*.

God is idolatry, then God must worship himself—and even though God is God, self-worship seems somehow improper or "narcissistic." However, if worship is understood as an expression of love, devotion, and self-donation, then the doctrine of the Trinity helps us to see how worship is a necessary component of the divine nature.

First John proclaims, "Whoever does not know love does not know God, because *God is love*" (4:8). The implications of those final three words ought not to be underestimated, especially when applied to the triune God. For example, there is an old saying about origins of the universe: "God created the world because he was lonely and wanted something to love." This is poor theology for many reasons. But, even poor theology can be motivated by a correct instinct. In this case, it is quite right that love is directional and must have an object. However, the Christian conviction that God exists eternally as Father, Son, and Spirit—one being in three persons, co-equal and co-eternal—helps to address the problem of directionality. God is an eternal communion of love between the persons of the Trinity, explaining nicely how God can be eternally loving while not being dependent on the universe as a remedy for loneliness.

Some scholars have offered helpful advice about how much we can say about the inner-life of the triune God: namely, we ought to be humble and tread lightly, being careful not to overextend ourselves when we make connections between this great mystery of the faith and other questions about the Christian life.[11] But this much seems necessary to say: if God is a communion of love between the divine persons, then the inner life of God provides a helpful image of what worship is intended to be and what it is intended to accomplish.

Jesus explored the theme of the divine love and our worship in John's Gospel at a moment when the stakes could not have been higher (John 14–17). He and the disciples had just finished sharing their last supper together, and he knew that in a matter of hours the greatest suffering of his life would begin. It was in that moment that Jesus chose to share an insight about the love shared between Father, Son, and Spirit—and therefore the sort of love that Christian love was intended to express and create. He did this through two powerful prayers; one for his disciples, and the other for those of us who would come later:

> "I pray also for those who will believe in me through their message, that all of them may be one, Father, just as you are in me

---

11. For an excellent critique of theologians' propensity to overextend themselves when applying the doctrine of the Trinity to other theological issues, see Kilby, "Perichoresis and Projection," 432–45.

and I am in you. May they also be in us so that the world may
believe that you have sent me. I have given them the glory that
you gave me, that they may be one as we are one—I in them
and you in me—so that they may be brought to complete unity.
Then the world will know that you sent me and have loved them
even as you have loved me. Father, I want those you have given
me to be with me where I am, and to see my glory, the glory you
have given me because you loved me before the creation of the
world" (17:20–24).

In Christ's final teaching before the cross we see a picture of the Trinity
at work: the Son glorifies the Father, who in turn glorifies the Son. Similarly, the Spirit glorifies the Son, and the Son lovingly sends the Spirit to
the Church as a gift. Here we see the triune God united in love and purpose—the purpose of our salvation. But, there is more. As the final prayer
for future believers reveals, Jesus' intent for the church is that we would
be united with the same sort of love that unites the Trinity, and that this
love would also unite us to God. God's intent for salvation is that the world
would be drawn into God's own inner life of love.

It is here that we see at its deepest level how worship and the mission of
God intersect. Put simply, worship in spirit and in truth—the kind of worship that transforms and unites our love to the divine love—is the mission
of God. In worship, God's kingdom comes and his will is done on earth as
it is in heaven.

Worship is a participation in a cosmic reality in which we join
with saints and angels in creation's song of praise directed toward its
Creator. What is more, worship is a participation in the divine nature,
connecting our worship to the essence of the Triune God who is love.
Worship, then, is the proper end and goal of mission, and worship has
an inescapably missional character. So, Baptists who justifiably are concerned to maintain the centrality of mission have every reason to take
the theology of worship seriously, because what is at stake in worship is
nothing less than the very heart of the mission of God in the world.

Conclusion

There is an important question that has gone unaddressed in this chapter:
if worship is so important, then what is the content of Christian worship?
Stated differently: if worship is a participation in the cosmic, eternal worship

of the triune God, then how do we join in the song? These questions point to the crucial issue of liturgy.

If worship is the "what," then liturgy describes the "how"—and when it comes to worship, "how" is an enormous question. Other chapters have engaged various aspects of these practical concerns, and without doubt, more work remains to be done. But, what is of paramount importance is that we actually do this theological work.

For a host of reasons, cultural and theological, Baptists have not always attended closely to questions of liturgy. In recent days it seems that there are two concerns that have driven the conversation. The first concern is pragmatic in nature. Many have shaped their worship practices according to the practical demands of "reaching people," adjusting worship services according to cultural tastes in order to stay relevant or to draw a crowd. The danger, of course, is that theological concerns are jettisoned in order to accommodate a different logic: that of the marketplace, or, doing what sells. But there's a second and equally dangerous temptation at work: doing what's easy. And what could be easier than refusing to think long and hard about what we are doing in worship and why we are doing it that way? Thinking liturgically is not easy—but it's worth it!

My hope is that this chapter, together with all the chapters in this volume, has buttressed the conviction that worship matters. What happens when we gather together is nothing less than a participation in eschaton and a foretaste of the eternal worship of the triune God—so what we do when we are gathered makes all the difference in the world.

an encouragement to their full worship participation. Consequently, their full participation encourages our fuller participation, and the cycle escalates and increases. Our physical and musical offering then becomes a part of the collective gift that the community offers to God through corporate worship.

Conclusion

The music of the church is as diverse as the people who serve God. Individuals and congregations throughout the world use music to draw together in community and to express their deepest thoughts, needs, and desires to God. Nothing has been more discussed in the last forty or so years as has music; however, much of the discussion has centered around issues of style while issues of liturgical involvement and function have been largely ignored. Within these discussions, music has sometimes been a divisive rather than a unifying element. Music is fully capable of unifying the body of Christ, and, in fact, music may be the church's best hope for Christian unity. Underneath the bickering and side-choosing, God seems to be raising up a new generation of worshipers who are far more concerned with the fully-worshiping body of Christ than with their individual preferences. If all who serve the church and sing its songs can lean into the reality that charity should be embodied in all music of the church, the future could indeed be abundant and well lit.

Appendix I

Worship Resources

THE COLLECTION OF WORSHIP resources provided in the Appendix are organized according to the Christian year—Advent, Christmas, Epiphany, Lent, Holy Week, Easter, Pentecost, and Ordinary Time. The symbolism rooted in the seasons of the Church Year resonates with the visual learning style that dominates in our culture. Rhetorical scholars have identified the present generation as an "oral-video" age. By combining the orality of the spoken word with the rich symbols and practices of the Christian year, our worship can be enhanced. All the senses are thus employed in the praise of God. The orders of worship and other worship practices are offered as suggestions for those congregations who would like to use some or all of the liturgical resources. All of the material in this appendix is optional and is not intended as a template or paradigm. None of it is required, and any congregation would be hard-pressed to use all of it.

The materials come from a number of sources. Generally, they are the product of the specific use by worshipping communities. The resources are thus suggestive in nature and our prayer is that they will be adapted, expanded, and used in ever more creative ways. The Orders of Worship are from Baptist congregations. The creeds and affirmations of faith are from Scripture and from the "Great Tradition" of the church catholic. The resources for the Christian year, baptism, and communion are a compilation of multiple sources.

We prayerfully request that pastors and worship leaders using these practices provide us with feedback, suggestions, and examples of additional liturgical resources to include in possible future editions.

A Basic Order of Worship

Entrance

Gathering: The people gather in the name of God for the praise of God.
    Prelude
    Chiming of the Trinity
    Meditation and private prayer
    Lighting of the candles
Greeting: The pastor greets the people in the name of Jesus Christ.
    Leader: The grace of the Lord Jesus Christ be with you.
    People: And also with you.
    Leader: The risen Christ is with us.
    People: Praise the Lord!
    This is the day that the Lord has made; let us rejoice and be glad in it.
    You have gathered from many places. Let us now praise the Lord
    together as one body.
Processional Hymn
Opening Prayer
Prayer of Confession
Pardon
Welcome and Passing of the Peace

Proclamation and Response

Prayer for Illumination
Scripture
    OT Lesson
    Psalter
    NT Epistle Lesson
Gospel Lesson
Anthem
Sermon
Response to the Word
Affirmation of Faith/Creed
    The Apostles' Creed
    The Nicene Creed
    Concerns and Prayers/Prayers of the People
    Pastoral Prayer
    The Lord's Prayer
    Offering

Sending Forth

Invitation to Christian Discipleship
Recessional Hymn
Dismissal with Blessing

ACTS OF WORSHIP FOR THE CHRISTIAN YEAR

Advent

Advent is the four week period that begins the Church year and comprises the four Sundays prior to Christmas Day. The theme of Advent is the coming of Christ as the baby of Bethlehem and the second coming as king of the world. There are a variety of worship practices that enable a congregation to celebrate Advent: lighting an advent wreath, a hanging of the greens service, a Chrismon tree, and an Advent devotional booklet.

Prayers and Readings for the Lighting of the Advent Candles

First Sunday   *Isaiah 60:2-3*

"For darkness shall cover the earth, and thick darkness the peoples; but the Lord will arise upon you, and his glory will appear over you. Nations shall come to your light, and kings to the brightness of your dawn." We light this candle as a symbol of our hope that Jesus will lead us out of darkness into light.

Second Sunday   *Luke 2:10*

But the angel said to them, "Do not be afraid; for see—I am bringing you good news of great joy for all the people." We light this candle and remember the angels who brought us good news of peace on earth and good will to all humankind. May we be the instruments of that peace and good will.

Third Sunday   Isaiah 35:10

And the ransomed of the Lord shall return, and come to Zion with singing; everlasting joy shall be upon their heads; they shall obtain joy and
gladness, and sorrow and sighing shall flee away.

Fourth Sunday   Isaiah 9:6–7

For a child has been born for us, a son given to us; authority rests upon
his shoulders; and he is named Wonderful Counselor, Mighty God, Everlasting Father, Prince of Peace. His authority shall grow continually, and
there shall be endless peace for the throne of David and his kingdom.
He will establish and uphold it with justice and with righteousness from
this time onward and forevermore. The zeal of the Lord of hosts will do
this. We light this candle as a symbol of the Prince of Peace. May we be a
people prepared for the coming of Jesus and his kingdom of peace.

Blessing of the Chrismon Tree

Precious Lord, we joyfully celebrate the birth of your Son, who has redeemed
us from the darkness of sin and made of the cross a tree of life and light. May
this tree, decorated in your signs, speak to us of the life-giving nature of the
cross of Christ. May we rejoice throughout this blessed Advent season in the
new life that shines in our lives. Amen.

Advent Prayers

Merciful God, You sent your messengers, the prophets, to preach repentance and prepare the way for our salvation. Give us the grace to heed their
warnings and to forsake our sins, that we may greet with joy the coming of
Jesus Christ, our Redeemer; who lives and reigns with you and the Holy
Spirit, one God, now and forevermore. Amen.

O Lord my God, I know that I am not worthy or sufficient that Thou
shouldest come under the roof of the house of my soul, for all is desolate and
fallen, and Thou hast not with me a place fit to lay Thy head. But as from
the highest heaven Thou didst humble Thyself for our sake, so now conform
Thyself to my humility.

And as Thou didst consent to lie in a cave and in a manger of dumb
beasts, so also consent to lie in the manger of my unspiritual soul and to
enter my defiled body.

And as Thou didst not disdain to enter and dine with sinners in the house of Simon the Leper, so consent also to enter the house of my humble soul which is leprous and sinful.

And as Thou didst not reject the woman, who was a harlot and a sinner like me, when she approached and touched Thee, so also be compassionate with me, a sinner, as I approach and touch Thee, and let the live coal of Thy most holy Body and precious Blood be for the sanctification and enlightenment and strengthening of my humble soul and body, for a relief from the burden of my many sins, for a protection from all diabolical practices, for a restraint and a check on my evil and wicked way of life, for the mortification of passions, for the keeping of Thy commandments, for an increase of Thy divine grace, and for the advancement of Thy Kingdom.

For it is not insolently that I draw near to Thee, O Christ my God, but as taking courage from Thy unspeakable goodness, and that I may not by long abstaining from Thy communion become a prey to the spiritual wolf.

Therefore, I pray Thee, O Lord, Who alone art holy, sanctify my soul and body, my mind and heart, my emotions and affections, and wholly renew me.

Root the fear of Thee in my members, and make Thy sanctification indelible in me. Be also my helper and defender, guide my life in peace, and make me worthy to stand on Thy right hand with Thy Saints: through the prayers and intercessions of Thy immaculate Mother, of Thy ministering Angels, of the immaculate Powers and of all the Saints who have ever been pleasing to Thee. Amen.

(John Chrysostom)

A Great Thanksgiving
for the Sacrament of Holy Communion During Advent

Musical Response:

Our Lord God is with us, lift your hearts and voices high,
let us give thanks to the Lord everywhere and at all times:
God, all glory be to you at this blessed Advent time,
for the gift of your own Son, born a poor child, peasant King.
For the love you sent to us, for the life he shared with us,
for the sacrifice he made, Lord of lords, and King of kings.

(Musical Response)

On the night he was betrayed the Lord Jesus took the bread,
blessed and broke it as he said, "Take and eat, this is my flesh."

After supper, took the cup, gave you thanks, and giving said,
"Drink this cup, it is my blood, poured for you and everyone."

(Musical Response)

When we eat this holy bread, when we drink this holy wine,
we his presence sense anew, and his victory await.
We remember and proclaim what your Son has done for us,
in his life and in his death, as he rises and ascends.

(Musical Response)

Now accept our sacrifice as surrender of ourselves.
Send your Holy Spirit down on us here and on our gifts.
Help us through this bread and wine to know the presence of our
Christ. Make us one with him today and with humankind, we pray.

(Musical Response)

Christmas and the Sundays after Christmas

Christmas, also known as the Feast of the Nativity, means "Christ Mass." The feast celebrates the birth and Incarnation of the Son of God, Jesus, on December 25th. Celebrate the Sundays after Christmas with a Nativity Scene, a festival of nine lessons and carols, the Christ candle, and a covenant renewal service.

Nativity Prayer of St. Augustine (AD 354–440)

Let the just rejoice,
for their justifier is born.
Let the sick and infirm rejoice,
For their saviour is born.
Let the captives rejoice,
For their Redeemer is born.
Let slaves rejoice,
for their Master is born.
Let free men rejoice,
For their Liberator is born.
Let All Christians rejoice,
For Jesus Christ is born.

Nativity Prayer of St. Ephraim the Syrian (AD 306–73)

The feast day of your birth resembles You, Lord
Because it brings joy to all humanity.
Old people and infants alike enjoy your day.
Your day is celebrated
from generation to generation.
Kings and emperors may pass away,
And the festivals to commemorate them soon lapse.
But your festival
will be remembered until the end of time.
Your day is a means and a pledge of peace.
At your birth heaven and earth were reconciled.
Since you came from heaven to earth on that day
You forgave our sins and wiped away our guilt.
You gave us so many gifts on the day of your birth:
A treasure chest of spiritual medicines for the sick;
Spiritual light for the blind;
The cup of salvation for the thirsty;
The bread of life for the hungry.
In the winter when trees are bare,
You give us the most succulent spiritual fruit.
In the frost when the earth is barren,
You bring new hope to our souls.
In December when seeds are hidden in the soil,
The staff of life springs forth from the virgin womb.

Nativity Prayer of St. Bernard of Clairvaux (AD 1090–1153)

Let Your goodness Lord appear to us, that we
made in your image, conform ourselves to it.
In our own strength
we cannot imitate Your majesty, power, and wonder
nor is it fitting for us to try.
But Your mercy reaches from the heavens
through the clouds to the earth below.
You have come to us as a small child
but you have brought us the greatest of all gifts,
the gift of eternal love.
Caress us with Your tiny hands,

embrace us with Your tiny arms
and pierce our hearts with Your soft, sweet cries.

The Season after Epiphany and The Baptism of Our Lord

The Epiphany celebrates the manifestation of Christ to the Gentiles, and the visit of the Magi to the Christ child. Other manifestations recalled on Epiphany are the miracle at Cana, and the Baptism of Jesus. Epiphany is celebrated on January 6.

Epiphany Hymn of St. Ambrose (AD 338–97)

Most High God!
Thou that enkindlest
the fires of the shining stars!
O Jesus!
Thou that art peace and life and light and truth,
hear and grant our prayers.
This present day has been made holy
by thy mystic baptism,
whereby thou didst sanctify
those waters of the Jordan,
which of old were thrice turned back.
It is holy by the star shining in the heavens,
whereby thou didst announce
thy Virginal Mother's delivery
and didst, on the same day,
lead the Magi to adore thee in thy crib.
It is holy too,
by thy changing the water
of the pitchers into wine;
which the steward of the feast,
knowing that he had not so filled them,
drew forth for the guests.
Glory be to thee, O Lord Jesus,
that didst appear on this Day!
And to the Father and to the Holy Spirit,
for everlasting ages. Amen.

Lent

Lent is the 40 day period of fasting, penitence, and sorrow, leading up to the feast of Easter, recalling Jesus' 40-day fast in the wilderness. Lent begins with Ash Wednesday, usually in February. These Lent prayers reflect the themes of fasting, penitence, and sorrow. Services during Holy Week may include Maundy Thursday with foot washing and Good Friday with a Tenebrae service.

Penitential Prayer of St. Augustine

O Lord,
The house of my soul is narrow;
enlarge it that you may enter in.
It is ruinous, O repair it!
It displeases Your sight.
I confess it, I know.
But who shall cleanse it,
to whom shall I cry but to you?
Cleanse me from my secret faults, O Lord,
and spare Your servant from strange sins.

Penitential Prayer of St. Ambrose of Milan

Lord, who hast mercy upon all,
take away from me my sins,
and mercifully kindle in me
the fire of thy Holy Spirit.
Take away from me the heart of stone,
and give me a heart of flesh,
a heart to love and adore Thee,
a heart to delight in Thee,
to follow and enjoy Thee, for Christ's sake. Amen.

Prayer of St. Ephraim the Syrian

O Lord and Master of my life,
give me not the spirit of laziness,
despair, lust of power, and idle talk. [Prostration]

But give rather the spirit of sobriety,
humility, patience and love to Thy servant. [Prostration]
Yea, O Lord and King,
grant me to see my own transgressions
and not to judge my brother,
for blessed art Thou unto ages of ages. Amen. [Prostration]

Eastern Sinner's Prayer (from John Chrysostom)

O my all-merciful God and Lord,
Jesus Christ, full of pity:
Through Your great love You came down
and became incarnate in order to save everyone.
O Savior, I ask You to save me by Your grace!
If You save anyone because of their works,
that would not be grace but only reward of duty,
but You are compassionate and full of mercy!
You said, O my Christ,
"Whoever believes in Me shall live and never die."
If then, faith in You saves the lost, then save me,
O my God and Creator, for I believe.
Let faith and not my unworthy works be counted to me, O my God,
for You will find no works which could account me righteous.
O Lord, from now on let me love You as intensely as I have loved sin,
and work for You as hard as I once worked for the evil one.
I promise that I will work to do Your will,
my Lord and God, Jesus Christ, all the days of my life and forever more.

Easter Sunday and the Sundays after Easter

Easter, also called *Pascha*, is the feast of Christ's resurrection from the dead. It is celebrated on the Sunday following Holy Week. Easter is also a 50-day season, often called Eastertide.

Call to Worship

Leader: Alleluia! Christ is risen!
People: Christ is risen indeed!

Leader: This is the Easter festival of life. We celebrate the birth of new possibilities, of re-creation and new life as gifts from God.

People: All creatures rejoice in the powerful work of God's salvation!

Leader: In Christ's resurrection, hope triumphs over despair!

People: Love triumphs over hate!

Leader: Good triumphs over evil!

People: Belief triumphs over doubt and life triumphs over death!

Leader: Glory and honor and praise to Christ who lives and reigns among us!

People: Alleluia to the Living Christ!

Leader: Christ is risen! ALL: Christ is risen indeed!

Lessons and Hymns of the Resurrection

The empty tomb	John 20:1–18	Appearance to Mary
In the garden	Matthew 28:1–10	Jesus with Mary and Mary
Walk to Emmaus	Luke 24:13–35	Appearance to travelers
The upper room	John 20:19–23	Appearance with disciples
The upper room	John 20:24–29	Jesus and Thomas
The Sea of Tiberias	John 21:1–19	Peter called to feed the sheep
Mount in Galilee	Matthew 28:16–20	The Great Commission
Jerusalem	Luke 24:36–49	The command to wait
The Ascension	Acts 1:4–11	Jesus ascends to heaven

Easter Prayer of St. Hippolytus of Rome (AD 190–236)

Christ is Risen: The world below lies desolate
Christ is Risen: The spirits of evil are fallen
Christ is Risen: The angels of God are rejoicing
Christ is Risen: The tombs of the dead are empty
Christ is Risen indeed from the dead,
the first of the sleepers,
Glory and power are his forever and ever.

Pentecost

Pentecost, also known as Whitsunday, celebrates the birthday of the Church, when the Holy Spirit came upon the Apostles in the Book of Acts. Pentecost is celebrated fifty days after Easter. These Pentecost Prayers relate to the themes of the Church and the Holy Spirit.

Call to Worship

Come, believers and faithful ones, sing your alleluias to God!
Praise God, who invades us with the rush of a mighty wind and fills us with fire.
Praise God, who out of love for humanity sent Jesus Christ to live among us.
Praise God, whose Spirit is poured out upon all flesh so that our sons and daughters might prophesy.
Praise God, who empowers us with gifts and calls us each by name.
Come, Holy Spirit. Dream dreams through us. Imagine with us.
Breathe, O breathe your loving Spirit into our world!

An Orthodox Prayer to the Holy Spirit

Glory to thee, O Lord, glory to thee!
Heavenly King, Comforter, Spirit of Truth,
Who art everywhere present and filleth all things,
Treasury of all good and giver of life,
Come and dwell within us;
Cleanse us from all unrighteousness,
And of thy goodness, save our souls.

Prayer of St. Bonaventure (AD 1221–1274)

Lord Jesus, as God's Spirit came down and rested upon you,
May the same Spirit rest on us,
Bestowing his sevenfold gifts.
First, grant us the gift of understanding,
By which your precepts may enlighten our minds.
Second, grant us counsel, by which we may follow
in your footsteps on the path of righteousness.
Third, grant us courage,
By which we may ward off the enemy's attacks.
Fourth, grant us knowledge,
By which we can distinguish good from evil.
Fifth, grant us piety,

By which we may acquire compassionate hearts.
Sixth, grant us fear,
By which we may draw back from evil
And submit to what is good.
Seventh, grant us wisdom,
That we may taste fully the life-giving sweetness of your love.

Evening Prayers

Pattern I

Our small salves, our big problems—these we place upon your altar!
The burning flame of your Temple of Silence
consumes us again and again . . . Tender your flame, O God.

> ~ *Howard Thurman,*
> *African-American pastor-scholar*
> *(d. April 10, 1981)*

Contemplative Song
Psalm & Prayers of the People
Benediction *(spoken together)*
> We will keep our hearts open to the light.
> Even when the light burns,
> when it is too bright, or too revealing.
> Even in darkness we will wait for the light,
> confident that it will come to cast its shaft
> across our path at the point of our need.
> And because God is the God of darkness as well as the light,
> we will be unafraid of the darkness.
> We will keep our hearts open to the light.

> ~ *Howard Thurman*

Pattern II

The cultivation of the spirit should be considered
with at least as much planning as the cultivation of corn.
If the field is of good soil and well plowed,
> if good seed is sown in it, if each day it gets sunshine and rain,
> if the four winds of heaven blow upon it,
> good ears of corn inevitably appear.

So it is with us.

If our mind is prepared and disciplined,

> if the wisdom of Jesus is sown in it, if each day it is set toward God
> and without worry and striving laid open to God's influence,
> fullness inevitably appears.

> > ~ *Muriel Lester,*
> > *Baptist contemplative/social reformer*
> > *(d. February 11, 1968)*

Contemplative Song

Psalm & Prayers of the People

Benediction

> Our job is big . . .
> It is to spread the Kingdom of God, the Rule of God.
> Our business is to stop war,
> to purify the world,
> to get it saved from poverty and riches,
> to help people to like each other,
> to heal the sick, and comfort the sad,
> to wake up those who have not yet found God,
> to create joy and beauty wherever we go
> to find God in everything and in everyone.

> > ~ *Muriel Lester*

Pattern III

Lord God Almighty, Father of your blessed and beloved child Jesus Christ,

> through whom we have received knowledge of you,
> God of angels and hosts and all creation,
> God of the whole race of the upright who live in your presence:

I praise you, I bless you, I glorify you,

> through the eternal heavenly high priest Jesus Christ,
> your beloved child,
> through whom be glory to you, with him and the Holy Spirit,
> now and for the ages to come. Amen.

> > ~ *Polycarp of Smyrna,*
> > *bishop & martyr*
> > *(d. February 23, 156)*

Contemplative Song
Psalm & Prayers of the People
Benediction

> May the God and Father of our Lord Jesus Christ,
> and the eternal High Priest himself, the Son of God Jesus Christ,
> **build us up in faith and truth and in all gentleness and in
> all freedom from anger and forbearance and
> steadfastness and patient endurance and purity.
> May God give to us a share and a place among his saints,
> and to all those under heaven who will yet believe in our
> Lord and God Jesus Christ and in his Father who raised
> him from the dead.**
> Pray for all the saints. Pray also for leaders, and for those who per-
> secute and hate you, and for the enemies of the cross, in order that
> your fruit may be evident among all people, that you may be perfect
> in Christ.

> > *~ adapted from a benediction by Polycarp of Smyrna*

CREEDS AND AFFIRMATIONS OF FAITH

Proto-Creedal Affirmations and Summaries of Faith Found in the Scriptures[1]

Deuteronomy 6:4–5: "Hear, O Israel: The Lord is our God, the Lord alone. You shall love the Lord your God with all your heart, and with all your soul, and with all your might."

Deuteronomy 26:5b–9: ". . . A wandering Aramean was my ancestor; he went down into Egypt and lived there as an alien, few in number, and there he became a great nation, mighty and populous. When the Egyptians treated us harshly and afflicted us, by imposing hard labor on us, we cried to the Lord, the God of our ancestors; the Lord heard our voice and saw our affliction, our toil, and our oppression. The Lord brought us out of Egypt with a mighty hand and an outstretched arm, with a terrifying display of power, and with signs and wonders; and he brought us into this place and gave us this land, a land flowing with milk and honey."

---

1. Other examples may be found, along with other ancient summaries and confessions from the early church, in Leith, *Creeds of the Churches*, 12–36. This book remains
an invaluable compendium of confessional statements from across the wide variety of
Christian communions, Protestant, Catholic, and Orthodox.

Micah 6:8: "He has told you, O mortal, what is good; and what does the Lord require of you but to do justice, and to love kindness, and to walk humbly with your God?"

Philippians 2:6–11: "who, though he was in the form of God, did not regard equality with God as something to be exploited, but emptied himself, taking the form of a slave, being born in human likeness. And being found in human form, he humbled himself and became obedient to the point of death— even death on a cross.

"Therefore God also highly exalted him and gave him the name that is above every name, so that at the name of Jesus every knee should bend, in heaven and on earth and under the earth, and every tongue should confess that Jesus Christ is Lord, to the glory of God the Father."

1 Corinthians 8:6: "yet for us there is one God, the Father, from whom are all things and for whom we exist, and one Lord, Jesus Christ, through whom are all things and through whom we exist."[2]

1 Corinthians 15:3–7: "For I handed on to you as of first importance what I in turn had received: that Christ died for our sins in accordance with the scriptures, and that he was buried, and that he was raised on the third day in accordance with the scriptures, and that he appeared to Cephas, then to the twelve. Then he appeared to more than five hundred brothers and sisters at one time, most of whom are still alive, though some have died. Then he appeared to James, then to all the apostles."[3]

1 Timothy 2:5–6: "For there is one God; there is also one mediator between God and humankind, Christ Jesus, himself human, who gave himself a ransom for all—this was attested at the right time."

2 Timothy 3:16: "Without any doubt, the mystery of our religion is great: He was revealed in flesh, vindicated in spirit, seen by angels, proclaimed among Gentiles, believed in throughout the world, taken up in glory."

2 Timothy 2:11–13: "The saying is sure: if we have died with him, we will also live with him; if we endure, we will also reign with him; if we deny him, he will also deny us; if we are faithless, he remains faithful—for he cannot deny himself."

Titus 2:11–14: "For the grace of God has appeared, bringing salvation to all, training us to renounce impiety and worldly passions, and in the

---

2. Blaising, "Creedal Formulation," makes a compelling case that this verse lies at the heart of the Nicaeno-Constantinopolitan Creed. Thus he argues the development of the Creed reflects not an abandonment of Scripture for a "merely human statement," but rather was deeply rooted in the desire to interpret Scripture faithfully.

3. McKnight, *The King Jesus Gospel*, 45–62, contends that these verses, which are a summary of faith, are the oldest condensation of the gospel.

present age to live lives that are self-controlled, upright, and godly, while we wait for the blessed hope and the manifestation of the glory of our great God and Saviour, Jesus Christ. He it is who gave himself for us that he might redeem us from all iniquity and purify for himself a people of his own who are zealous for good deeds."[4]

Post-biblical Creeds

The Apostles' Creed" (early 2nd century to AD 700)

I believe in God, the Father almighty, creator of heaven and earth.
I believe in Jesus Christ, his only Son, our Lord.
He was conceived by the power of the Holy Spirit and born of the Virgin Mary.
He suffered under Pontius Pilate, was crucified, died, and was buried.
He descended to the dead. On the third day he rose again.
He ascended into heaven, and is seated at the right hand of the Father.
He will come again to judge the living and the dead.
I believe in the Holy Spirit,
> the holy catholic Church,
> the communion of saints,
> the forgiveness of sins,
> the resurrection of the body,
> and the life everlasting.[5]

The Nicaeno-Constantinopolitan Creed, commonly called "The Nicene Creed" (AD 381)

We believe in one God,
> the Father, the Almighty,
> maker of heaven and earth,
> of all that is, seen and unseen.

4. This is a particularly important example for Baptists. In *Christianismus Primitivus*, 2.1.1 (35–36), Thomas Grantham discusses how truly to define the Christian religion. After giving, and then dismissing as inadequate, a couple possibilities, he says, "in mine Opinion, we have a more compleat (sic) definition of Religion (especially as it concerns Christianity, the Religion now to be considered) by the Apostle Paul himself, Tit. 2.11,12.13,14." In these verses, he continues, "the Apostle layeth the Foundation of a Religious Life, and the Glory consequent to it." This is a fine definition of the function of creeds as well.

5. *Book of Common Prayer*, 304.

We believe in one Lord, Jesus Christ,
    the only Son of God,
    eternally begotten of the Father,
    God from God, Light from Light,
    true God from true God,
    begotten, not made,
    of one Being with the Father.
    Through him all things were made.
    For us and for our salvation
    he came down from heaven:
    by the power of the Holy Spirit
    he became incarnate from the Virgin Mary,
    and was made man.
    For our sake he was crucified under Pontius Pilate;
    he suffered death and was buried.
    On the third day he rose again
    in accordance with the Scriptures;
    he ascended into heaven
    and is seated at the right hand of the Father.
    He will come again in glory to judge the living and the dead,
    and his kingdom will have no end.
We believe in the Holy Spirit, the Lord, the giver of life,
    who proceeds from the Father (and the Son).
    With the Father and the Son he is worshiped and glorified.
    He has spoken through the Prophets.
    We believe in one holy catholic and apostolic Church.
    We acknowledge one baptism for the forgiveness of sins.
    We look for the resurrection of the dead,
    and the life of the world to come. Amen.[6]

Contemporary Confessions Suitable for Liturgical Use

A New Creed (United Church of Canada, 1968)

We are not alone,
    we live in God's world.
We believe in God,
    who has created and is creating,
    who has come in Jesus

6. *Book of Common Prayer*, 358–59.

the Word made flesh,
    to reconcile and make new,
    who works in us and others
    by the Spirit.
We trust in God.
We are called to be the Church:
    to celebrate God's presence,
    to live with respect in Creation,
    to love and serve others,
    to seek justice and resist evil,
    to proclaim Jesus, crucified and risen,
    our judge and our hope.
In life, in death, in life beyond death,
    God is with us.
We are not alone.
Thanks be to God.[7]

A Brief Statement of Faith of the Presbyterian Church (USA) (1983)

In life and in death we belong to God.
Through the grace of our Lord Jesus Christ,
the love of God,
and the communion of the Holy Spirit,
we trust in the one triune God, the Holy One of Israel,
whom alone we worship and serve.

We trust in Jesus Christ,
Fully human, fully God.
Jesus proclaimed the reign of God:
preaching good news to the poor
and release to the captives,
teaching by word and deed
and blessing the children,
healing the sick
and binding up the brokenhearted,
eating with outcasts,
forgiving sinners,
and calling all to repent and believe the gospel.
Unjustly condemned for blasphemy and sedition,

7. United Church of Canada, "A New Creed," onliine: http://www.united-church.ca/beliefs/creed, accessed 26 June 2012.

Jesus was crucified,
suffering the depths of human pain
and giving his life for the sins of the world.
God raised Jesus from the dead,
vindicating his sinless life,
breaking the power of sin and evil,
delivering us from death to life eternal.

We trust in God,
whom Jesus called Abba, Father.
In sovereign love God created the world good
and makes everyone equally in God's image
male and female, of every race and people,
to live as one community.
But we rebel against God; we hide from our Creator.
Ignoring God's commandments,
we violate the image of God in others and ourselves,
accept lies as truth,
exploit neighbor and nature,
and threaten death to the planet entrusted to our care.
We deserve God's condemnation.
Yet God acts with justice and mercy to redeem creation.
In everlasting love,
the God of Abraham and Sarah chose a covenant people
to bless all families of the earth.
Hearing their cry,
God delivered the children of Israel
from the house of bondage.
Loving us still,
God makes us heirs with Christ of the covenant.
Like a mother who will not forsake her nursing child,
like a father who runs to welcome the prodigal home,
God is faithful still.

We trust in God the Holy Spirit,
everywhere the giver and renewer of life.
The Spirit justifies us by grace through faith,
sets us free to accept ourselves and to love God and neighbor,
and binds us together with all believers
in the one body of Christ, the Church.
The same Spirit

who inspired the prophets and apostles
rules our faith and life in Christ through Scripture,
engages us through the Word proclaimed,
claims us in the waters of baptism,
feeds us with the bread of life and the cup of salvation,
and calls women and men to all ministries of the church.
In a broken and fearful world
the Spirit gives us courage
to pray without ceasing,
to witness among all peoples to Christ as Lord and Savior,
to unmask idolatries in Church and culture,
to hear the voices of peoples long silenced,
and to work with others for justice, freedom, and peace.
In gratitude to God, empowered by the Spirit,
we strive to serve Christ in our daily tasks
and to live holy and joyful lives,
even as we watch for God's new heaven and new earth,
praying, "Come, Lord Jesus!"
With believers in every time and place,
we rejoice that nothing in life or in death
can separate us from the love of God in Christ Jesus our Lord.

Glory be to the Father, and to the Son, and to the Holy Spirit. Amen.[8]

The Masai Creed

We believe in the one High God, who out of love created the beautiful world and everything good in it. He created man and wanted man to be happy in the world. God loves the world and every nation and tribe on the earth. We have known this High God in the darkness, and now we know him in the light. God promised in the book of his word, the Bible, that he would save the world and all nations and tribes.

We believe that God made good his promise by sending his son, Jesus Christ, a man in the flesh, a Jew by tribe, born poor in a little village, who left his home and was always on safari doing good, curing people by the power of God, teaching about God and man, showing that the meaning of religion is love. He was rejected by his people, tortured and nailed hands and feet to a cross, and died. He was buried in the grave, but the hyenas did

---

8. *Constitution of the Presbyterian Church (U.S.A.)*, 275–76. This is admittedly long, but portions may be excerpted from it for use in worship.

not touch him, and on the third day, he rose from that grave. He ascended to the skies. He is the Lord.

We believe that all our sins are forgiven through him. All who have faith in him must be sorry for their sins, be baptized in the Holy Spirit of God, live the rules of love, and share the bread together in love, to announce the good news to others until Jesus comes again. We are waiting for him. He is alive. He lives. This we believe. Amen.

The Nanzan Creed for Christians in an Interreligious World

We believe that the poor [in spirit] are blessed, for the kingdom of heaven is theirs; that those who mourn are blessed, for they will be comforted; that the meek are blessed, for they will inherit the earth; that those who hunger and thirst after righteousness are blessed; for they will be satisfied; that the merciful are blessed, for they shall obtain mercy; that the pure in heart are blessed, for they shall see God; that the peacemakers are blessed, for they will be called the children of God; that those who are persecuted for righteousness' sake are blessed, for theirs is the kingdom of heaven. We believe that we should love our enemies, do good to those who hate us, bless those who curse us, and pray for those who abuse us.

We believe that we should not judge, and we will not be judged; that we should not condemn, and we will not be condemned; that we should forgive, and we will be forgiven; that we should give, and [in like measure] it will be given to us.

We believe that we should not lay up for ourselves treasures on earth, but should lay up treasures in heaven, for where our treasures are, there will our hearts be also. We believe that we should not be anxious about our lives, about what we shall eat or what we shall drink or what we shall wear, but should seek first the kingdom of God and its righteousness.
We believe that we should love the Lord our God with all our hearts, and with all our souls, and with all our minds, that we should love our neighbors as ourselves, and that all laws and prophecies depend on this.

A Celtic Creed

We believe in God above us, maker and sustainer of all life, of sun and moon, of water and earth, of male and female. We believe in God beside us, Jesus

Christ, the Word made flesh, born of woman, servant of the poor, tortured and nailed to a tree. A man of sorrows, he died forsaken. He descended into the earth to the place of death. On the third day he rose from the tomb. He ascended into heaven, to be everywhere present, and his kingdom will come on earth. We believe in God within us, the Holy Spirit of Pentecostal fire, life-giving breath of the Church, Spirit of healing and forgiveness, source of resurrection and of eternal life. *Amen.*

THE SACRAMENT OF HOLY COMMUNION

Worship Practices for the Sacrament of Holy Communion

At the last supper, Jesus gave thanks over the bread and cup. As a biblical people, it follows that we too would take the opportunity to bless the elements and to give thanks and praise to God. By praying the Great Thanksgiving, the pastor can tell the grand story of faith from creation to culmination of a new heaven and a new earth. The prayer of great thanksgiving recounts the mighty acts of God. This metanarrative, repeated in worship, along with the passing of the bread and the cup, forms disciples who know the story of their salvation.

"The Bible tells a coherent story." The prayer of Great Thanksgiving allows the preacher to creatively tell this story in every celebration of the sacrament of Holy Communion. In a church culture, where biblical illiteracy abounds, this opportunity to tell the old, old story is too important to ignore.

There are numerous summaries of the story of faith in the biblical record that may be used to write the Great Thanksgiving (cf. Deut 6:20–24; 26:5–9; Josh 24:2–13; Neh 9:6–37; Ps 78; 105; 135:8–12; 135; Acts 7:2–50; 10:36–41). Acts 13:17–41 is a pivotal passage because it begins with the patriarchs and ends with the resurrection of Jesus and the preaching of the apostolic message. The book of Revelation offers an overview of the story from the perspective of its end, but even here the end is anticipated from within the still-continuing story. The historical elements of the Great Thanksgiving include the following: Creation; Sin; Fall; God's covenant love; Exodus; covenant to be our God; message of salvation from the prophets; Holy, holy, holy, Jesus Christ—Isaiah 61; His ministry of healing, preaching, and teaching; His suffering, death, and resurrection; deliverance from our sins; new covenant by water and the Spirit; ascension and promise to be with us; words of institution; our offering in praise and thanksgiving; the mystery of faith (Christ has died; Christ is risen; Christ will come again); prayer for the work of the Holy Spirit; transforming our lives with Christ.

A portion of the Great Thanksgiving can reflect the seasons of the church year. After the people have said or sung the "Holy, holy, holy," there is a place for the pastor to add stories that relate to the season. Examples of these variations on the basic theme are included below.

A Basic Pattern for the Great Thanksgiving

The Lord be with you.
And also with you.
Lift up your hearts.
We lift them to the Lord.
Let us give thanks and praise to the Lord our God.
It is right to give God thanks and praise.

Holy and almighty God: In your covenant love you created us in your image to share the ecstasy of aliveness with us. Yet we fell into sin through disobedience to your Word. You responded by loving us still and sent us the message of a way home through your prophets. Then you sent Jesus, the only begotten Son, in your grace, to walk among us and be one of us, to live and die as one of us, to reconcile us to you, the God and Father of all.
Through his death on the cross, Jesus offered himself in obedience to your will, and once and for all sacrifice for the whole world.

The Great Thanksgiving for Advent

Holy are you, and blessed is your Son Jesus Christ, whom you sent in the fullness of time to be a light to the nations, the joy and hope of the world, and the peace of all humankind. You scatter the proud in the imaginations of their hearts and have mercy on those who fear you from generation to generation. You put down the mighty from their thrones and exalt those of low degree. You fill the hungry with good things, and the rich you send empty away. Your Son came among us as a servant, to be God with us. He humbled himself in obedience to your will and freely accepted death on a cross.

The Great Thanksgiving for Christmas Eve

Holy are you, and blessed is your Son Jesus Christ. As Mary and Joseph went from Galilee to Bethlehem where there was no room, so Jesus went from Galilee to Jerusalem and was despised and rejected. As in the poverty of a manger Jesus was born, and under the shadow of the oppression of Herod, so you gave birth to your Church.

The Great Thanksgiving for Epiphany

Holy are you, and blessed is your Son, Jesus Christ, in whom you revealed the truth, our light and our salvation. You sent a star to guide wise men to where Jesus was born; and in your signs and witnesses, in every age and through all the world, you have led your people from foreign lands to his light. In his baptism and in table fellowship he took his place with sinners. Your Spirit anointed him to preach good news to the poor, to proclaim release to the captives and recovering of sight to the blind, to set at liberty those who are oppressed, and to announce that the kingdom of God had arrived.

The Great Thanksgiving for Lent

Holy are you, and blessed is your Son Jesus Christ. When you gave him to save us from our sin, your Spirit led him into the wilderness, where he fasted forty days and forty nights to prepare for his mission. When he suffered and died on a cross for our sin, you raised him to life, presented him alive to the apostles during forty days, and exalted him at your right hand.

Great Thanksgiving for Easter

Holy are you, and blessed is your Son Jesus Christ. When you gave him to the throes of death, your Spirit raised him from the dead. You breathed into him the breath of life and returned him to his disciples before, after fifty days, you exalted him at your right hand.

The Great Thanksgiving for Pentecost

Holy are you, and blessed is your Son Jesus Christ. At his baptism, the heavens opened, your Spirit descended and declared him to be your Son. Led by your Spirit into the wilderness, he was strengthened by the same Spirit to resist the temptations of the devil. Your Spirit anointed him to preach good news to the poor, to proclaim release to the captives and the recovering of sight to the blind, to set at liberty those who are oppressed, and to announce the arrival of your kingdom and the salvation of your people. As he promised on the day he ascended, your Spirit empowered and gave birth to your

Church. On this the Day of Pentecost the Holy Spirit baptized us with fire and gave to us the gift of understanding your gospel.

THE SACRAMENT OF BAPTISM

Baptists, of all the varieties of Christians, should celebrate the sacrament of baptism in the most meaningful and powerful of ways. The use of symbols, blessings, readings, litanies, prayers, and confessions of faith may all be used in ways that lift up the deep spiritual meaning of baptism. The resources provided here are suggestive of ways that churches may celebrate the Sacrament of Baptism.

Suggested Scripture Readings:

> Mark 1:6–11 or Matt 3:13–17
> Rom 6:3–5
> Matt 28:18–20
> Gal 3:26–28
> 1 Pet 3:18–22

Baptism Litany

Affirmation

Leader: We have come to celebrate the baptism of this disciple of Jesus Christ. What do you want her to know?
People: That we thank God for her faith in Jesus as Savior and Lord, and that we happily welcome her into our church family; that her joys and sorrows will be our own; that we will do the work of Christ together, prayerfully, compassionately and courageously.

Act of Baptism

Blessing

Leader: Let us pronounce the baptismal blessing together.
People: We celebrate the joy of our salvation. We praise God for the life, death and resurrection of the Son. We share in your joy and celebrate the grace of God that empowers and sustains us.

Prayers:

Eternal God,
your Spirit hovered over the waters in creation,
you brought your people through the parting of the desert sea,
and your Son came to John to be baptized.
Pour out your Spirit on those
whom now you meet in these waters,
that they may enter Christ's tomb and be reborn,
that they may die to all that is death
and be born to a new and living hope.
This we ask through the same Jesus Christ,
who lives and reigns with you in unity with the Holy Spirit,
One God for ever and ever. Amen.[9]

Eternal Spirit, heavenly Dove,
On these baptismal waters move;
That we through energy divine,
May have the substance with the sign.[10]

Grant, O Lord, that all who are baptized into the death of Jesus Christ your Son may live in the power of his resurrection and look for him to come again in glory; who lives and reigns now and for ever. Amen.[11]

We thank you, Almighty God, for the gift of water. Over it the Holy Spirit moved in the beginning of creation. Through it you led the children of Israel out of their bondage in Egypt into the land of promise. In it your Son Jesus received the baptism of John and was anointed by the Holy Spirit as the Messiah, the Christ, to lead us, through his death and resurrection, from the bondage of sin into everlasting life.

We thank you, Father, for the water of Baptism. In it we are buried with Christ in his death. By it we share in his resurrection. Through it we are reborn by the Holy Spirit. Therefore in joyful obedience to your Son, we bring into his fellowship those who come to him in faith, baptizing them in the name of the Father, and of the Son, and of the Holy Spirit. Amen.[12]

---

9. Ellis and Blyth, *Gathering for Worship*, 69.

10. Clay, *Hymns and Spiritual Songs,* cited in Thompson, "Re-envisioning Baptist Identity," 291–92.

11. *Book of Common Prayer*, 306.

12. Ibid., 306–7.

Hymns

"Baptized in Water"

Baptized in water, Sealed by the Spirit, Cleansed by the blood of Christ, our King;
Heirs of salvation, Trusting His promise, Faithfully now God's praise we sing.
Baptized in water, Sealed by the Spirit, Dead in the tomb with Christ, our King;
One with His rising, Freed and forgiven, Thankfully now God's praise we sing.
Baptized in water, Sealed by the Spirit, Marked with the sign of Christ, our King;
Born of one Father, We are His children, Joyfully now God's praise we sing.[13]

"Come, Holy Spirit, Dove Divine"

Come, Holy Spirit, Dove divine,
On these baptismal waters shine,
And teach our hearts, in highest strain,
To praise the Lamb for sinners slain.
We love Your Name, we love Your laws,
And joyfully embrace Your cause;
We love Your cross, the shame, the pain,
O Lamb of God, for sinners slain.
We sink beneath the water's face,
And thank You for Your saving grace;
We die to sin and seek a grave
With You, beneath the yielding wave.
And as we rise with You to live,
O let the Holy Spirit give
The sealing unction from above,
The joy of life, the fire of love.[14]

13. Michael Saward, "Baptized in Water," in *The Baptist Hymnal*, #362.

14. Adoniram Judson, "Come, Holy Spirit, Dove Divine," in ibid., #364. The words from the prayer by Eleazer Clay, cited above, could be substituted for verse one in Judson's version. Clay explicitly relates the substance with the sign in a way that Judson does not.

Occasional Services

Hanging of the Greens

PREPARING OUR HEARTS

GATHERING SONG

WELCOME & CALL TO WORSHIP

(A child comes forward with the appropriate symbols after each responsive verse.)

> Leader: How shall we prepare this house of worship for the coming of the King?
>
> **People: With branches of cedar, the tree of royalty.**
>
> Leader: How shall we prepare this house of worship for the coming of Christ?
>
> **People: With garlands of pine and fir, whose leaves are ever living, evergreen.**
>
> Leader: How shall we prepare this house of worship for the coming of our Savior?
>
> **People: With wreaths of holly and ivy, telling of his passion, death, and resurrection.**
>
> Leader: How shall we prepare our hearts for the coming of the Son of God?
>
> **People: By hearing again the words of the prophets, who foretold the saving work of God.**

Leader: For God did not send the Son into the world to condemn the world, but that the world through him might be saved.

ALL: **Glory to God in the highest!**

OPENING SONG

THE PROPHET SPEAKS OF A CHILD—ISA 9:2, 6–7

MUSICAL OFFERING

THE PEACEFUL KINGDOM—ISA 11:1–9

CONGREGATIONAL SONG

THE SONG OF MARY—LUKE 1:46–55

ANTHEM

LORD, WHEN DID WE SEE YOU?—MATT 25:31–46

SENDING SONG

BLESSING & SENDING

Ash Wednesday

"When on Ash Wednesday we hear the words, 'Remember, you are dust,' we are also told that we are brothers and sisters of the incarnate Lord. In these words we are told that we are: nothingness that is filled with eternity; death that teems with life; futility that redeems; dust that is God's life forever."
-Karl Rahner

PRELUDE

OLD TESTAMENT LESSON—JOEL 2:1–2; 12–13

INVITATION TO WORSHIP

Bless the Lord who forgives all our sins.
God's mercy endures for ever.

HYMN OF REPENTANCE

PSALTER—Ps 51:1–17

Musical Response

Leader: Have mercy on me, O God, according to your steadfast love;

People: According to your abundant mercy blot out my transgressions.

Leader: Wash me thoroughly from my iniquity, and cleanse me from my sin.

People: For I know my transgressions, and my sin is ever before me.

Leader: Against you, you alone, have I sinned, and done what is evil in your sight, so that you are justified in your sentence and blameless when you pass judgment.

People: Indeed, I was born guilty, a sinner when my mother conceived me. [Musical Response]

Leader: You desire truth in the inward being; therefore teach me wisdom in my secret heart.

People: Purge me with hyssop, and I shall be clean; wash me, and I shall be whiter than snow.

Leader: Let me hear joy and gladness; let the bones that you have crushed rejoice.

People: Hide your face from my sins, and blot out all my iniquities. [Musical Response]

Leader: Create in me a clean heart, O God, and put a new and right spirit within me.

People: Do not cast me away from your presence, and do not take your holy spirit from me.

Leader: Restore to me the joy of your salvation, and sustain in me a willing spirit.

People: Then I will teach transgressors your ways, and sinners will return to you.

Leader: Deliver me from bloodshed, O God, O God of my salvation, and my tongue will sing aloud of your deliverance.

People: **O Lord, open my lips, and my mouth will declare your praise.**

Leader: For you have no delight in sacrifice; if I were to give a burnt offering, you would not be pleased.

People: **The sacrifice acceptable to God is a broken spirit; a broken and contrite heart, O God, you will not despise. [Musical Response]**

NEW TESTAMENT EPISTLE LESSON—2 COR 5:20B–6:10

MUSICAL OFFERING

GOSPEL LESSON—MATT 6:1–6, 16–21

THE CALL TO CONFESSION

Let the wicked forsake their ways, the unrighteous their thoughts; let them return unto the Lord. God will have mercy and abundantly pardon.
The sacrifices to God are a broken spirit, a broken and contrite heart.

THE PRAYER OF CONFESSION

Let us pray.
Most holy and merciful God, we confess to you and to one another, and to the whole communion of saints in heaven and on earth, that we have sinned by our own fault in thought, word, and deed, by what we have done and by what we have left undone.

We have not loved you with our whole heart, our mind, and strength. We have not loved our neighbors as ourselves. We have not forgiven others as we have been forgiven.
Have mercy on us, O God.

We have been dead to your call to serve as Christ served us. We have not been true to the mind of Christ. We have grieved your Holy Spirit.
Have mercy on us, O God.

All our past unfaithfulness: the pride, hypocrisy, and impatience in our lives,
we confess to you, O God.

Our negligence in prayer and worship and our failure to commend the faith that is in us,
we confess to you, O God.

Our self-indulgent appetites when we already have enough and some to spare and our neglect of the needs of others,
we confess to you, O God.

For all false judgments, for uncharitable thoughts toward our neighbors, and for our prejudice and contempt toward those who differ from us,
accept our repentance.

For our participation in the divisions of our community and our world; for our failure to act on behalf of peace and justice,
accept our repentance.
For our failure to see our sins as an affront to you; for our failure to accept the forgiveness you offer,
accept our repentance.
Restore us, O God, for we are sinners, poor and needy.
Hear our prayer, O God, for your mercy is great.

SILENT PRAYERS

ASSURANCE OF PARDON

If we confess our sin, God who is faithful and just will forgive our sins and cleanse us from all unrighteousness.—1 Jn 1:9

HYMN OF ASSURANCE

MEDITATION

INVITATION TO THE OBSERVANCE OF LENTEN DISCIPLINE

THANKSGIVING OVER THE ASHES

Almighty God, you have created us out of the dust of the earth. Grant that these ashes may be to us a sign of our mortality and penitence, so that we may remember that only by your gracious gift are we given everlasting life; through Jesus Christ our Savior. Amen.

IMPOSITION OF ASHES

This ancient tradition, going back at least to the tenth century, communicates the human condition before God. From dust we were created; to dust shall we return.
Hymns during the imposition of the ashes

HYMN OF MERCY

BENEDICTION

Maundy Thursday

> The Thursday before Easter is called "Maundy" based on Christ's command, which in Latin is the word *mandatum*, that his disciples should love one another. In fourth-century Jerusalem there were special services at the Mount of Olives and Gethsemane, and in North Africa an evening Eucharist commemorating the Last Supper. By the sixth century in the West, the Blessing of Oils and the Reconciliation of Penitents took place on this day. By the Middle Ages the stripping and washing of altars and the *pedilavium* (foot washing) were added. The latter ceremony was sometimes performed by sovereigns, and the modern English Royal Maundy Service is a modified survival of this.
>
> (from *Dictionary of the Christian Church*)

The Gathering

The history of humanity is a story of occasional leaps in the right direction, followed by a return to the old ways. We go ahead two steps, back three. We don't always see where we are going or that God is with us. We join the Jews in the wilderness and Jesus on the streets of his time and place. Tonight we enter the upper room with the disciples, there to be with our Master for one last time before his ultimate sacrifice. We know that, like the disciples, we will affirm and deny. May we, also like the disciples, finally come to that moment when we meet a risen Master and journey to the Kingdom at his side.

WORDS OF PREPARATION

THE PRELUDE

CALL TO WORSHIP

This is the day
>   that Christ the Lamb of God
>   gave himself into the hands of those who would slay him.

This is the day
>   **that Christ gathered with his disciples in the upper room.**
>   This is the day

that Christ took a towel and washed the disciples' feet,
giving us an example that we should do to others
as he has done to us.

This is the day
    that Christ our God gave us this holy feast,
    that we who eat this bread and drink this cup
    may here proclaim his holy sacrifice
    and be partakers of his resurrection
    and at the last day may reign with him in heaven.

HYMN

INVITATION TO CONFESSION

The grace of the Lord Jesus Christ be with you.
And also with you.
My sisters and brothers,
Christ shows us his love by becoming a humble servant.
Let us draw near to God and confess our sin in the
truth of God's Spirit.

PRAYER OF CONFESSION

Loving God, you are faithful and forgiving:
help us now to grasp the nature of your love.
Help us to pray honestly
as we make our confession and seek your forgiveness.
Where we have failed to love, and have loved to hurt:
Where we have spoken harsh words to others,
and have been quick to take offense ourselves:
Where we have scorned difference
and have been indifferent to those in need:
Where we have prayed and sung about injustice,
and have ignored the injustice around us:
Merciful God, unlike us, you are true to your word.
When we cry to you in sorrow and repentance,
you hear our cries and are swift to forgive.
For your faithful love we praise you.
Amen.

SILENT CONFESSION

One of the messages of Holy Week is that sooner or later every disciple will betray Jesus. We will betray him in the workplace when it will cost too much to think like a Christian, and in our homes when the anger is so great that we hurt those who trust us, and in the sacred commitments we make that we simply cannot keep.—Craig Barnes

WORDS OF ASSURANCE

OLD TESTAMENT LESSON—Ex 12:1–4, 11–14

THE LAST SUPPER

Invitation to the Table
Sharing the Bread and the Cup
Prayer of Thanksgiving
The Lord's Prayer *(Debts & Debtors)*

HYMN

GOSPEL LESSON—John 13:1–17

MEDITATION

INVITATION TO THE SERVICE OF FOOTWASHING

SERVICE OF FOOTWASHING

Footwashing is a powerful symbolic response to the Word, dramatizing the servanthood of Jesus, both on the night before his death and in his continuing presence in our midst. Footwashing involves imitating Jesus' actions and acting on his commandment to love one another. As you feel comfortable, feel free to move forward to one of the footwashing stations to wash another person's foot and have your foot washed (i.e., to serve and be served).

GOSPEL LESSON—John 13:21–30

SONG OF WAITING

After the song is sung the congregation will be asked to begin leaving in silence, reflecting on the meaning of the events of Christ's life and ministry we have remembered tonight.

Good Friday

MUSIC OF THE PASSION

JESUS, BETRAYED AND ARRESTED
John 18:1–14

HYMN

JESUS, DENIED AND INTERROGATED
John 18:15–27

PRAYERS OF MERCY

In your mercy, God, hear our prayer.
O Jesus, stretch forth your wonderful hands over your people to heal and to restore, and to draw us to yourself and to one another in love.
Merciful God, we meet each other today at this cross as inhabitants of one world—
As those who inflict wounds on each other: **be merciful to us.**
As those who deny justice to others: **be merciful to us.**
As those who seize wealth: **be merciful to us.**
As those who put others on trial: **be merciful to us.**
As those afraid of this world's torment: **be merciful to us.**
Giver of life, we wait with you to bear hope to earth's darkest places—
Where justice is destroyed: **let righteousness rule.**
Where hope is crucified: **let faith persist.**
Where war is rampant: **let peace reign.**
Where truth is denied: **let the struggle continue.**
Where sorrow lingers: **let your light shine.**
God, reach into this silent darkness with your love; deepen the terror of this moment into new hope; relieve the hideous cries with your voice of peace that here we may know your salvation, your glory, your future in Jesus Christ, the crucified Lord.
In your mercy, God, hear our prayer.
O Jesus, stretch forth your wonderful hands over your people to heal and to restore, and to draw us to yourself and to one another in love.

JESUS, INTERROGATED AND CONDEMNED
John 18:28—19:16a

MEDITATION

JESUS, CRUCIFIED AND KILLED

John 19:16b-37

STRIPPING OF THE ALTAR

SUNG RESPONSE: Jesus, remember me, when you come into your kingdom. (2x)

O my people, O my Church, what have I done to you, or in what way have I offended you? I led you forth from the land of Egypt and delivered you by the waters of baptism, but you have prepared a cross for your Savior. **(Response)**

I led you through the desert forty years and fed you with manna; I brought you through times of persecution and of renewal and gave you my body, the bread of heaven; but you have prepared a cross for your Savior. **(Response)** I made your branches of my vineyard and gave you the water of salvation, but when I was thirsty you gave me vinegar and gall and pierced with the spear the side of your Savior. **(Response)**

I went before you in a pillar of cloud but you have led me to the judgment hall of Pilate. I brought you to a land of freedom and prosperity, but you have scourged, mocked and beaten me. **(Response)**

I gave you a royal scepter, and bestowed the keys of the kingdom, but you have given me a crown of thorns. I raised you on high with great power, but you have hanged me on the cross. **(Response)**

My peace I gave, which the world cannot give, and washed your feet as a servant, but you draw the sword to strike in my name and seek high places in my kingdom. **(Response)**

I accepted the cup of suffering and death for your sakes, but you scatter and deny and abandon me. I sent the Spirit of truth to lead you, but you close your hearts to guidance. **(Response)**

I called you to go and bring forth fruit, but you cast lots for my clothing. I prayed that you all may be one, but you continue to quarrel and divide. **(Response)**

I grafted you into the tree of my chosen people Israel, but you turned on them with persecution and mass murder. I made your joint heirs with them of my covenants, but you made them scapegoats for your own guilt. **(Response)**

I came to you as the least of your brothers and sisters. I was hungry, but you gave me no food, thirsty but you gave me no drink. I was a stranger, but you did not welcome me, naked but you did not clothe me, sick and in prison, but you did not visit me. **(Response)**

HYMN

JESUS, BURIED

John 19:38–42

THE DARKNESS

Bibliography

Adam, Adolf. *The Liturgical Year: Its History & Its Meaning after the Reform of the Liturgy.* Collegeville, MN: Liturgical, 1990.

Allen, Charlotte. "The Do-It-Yourself Doctrine." Religion, *Los Angeles Times*, 23 May 2004. Online: http://articles.latimes.com/2004/may/23/opinion/op-allen23.

Althaus, Paul. *The Theology of Martin Luther.* Philadelphia: Fortress, 1966.

Anglican Communion Office and Baptist World Alliance. *The Report of the International Conversations between the Anglican Communion and the Baptist World Alliance: Conversations Around the World, 2000–2005.* London: Anglican Communion Office, 2005.

Aquinas, Thomas. *Summa Theologiae.* Translated by the Fathers of the English Dominican Province. New York: Benziger Brothers, 1914.

Augustine. *Confessions.* Translated by Henry Chadwick. New York: Oxford University Press, 1991.

———. *On Christian Teaching.* Translated by R. P. H. Green. New York: Oxford University Press, 1997.

———. *Saint Augustine: Expositions on the Book of Psalms.* In vol. 8 of *The Nicene and Post-Nicene Fathers*, Series 1. Edited by Philip Schaff. 1886–1889. 14 vols. Repr. Peabody, MA: Hendrickson, 1994.

Aune, David E. *Revelation 1–5.* Word Biblical Commentary 52A. Dallas: Word, 1997.

Baldovin, John. "The Liturgical Year: Calendar for a Just Community." In *Between Memory and Hope: Readings on the Liturgical Year*, edited by Maxwell E. Johnson, 429–44. Collegeville, MN: Liturgical, 2000.

Baptism, Eucharist and Ministry. Faith and Order Paper 111. Geneva: World Council of Churches, 1982.

The Baptist Hymnal. Nashville: Convention, 1991.

Barker, Margaret. *Christmas: The Original Story.* London: SPCK, 2008.

———. *Creation: A Biblical Vision for the Environment.* New York: T. & T. Clark, 2010.

———. *The Gate of Heaven: The History and Symbolism of the Temple in Jerusalem.* Sheffield: Sheffield Phoenix, 2008.

———. *The Great High Priest: The Temple Roots of Christian Liturgy.* New York: T. & T. Clark, 2003.

———. *Temple Themes in Christian Worship.* New York: T. & T. Clark, 2007.

Barnhart, Bruno. *The Good Wine: Reading John from the Center.* Eugene, OR: Wipf & Stock, 2008.

Bauerschmidt, Frederick C. *Holy Teaching, Introducing the* Summa Theologiae *of St. Thomas Aquinas.* Grand Rapids: Brazos, 2005.

Berry, Wendell. *Standing by Words*. San Francisco: North Point, 1983.

Blaising, Craig A. "Creedal Formulation as Hermeneutical Development: A Reexamination of Nicaea." *Pro Ecclesia* 19/4 (2010) 371–88.

Boersma, Hans. *Heavenly Participation: The Weaving of a Sacramental Tapestry*. Grand Rapids: Eerdmans, 2011.

Bond, L. Susan. *Contemporary African American Preaching: Diversity in Theory and Style*. St. Louis: Chalice, 2003.

Bonhoeffer, Dietrich. *Life Together*. Translated by John W. Doberstein. New York: Harper & Row, 1954.

———. *Life Together / Prayerbook of the Bible*. Edited by Geoffrey Kelly. Translated by Daniel W. Bloesch and James H. Burtness. Dietrich Bonhoeffer Works 5. Minneapolis: Fortress, 2005.

———. *Worldly Preaching: Lectures on Homiletics*. Edited and translated by Clyde E. Fant. New York: Nelson, 1975.

Bonneau, Normand. *The Sunday Lectionary: Ritual Word, Paschal Shape*. Collegeville, MN: Liturgical, 1998.

Book of Common Prayer. Oxford: Oxford University Press, 1979.

Book of Common Worship. Louisville: Westminster John Knox, 1993.

Bourgeault, Cynthia. *The Wisdom Jesus: Transforming Heart and Mind—a New Perspective on Christ and His Message*. Boston: Shambhala, 2008.

Brackney, William H. "Doing Baptism Baptist Style: Documents for Faith and Witness." Last modified January 31, 2007. Online: http://www.baptisthistory.org/pamphlets/ baptism.htm.

Bradley, C. Randall. *From Memory to Imagination: Reforming the Church's Music*. Grand Rapids: Eerdmans, 2012.

Bradshaw, Paul F., editor. *The New Westminster Dictionary of Liturgy and Worship*. Philadelphia: Westminster John Knox, 2002.

Brown, Frank Burch. *Inclusive yet Discerning: Navigating Worship Artfully*. Grand Rapids: Eerdmans, 2009.

Brueggemann, Walter. *Prayers for a Privileged People*. Nashville: Abingdon, 2008.

Budde, Michael L. *The Borders of Baptism, Identities, Allegiances, and the Church*. Eugene, OR: Cascade, 2011.

Bunyan, John. "The Pilgrim's Progress." In *The Works of John Bunyan*, edited by George Offor, 3:1–210. Glasgow: Blackie & Son, 1862.

Burgess, John P. "Going Creedless: Alternative Christianities." *Christian Century* 121/11 (2004) 24–28.

Burleson, Blake, and Michael Sciretti Jr., editors. *Entempling: Baptist Wisdom for Contemplative Prayer*. Telephone, TX: Praxis, 2012.

Burrows, David. *Sound, Speech and Music*. Amherst: University of Massachusetts Press, 1990.

Buttrick, David. *Homiletics*. Philadelphia: Fortress, 1987.

Byars, Ronald P. "Creeds and Prayers: Ecclesiology." In *A More Profound Alleluia: Theology and Worship in Harmony*, edited by Leanne Van Dyk, 83–108. Grand Rapids: Eerdmans, 2005.

Calvin, John. *Institutes of the Christian Religion*. Edited by John T. McNeill. Translated by Ford Lewis Battles. 2 vols. Library of Christian Classics 20. Philadelphia: Westminster, 1960.

Chan, Simon. *Liturgical Theology: The Church as Worshiping Community*. Downers Grove, IL: InterVarsity, 2006.

Charry, Ellen T. *By the Renewing of Your Minds: The Pastoral Function of Christian Doctrine*. New York: Oxford University Press, 1997.

Childress, Kyle. "Proper Work: Wendell Berry and the Practice of Ministry." In *Wendell Berry and Religion: Heaven's Earthly Life*, edited by Joel James Shuman and L. Roger Owens, 71–81. Lexington: University Press of Kentucky, 2009.

Chrysostom, John. *Chrysostom: Homilies on Galatians, Ephesians, Philippians, Colossians, Thessalonians, Timothy, Titus, and Philemon*. In vol. 13 of *The Nicene and Post-Nicene Fathers*, Series 1. Edited by Philip Schaff. 1886–1889. 14 vols. Repr. Peabody, MA: Hendrickson, 1994.

Clay, Eleazar. *Hymns and Spiritual Songs, Selected From Several Approved Authors*. Richmond, VA: Dixon, 1793.

Clément, Olivier. *The Roots of Christian Mysticism: Texts from the Patristic Era with Commentary*. Hyde Park, NY: New City, 1993.

Cobb, Peter G. "The History of the Christian Year" in *The Study of Liturgy*, rev. ed., edited by Cheslyn Jones et al., 455–71. New York: Oxford University Press, 1992.

Collins, Hercules. "An Orthodox Catechism: Being the Sum of Christian Religion, Contained in the Law and Gospel." London: n.p., 1680.

Commission of Faith and Order from the World Council of Churches. *One Lord, One Baptism*. Minneapolis: Augsburg, 1960.

Connolly, Myles. *Mr. Blue*. New York: Macmillan, 1928. Reprint, Chicago: Loyola Press, 2004.

Conroy, Pat. *My Reading Life*. New York: Doubleday, 2010.

The Constitution of the Presbyterian Church (U.S.A.). Louisville: Office of the General Assembly, 1994.

Cothen, Grady C. "Truths or Truth: Creed or Scripture." In *Soul Freedom: Baptist Battle Cry*, edited by Grady C. Cothen and James M. Dunn, 89–98. Macon, GA: Smyth & Helwys, 2000.

Cross, Anthony R. *Baptism and the Baptists: Theology and Practice in Twentieth-Century Britain*. Waynesboro, GA: Paternoster, 2000.

Cunningham, David S. *These Three are One: The Practice of Trinitarian Theology*, Malden, MA: Blackwell, 1998.

Daniélou, Jean. "Le symbolisme des rites baptismaux." *Dieu vivant 1* (1945) 17–43.

Davis, Ellen F. "Teaching the Bible Confessionally in the Church." In *The Art of Reading Scripture*, edited by Ellen F. Davis and Richard B. Hays, 9–23. Grand Rapids: Eerdmans, 2003.

Dawn, Marva J. *Reaching Out without Dumbing Down: A Theology of Worship for this Urgent Time*. Grand Rapids: Eerdmans, 1995.

deConick, April. "What is Early Jewish and Christian Mysticism?" In *Paradise Now: Essays on Early Jewish and Christian Mysticism*, edited by April deConick, 1–24. Atlanta: SBL, 2006.

Deweese, Charles W., editor. *Defining Baptist Convictions: Guidelines for the Twenty-First Century*. Franklin: Providence House, 1996.

Dix, Gregory. *The Shape of the Liturgy*. London: Black, 1964.

Dunn, James M. "No Freedom For the Soul With A Creed." In *Soul Freedom: Baptist Battle Cry*, edited by Grady C. Cothen and James M. Dunn, 83–88. Macon, GA: Smyth & Helwys, 2000.

Ecumenical Patriarch Bartholomew. "Sacrifice: The Mission Dimension." In *The Adriatic Sea: A Sea at Risk, a Unity of Purpose*, edited by Neal Ascherson and Andrew Marshall, 217–20. Athens, Greece: Religion, Science and the Environment, 2003.

Ehmann, Lain Chroust. "The Health Benefits of Touch." Online: http://www.beliefnet.com/healthandhealing/getcontent.aspx?cid=13623.

Elior, Rachel. *The Three Temples: On the Emergence of Jewish Mysticism*. Translated by David Louvish. Portland: Littman Library of Jewish Civilization, 2005.

Ellis, Christopher J. "Believer's Baptism and the Sacramental Freedom of God." In *Reflections on the Water: Understanding God and the World through the Baptism of Believers*, edited by Paul S. Fiddes, 23–45. Macon, GA: Smyth & Helwys, 1996.

———. *Gathering: A Theology and Spirituality of Worship in Free Church Tradition*. London: SCM, 2004.

Ellis, Christopher J., and Myra Blyth, editors. *Gathering for Worship: Patterns and Prayers for the Community of Disciples*. Norwich: Canterbury, 2005.

Estep, W. R. "Baptists and Authority: The Bible, Confessions, and Conscience in the Development of Baptist Identity." *Review and Expositor* 84/4 (1987) 599–615.

Ferguson, Everett. *Baptism in the Early Church: History, Theology, and Liturgy in the First Five Centuries*. Grand Rapids: Eerdmans, 2009.

Fiddes, Paul S. "Baptism and Creation." In *Reflections on the Water: Understanding God and the World through the Baptism of Believers*, edited by Paul S. Fiddes, 47–67. Macon, GA: Smyth & Helwys, 1996.

Flett, John G. *The Witness of God: The Trinity, Missio Dei, Karl Barth, and the Nature of Christian Community*. Grand Rapids: Eerdmans, 2010.

Fowler, Stanley K. *More Than a Symbol: The British Baptist Recovery of Baptismal Sacramentalism*. Eugene, OR: Wipf & Stock, 2007.

Freeman, Curtis W. "'To Feed Upon by Faith': Nourishment from the Lord's Table." In *Baptist Sacramentalism*, edited by Anthony R. Cross and Philip E. Thompson, 194–210. Milton Keynes, UK: Paternoster, 2003.

Fuller, Andrew G. "An Inquiry into the Right of Private Judgment on Matters of Religion." In *The Complete Works of the Rev. Andrew Fuller*, 2:628–29. Boston: Lincoln, Edmands, 1833.

———. "On Creeds and Subscriptions." In *The Complete Works of the Rev. Andrew Fuller*, 2:629–31. Boston: Lincoln, Edmands, 1833.

Gaddy, C. Welton. *The Gift of Worship*. Nashville: Broadman, 1992.

Gaustad, Edwin S. "The Backus-Leland Tradition." In *Baptist Concepts of the Church*, edited by Winthrop S. Hudson, 106–34. Philadelphia: Judson, 1959.

George, Timothy. "The Spirituality of the Radical Reformation." In *Christian Spirituality: High Middle Ages and Reformation*, edited by Jill Rait, 334–71. New York: Crossroad, 1989.

Grant, Robert M. *Irenaeus of Lyons*. New York: Routledge, 1997.

Grantham, Thomas. *Christianismus Primitivus: Or, The Ancient Christian Religion*. London: Smith, 1678.

———. "Christianismus Primitivus." In *Baptist Roots: A Reader in the Theology of a Christian People*, edited by Curtis W. Freeman, James W. McClendon Jr., and C. Rosalee Velloso Ewell, 89–97. Valley Forge, PA: Judson, 1999.

———. *Hear the Church: Or, An Appeal to The Mother of Us All*. London: n.p., 1687.

———. *St. Paul's Catechism*. London: n.p., 1687.

Habel, Norman C., et al., editors. *The Season of Creation: A Preaching Commentary.* Minneapolis: Fortress, 2011.

Halbrooks, G. Thomas. "Why I am a Baptist." In *Being Baptist Means Freedom,* edited by Alan Neely, 1–8. Charlotte: Southern Baptist Alliance, 1988.

Harmon, Kathleen. *The Mystery We Celebrate, the Song We Sing: A Theology of Liturgical Music.* Collegeville, MN: Liturgical, 2008.

Harvey, Barry. "Re-Membering the Body: Baptism, Eucharist and the Politics of Disestablishment." In *Baptist Sacramentalism,* edited by Anthony R. Cross and Philip E. Thompson, 96–116. Milton Keynes, UK: Paternoster, 2003.

Hatch, Nathan O. *The Democratization of American Christianity.* New Haven: Yale University Press, 1989.

Hauerwas, Stanley. "Only Theology Overcomes Ethics; or, What 'Ethicists' Must Learn from Jenson." In *Trinity, Time, and Church: A Response to the Theology of Robert W. Jenson,* edited by Colin E. Gunton, 252–68. Grand Rapids: Eerdmans, 2000.

———. *Working with Words: On Learning to Speak Christian.* Eugene, OR: Cascade, 2011.

Haymes, Brian. "Towards a Sacramental Understanding of Preaching." In *Baptist Sacramentalism,* edited by Anthony R. Cross and Philip E. Thompson, 263–70. Milton Keynes, UK: Paternoster, 2003.

Heim, S. Mark. *The Depth of the Riches: A Trinitarian Theology of Religious Ends.* Grand Rapids: Eerdmans, 2001.

Hemming, Laurence Paul. "Transubstantiating Our Selves." *Heythrop Journal* 44 (2003) 418–39.

Hickman, Hoyt L., et al. *The New Handbook of the Christian Year.* Nashville: Abingdon, 1992.

Hinson, E. Glenn. "Baptists and Spirituality: A Community at Worship." *Review and Expositor* 34/4 (1987) 649–58.

———. "The Baptist Experience in the United States." *Review and Expositor* 79/2 (1982) 217–30.

———. "Creeds and Christian Unity: A Southern Baptist Perspective." *Journal of Ecumenical Studies* 23/1 (1986) 25–36.

Hoffman, Shirl James. "Sports Fanatics." *Christianity Today* 54/2 (2010). Online: http://www.christianitytoday.com/ct/2010/february/3.20.html?start=1.

International Theological Commission. "The Hope of Salvation for Infants who Die without Being Baptised." Last modified May 7, 2007. Online: http://www.vatican.va/roman_curia/congregations/cfaith/cti_documents/rc_con_cfaith_doc_20070419_un-baptised-infants_en.html.

Jennings, Jr., Theodore W. *Loyalty to God: The Apostles Creed in Life and Liturgy.* Nashville: Abingdon, 1992.

Jensen, Robin M. *Living Water, Images, Symbols, and Settings of Early Christian Baptism.* Boston: Brill, 2011.

Jenson, Robert W. "The Kingdom of America's God." In *Essays in Theology of Culture,* 50–66. Grand Rapids: Eerdmans, 1995.

———. *On Thinking the Human: Resolutions of Difficult Notions.* Grand Rapids: Eerdmans, 2003.

Johnson, Luke Timothy. *The Creed.* New York: Doubleday, 2003.

Johnson, Maxwell E., editor. *Between Memory and Hope: Readings on the Liturgical Year.* Collegeville, MN: Liturgical, 2000

Kaam, Adrian van. *The Vowed Life*. Denville, NJ: Dimension, 1968.

Keach, Benjamin. *A Feast of Fat Things Full of Marrow*. London: Printed by B. H., 1696.

———. *The Glory of a True Church, And its Discipline display'd*. London: n.p., 1697.

———. *Spiritual Melody, Containing near Three Hundred Sacred Hymns*. London: Hancock, 1691.

Keating, Thomas. *The Mystery of Christ: The Liturgy as Spiritual Experience*. New York: Continuum, 2003.

Kilby, Karen. "Perichoresis and Projection: Problems with Social Doctrines of the Trinity." *New Blackfriars* 81 (2000) 432–45.

Kirk, Andrew. *What is Mission?: Theological Explorations*. Minneapolis: Fortress, 2000.

Knowles, David. *The Evolution of Medieval Thought*. London: Longman, 1962.

Knox, David Broughton. "The Nature of Worship." *Churchman* 71/2 (1957) 64–67.

Kurz, Joel R. "The Gifts of Creation and the Consummation of Humanity: Irenaeus of Lyons' Recapitulatory Theology of the Eucharist." *Worship* 83/2 (2009) 112–32.

Larkin, Philip. "Church Going." In *The Norton Anthology of Modern Poetry*, edited by Richard Ellmann and Robert O'Clair, 1015. New York: Norton, 1973.

Leith, John H., editor. *Creeds of the Churches: A Reader in Christian Doctrine from the Bible to the Present*. 3rd ed. Richmond, VA: Knox, 1982.

Leland, John. "Letter to Thomas Bingham, Esq., July 1833." In *The Writings of the Late Elder John Leland*, edited by L.F. Greene, 642–44. New York: Wood, 1845. Reprint, New York: Arno, 1969.

Leonard, Bill J. *Baptist Ways: A History*. Valley Forge, PA: Judson, 2003.

"The London Confession, 1644." In *Baptist Confessions of Faith*, rev. ed., edited by William L. Lumpkin, 144–71. Valley Forge, PA: Judson, 1969.

Long, Thomas G. *The Witness of Preaching*. 2nd ed. Louisville: Westminster John Knox, 2005.

Lubac, Henri de. *Catholicism: Christ and the Common Destiny of Man*. Translated by Lancelot C. Sheppard and Elizabeth Englund. San Francisco: Ignatius, 1988.

———. *Corpus Mysticum: The Eucharist and the Church in the Middle Ages*. Translated by Gemma Simmonds, Richard Price, and Christopher Stephens. Notre Dame: University of Notre Dame Press, 2007.

———. *The Splendour of the Church*. Translated by Michael Mason. London: Sheed & Ward, 1956.

Lumpkin, William L., and Bill J. Leonard, editors. *Baptist Confessions of Faith*. 2nd rev. ed. Valley Forge, PA: Judson, 2011.

Luther, Martin. *The Large Catechism*. Translated by Robert H. Fischer. Philadelphia: Fortress, 1959.

———. "The Pagan Servitude of the Church." In *Martin Luther: Selections from His Writings*, edited by John Dillenberger, 249–359. New York: Doubleday, 1962.

Maclaren, Alexander. "In the Name of Christ . . . By the Power of the Spirit." In *The Life of Baptists in the Life of the World: 80 Years of the Baptist World Alliance*, edited by Walter B. Shurden, 16–18. Nashville: Broadman, 1985.

Maring, Norman H. "The Individualism of Francis Wayland." In *Baptist Concepts of the Church*, edited by Winthrop S. Hudson, 135–69. Philadelphia: Judson, 1959.

Marney, Carlyle. "A Come-and-Go Affair." In *The Twentieth Century Pulpit*, edited by James W. Cox, 135–40. Nashville: Abingdon, 1978.

Marshall, Molly T. *Joining the Dance: A Theology of the Spirit*. Valley Forge, PA: Judson, 2003.

"The Martyrdom of Polycarp." In *The Apostolic Fathers in English,* translated and edited by Michael W. Holmes, 3rd ed., 147–56. Grand Rapids: Baker Academic, 2006.

McBeth, H. Leon. *The Baptist Heritage: Four Centuries of Baptist Witness.* Nashville: Broadman, 1987.

McClendon Jr., James W. "Baptism as a Performative Sign." *Theology Today* 23/3 (1966) 403–16.

———. *Biography as Theology: How Life Stories Can Remake Today's Theology.* Philadelphia: Trinity, 1990.

———. *Doctrine.* Vol. 2 of *Systematic Theology.* Nashville: Abingdon, 1994.

———. *Ethics.* Rev. ed. Vol. 1 of *Systematic Theology.* Nashville: Abingdon, 2002.

———. *Making Gospel Sense to a Troubled Church.* Cleveland: Pilgrim, 1995.

———. *Witness.* Vol. 3 of *Systematic Theology.* Nashville: Abingdon, 2000.

McCue, James F. "The Doctrine of Transubstantiation from Berengar of Tours through Trent: The Point at Issue." *Harvard Theological Review* 61/3 (1968) 385–431.

McElrath, Hugh T. "Turning Points in the Story of Baptist Church Music." *Baptist History and Heritage* 19/1 (1984) 4–16.

McKnight, Scot. *The King Jesus Gospel: The Original Good News Revisited.* Grand Rapids: Zondervan, 2011.

Moffitt, David M. *Atonement and the Logic of Resurrection in the Epistle to the Hebrews.* Supplements to Novum Testamentum 14. Leiden: Brill, 2011.

Mullins, E.Y. *The Axioms of Religion: A New Interpretation of the Baptist Faith.* Philadelphia: American Baptist Publication Society, 1908.

———. "The Baptist Conception of Religious Liberty." In *The Life of Baptists in the Life of the World: 80 Years of the Baptist World Alliance,* edited by Walter B. Shurden, 57–64. Nashville: Broadman, 1985.

Neely, Alan, editor. *Being Baptist Means Freedom.* Charlotte: Southern Baptist Alliance, 1988.

A New Catechism, Catholic Faith for Adults. New York: Seabury, 1969.

Newman, Elizabeth. "The Lord's Supper: Might Baptists Accept a Theory of Real Presence?" In *Baptist Sacramentalism,* edited by Anthony R. Cross and Philip E. Thompson, 211–27. Milton Keynes, UK: Paternoster, 2003.

———. *Untamed Hospitality: Welcoming God and Other Strangers.* Grand Rapids: Brazos, 2007.

O'Connor, Flannery. *The Habit of Being.* Edited by Sally Fitzgerald. New York: Farrar, Strauss, & Giroux, 1979.

"The Orthodox Creed." In *Baptist Confessions of Faith,* edited by William L. Lumpkin, rev. ed., 295–334. Valley Forge, PA: Judson, 1969.

Patrologia graeca. Edited by J.-P. Migne. 162 vols. Paris. 1857–1886.

Patrologia latina. Edited by J.-P. Migne. 217 vols. Paris. 1844–1864.

Pelikan, Jaroslav. *Credo: Historical and Theological Guide to the Creeds and Confessions of Faith in the Christian Tradition.* New Haven: Yale University Press, 2003.

Perelman, Chaim, and L. Olbrechts-Tyteca. *The New Rhetoric: A Treatise on Argumentation.* Notre Dame: University of Notre Dame Press, 1969.

Peterson, Eugene. *Under the Unpredictable Plant: An Exploration in Vocational Holiness.* Grand Rapids: Eerdmans, 1992.

Plato. *Gorgias.* Translated by Walter Hamilton. New York: Penguin, 1960.

Porter, H. Boone. "Day of the Lord: Day of Mystery." In *Between Memory and Hope: Readings on the Liturgical Year*, edited by Maxwell E. Johnson, 49–58. Collegeville, MN: Liturgical, 2000.

Porter, Stanley E. "Baptism in Acts: The Sacramental Dimension." In *Baptist Sacramentalism*, edited by Anthony R. Cross and Philip E. Thompson, 117–28. Waynesboro, GA: Paternoster, 2003.

Poteat, William H. *A Philosophical Daybook*. Columbia: University of Missouri Press, 1990.

Priestly, David S. "From Theological Polemic to Nonpolemical Theology: The Absence of Denominational Apology in the Systematic Theologies by Nineteenth Century American Baptists." ThD diss., Lutheran School of Theology, Chicago, 1986.

Regan, Paul. "Pneumatological and Eschatological Aspects of Liturgical Celebration." *Worship* 51 (1977): 346–47.

Robinson, Ezekiel Gilman. "The Relation of the Church and the Bible." In *The Madison Avenue Lectures*, 387–419. Philadelphia: American Baptist, 1867.

Roll, Susan K. "The Origins of Christmas: The State of the Question." In *Between Memory and Hope: Readings on the Liturgical Year*, edited by Maxwell E. Johnson, 273–90. Collegeville, MN: Liturgical, 2000.

Saliers, Don E. "Sounding the Symbols of Faith: Exploring the Nonverbal Language of Christian Worship." In *Music in Christian Worship: At the Service of the Liturgy*, edited by Charlotte Y. Kroeker, 17–26. Collegeville, MN: Liturgical, 2005.

———. *Worship as Theology: Foretaste of Glory Divine*. Nashville: Abingdon, 1994.

Schmemann, Alexander. *The Eucharist*. Crestwood, NY: St. Vladimir's Seminary Press, 1988.

Searle, Mark. "Sunday: The Heart of the Liturgical Year." In *Between Memory and Hope: Readings on the Liturgical Year*, edited by Maxwell E. Johnson, 59–76. Collegeville, MN: Liturgical, 2000.

Shea, John. *The Spiritual Wisdom of the Gospels for Preachers and Teachers*. 4 vols. Collegeville, MN: Liturgical, 2004–2010.

Sherman, Cecil E. "Freedom of the Individual to Interpret the Bible." In *Being Baptist Means Freedom*, edited by Alan Neely, 9–24. Charlotte: Southern Baptist Alliance, 1988.

Shurden, Walter B. "The Baptist Identity and the Baptist Manifesto." *Perspectives in Religious Studies* 25/4 (1998) 321–40.

———. *The Baptist Identity: Four Fragile Freedoms*. Macon, GA: Smyth & Helwys, 1993.

———. "The Southern Baptist Synthesis: Is It Cracking?" *Baptist History and Heritage* 16 (1981) 2–11.

Smith, James K. A. *Desiring the Kingdom: Worship, Worldview, and Cultural Formation*. Vol. 1 of *Cultural Liturgies*. Grand Rapids: Baker Academic, 2009.

Smith, T. C. "Baptism." In *Encyclopedia of Southern Baptists*, edited by Norman Wade Cox, 1:106–9. Nashville: Broadman, 1958.

Southern Baptist Convention. "1963 Baptist Faith and Message." The Baptist Start Page. Online: http://www.baptiststart.com/print/1963_baptist_faith_message.html.

———. "The Baptist Faith and Message [2000]." SBC.net. Online: http://www.sbc.net/bfm/bfm2000.asp.

Strong, Augustus Hopkins. *Systematic Theology: A Compendium and Commonplace Book Designed for the Use of Theological Students.* Philadelphia: Griffith & Rowland, 1912.

Taft, Robert F. "The Liturgical Year: Studies, Prospects, Reflection." In *Between Memory and Hope: Readings on the Liturgical Year,* edited by Maxwell E. Johnson, 3–24. Collegeville, MN: Liturgical, 2000.

Talley, Thomas J. "Liturgical Time in the Ancient Church: The State of Research." In *Between Memory and Hope: Readings on the Liturgical Year,* edited by Maxwell E. Johnson, 25–48. Collegeville, MN: Liturgical, 2000.

———. *The Origins of the Liturgical Year.* Collegeville, MN: Liturgical Press, 1991.

Taylor, Barbara Brown. *The Preaching Life.* Boston: Cowley, 1993.

Thompson, Philip E. "Dimensions of Memory: Challenges and Tasks in the Baptist Recovery of Tradition." In *Tradition and the Baptist Academy,* edited by Roger A. Ward and Philip E. Thompson, 46–66. Milton Keynes, UK: Paternoster, 2011.

———. "Memorial Dimensions of Baptism." In *Dimensions of Baptism: Biblical and Theological Studies,* Journal for the Study of the New Testament Supplement 234, edited by Stanley E. Porter and Anthony R. Cross, 204–324. London: Sheffield Academic, 2002.

———. "Re-envisioning Baptist Identity: Historical, Theological, and Liturgical Analysis." *Perspectives in Religious Studies* 27/3 (2000) 287–302.

———. "Sacraments and Religious Liberty: From Critical Practice to Rejected Infringement." In *Baptist Sacramentalism,* edited by Anthony R. Cross and Philip E. Thompson, 36–54. Milton Keynes, UK: Paternoster, 2003.

———. "Seventeenth-Century Baptist Confessions in Context." *Perspectives in Religious Studies* 29/4 (2002) 335–48.

Turney, Edmund, editor. *Baptismal Hymns.* New York: Sheldon, 1862.

United States Catholic Conference. *Catechism of the Catholic Church.* Mahwah, NJ: Paulist, 1994.

Van Dyk, Leanne. "A Conversation with the Ecumenical Creeds." In *Conversations With the Confessions: Dialogue in the Reformed Tradition,* edited by Joseph D. Small, 17–31. Louisville: Geneva, 2005.

Wayland, Francis. *Notes on the Principles and Practices of Baptist Churches.* New York: Sheldon, Blakeman, 1857.

Weaver, C. Douglas. "Baptists and Denominational Identity and the Turn Toward Creedalism: 2000." In *Turning Points in Baptist History: a festschrift in honor of Harry Leon McBeth,* edited by Michael E. Williams and Walter B. Shurden, 288–301. Macon, GA: Mercer University Press, 2011.

Webster, John. "Confession and Confessions." In *Nicene Christianity: The Future for a New Ecumenism,* edited by Christopher R. Seitz, 119–32. Grand Rapids: Brazos, 2001.

West, Fritz. "Readings, Scripture." In *The Encyclopedia of Christianity,* edited by Erwin Fahlbusch, 4:491–96. Grand Rapids: Eerdmans, 2008.

Williams, Rowan. *Tokens of Trust: An Introduction to Christian Belief.* Louisville: Westminster John Knox, 2007.

Winkler, Gabriele. "The Appearance of the Light at the Baptism of Jesus and the Origins of the Feast of Epiphany: An Investigation of Greek, Syriac, Armenian, and Latin Sources." In *Between Memory and Hope: Readings on the Liturgical Year,* edited by Maxwell E. Johnson, 291–348. Collegeville, MN: Liturgical, 2000.

Wolterstorff, Nicholas P. "Thinking about Church Music." In *Music in Christian Worship: At the Service of the Liturgy*, edited by Charlotte Y. Kroeker, 3–16. Collegeville, MN: Liturgical, 2005.

Wood, Susan K. *One Baptism, Ecumenical Dimensions of the Doctrine of Baptism*. Collegeville, MN: Liturgical, 2009.

World Council of Churches. *One Lord, One Baptism*. Commission on Faith and Order. London: SCM, 1960.

Wright, John. *Telling God's Story: Narrative Preaching for Christian Formation*. Downers Grove, IL: InterVarsity, 2007.

Yoder, John Howard. "The New Humanity as Pulpit and Paradigm." In *For the Nations: Essays Evangelical and Public*, 37–50. Grand Rapids: Eerdmans, 1997.